est man
story

...hnson
... man in
... Olympic
... yester-
... time of

...h-rival,
...ho fin-
...ning his
... of 9.92

...ing line
...phantly
...rust his
...ard —
...blished

himself as the world's No 1 sprinter.

For the first time in history, four competitors finished under 10 seconds.

Johnson and Lewis were followed by Linford Christie, of Britain, in 9.97 seconds and American Calvin Smith in 9.99 seconds.

Lewis, who boasted before the Games that he would never again lose to Johnson, was first to shake the winner's hand.

● **FULL STORY: P69**

...SON.

...rn in
...es in

...ll-time

...s: ·

...HTS:
...sterday)
...me on

YESTERDAY'S TIME:
9.79 seconds — new world record.

CHARACTER TRAITS:
Dedicated to training and otherwise quiet — the complete opposite of Carl Lewis' Hollywood image. Still carries a slight child-hood stammer. Lewis has accused him of drug-taking to enhance his performance.

OLYMPIC REPORT Canada's Big Ben conquers the world

Toast of the track world

Race of the Century · step by step

strength and power to accelerate over the first 40 metres. To be safe, he must be a metre and a half ahead of Lewis after 40."

Third: "Then, very importantly, he has to maintain his speed endurance as he did in his greatest race, at Rome. You see, to

Johnson had followed the script Gowan has now outlined when to overcome Lewis at the 1987 global championships in Rome and etched a clocking of 9.83 seconds into the history of sport. And the Toronto ath-

Tonight places Gold vs. Watch

KEN McKEE
TV, radio
sports

HE SQUEAKS IN

Ben Johnson sure did it the hard way today. He finished third in heat two and had to wait for results of other five heats be-

WORLD'S FASTEST MAN*

WORLD'S FASTEST MAN*

THE INCREDIBLE LIFE OF
BEN JOHNSON

MARY ORMSBY

sh.
SUTHERLAND HOUSE

TORONTO, 2024

Sutherland House
416 Moore Ave., Suite 205
Toronto, ON M4G 1C9

Sutherland House and logo are registered
trademarks of The Sutherland House Inc.

First edition, April 2024

If you are interested in inviting one of our authors to a live event or
media appearance, please contact sranasinghe@sutherlandhousebooks.com
and visit our website at sutherlandhousebooks.com for more
information about our authors and their schedules.

We acknowledge the support of the Government of Canada.

Manufactured in Turkey
Cover designed by Serina Mercier, Shalomi Ranasinghe, and Jordan Lunn
Cover Photo Credit to Getty Images
Typeset by Karl Hunt

Library and Archives Canada Cataloguing in Publication
Title: World's fastest man : the incredible life of Ben Johnson / Mary Ormsby.
Names: Ormsby, Mary, author.
Description: In title the word "man" is followed by an asterisk.
Identifiers: Canadiana (print) 20230596991 | Canadiana (ebook) 20230597009 |
ISBN 9781990823732 (hardcover) | ISBN 9781990823749 (EPUB)
Subjects: LCSH: Johnson, Ben, 1961- | LCSH: Sprinters—Canada—Biography. |
LCSH: Doping in sports. | LCGFT: Biographies.
Classification: LCC GV1061.15.J63 O76 2024 |
DDC 796.42/2092—dc23

ISBN 978-1-990823-73-2
eBook 978-1-990823-74-9

CONTENTS

CHAPTER ONE

46 STRIDES

Ben Johnson gazed down lane six at Jamsil Olympic Stadium from behind his starting blocks. He gently shook each sculpted leg, massive quadriceps rippling. The short path ahead, the one that would define his future, glistened under a hot Seoul sun.

On this day, September 24, 1988, the Canadian would take 9.79 seconds to sear his name into Olympic legend as the fastest human ever to run 100 meters, winning a historic showdown that would forever be synonymous with his name.

But before that could happen, the reigning world champion needed to block out distractions: foremost, the showboating presence of defending Olympic champion Carl Lewis, Johnson's embittered rival. So deep was their hostility that the two had nearly come to blows after a close race in Spain the year before.

Johnson registered mild surprise that his loathed American opponent was in lane three, not next to him, in the gold medal race. No matter. After the starter's pistol fired, it would be close enough for Johnson to keep an eye on the man who'd won four events at the 1984 games in Los Angeles and who coveted more gold in Seoul.

When Lewis invited a pre-race handshake, visceral resolve flooded the Toronto sprinter, their palms barely touching.

"Stay away from me," Johnson silently fumed at the man who loathed him back. "This is my time, not yours."

The twenty-six-year-old also pushed aside thoughts of the spoils riding on a victory in this high-stakes race. There would be cash—lots of it. About $10 million in sponsorships and endorsements and at least another $10 to $15 million more over his lifetime. There would be respect. His detractors, including Lewis who'd publicly hinted that Johnson bolstered his speed with banned performance-enhancing drugs, would be dismissed as spiteful losers, jealous of his dominance. There would be vindication. His twelve-year relationship with coach Charlie Francis, who'd long rankled Canadian track officials for calling out their leadership as meek and regressive, would be established as the prototype for success. And there was an intensely personal element too. Though seventy thousand people packed the stadium and two billion more across the planet crowded around televisions to witness the event, including those throughout his birth country, Jamaica, Johnson was determined to win for one person: his mother.

Gloria Johnson had raised her six children alone in a rough Toronto neighborhood. For years, she had worked minimum-wage jobs that barely covered her bills. Today, she was in the Olympic stands, hands clasped in prayer. Her presence gave Johnson "an extra push."

"This is for you, Mum."

He did several practice starts out of the blocks, the first few steps a touch below the top speed he'd use in the race. As Johnson jogged lightly back to the start, the crowd's murmur rose. The atmosphere was electric. His coming battle with Lewis had been hyped ever since Johnson had faltered a month earlier in a Zurich race, losing to the American for the first time in three years. Lewis cranked up the mind games after his Swiss triumph, crowing to reporters that he'd never again lose to Johnson. Seoul was the rematch.

After their warm-up, moments before the start, the runners gathered in the call room under the stands. They pulled on their national team sweats and waited for Olympic officials to escort them back into the stadium for formal introductions to the crowd. Tense and silent, the call room was the last chance for the athletes to focus their thoughts for a minute or two. Johnson deliberately destroyed the mood, swaggering into bark:

"Which one of you guys is going to be second?"

He cackled when the angry men, including Lewis, glared at him. "Looking like they wanted to choke me and kill me," he said.

No one answered. Johnson blithely laced up his black-and-gold Diadora spikes, zippered his Canadian tracksuit, and joined the procession onto the track.

The press, mostly wire service and newspaper reporters, were crammed into a section of stands far from the finish line. I was there as part of the *Toronto Star* team. My job was to write a "sidebar" off the race on whoever was (a) not Ben Johnson and (b) not the gold medalist. Resting on a skinny shelf at my seat was my primitive laptop, a durable Tandy 200 that ran on AA batteries and miraculously transmitted copy through a cable plugged into a phone jack. An American reporter in the row below me had her Tandy 200 flipped open, and I couldn't help but see what she'd typed on the screen, predicting the finish: Carl Lewis had swatted down rival Ben Johnson to win back-to-back Olympic gold in the 100 meters. Could be. We'd know soon enough.

The official starter summoned the eight runners to the line after they'd had their last quick warm-up: a few starts, some stretching, and double-checking that laces were tied tightly. Johnson was calm. Focused. Ready. A double-bronze medalist at the 1984 games in Los Angeles, he was experienced in handling Olympic pressure. He also knew everything about his competition without even turning his head.

Brazil's Robson da Silva was in lane one, next to Jamaican Raymond Stewart. Lewis, one of a trio of Americans in the final, stood tall in lane three beside the British star Linford Christie. Calvin Smith of the United States, a former world-record holder, drew lane five. Clad in Team Canada red, Johnson held lane six with teammate Desai

Williams, also coached by Francis, in lane seven. American Dennis Mitchell rounded out the field in the far lane eight.

Johnson shook his legs once more, then curled his 172-pound frame into the starting blocks to take his mark. His chunky gold-chain necklace, a $9,000 gift to himself from a Cartier jewelry store in Rome, swung away from his throat, arcing downward. He placed his hands wide across the ocher lane, fingers just behind the thick white line, and elbows slightly bent.

Of all the meticulous pre-race preparations Johnson ticked off on his mental to-do list that day, passing the post-race drug screening of his urine was not one of them. Why would it be? Johnson had never failed an anti-doping test in the eight years he'd used prohibited muscle-building anabolic steroids. Secure in the knowledge that his sport rarely risked exposing its superstars as drug cheats—testing was spotty at international meets while steroid use among runners and throwers was rife—he had no reason to believe his fool-the-laboratory streak would end in Seoul.

Nobody did.

* * *

The loudspeaker call for the men's 100-meter finalists to assemble in Jamsil Stadium woke Johnson. He had been sleeping on a massage table under a tent at the adjacent warm-up track.

Determined to recover every bit of energy following the semifinals nearly three hours earlier, the sprinter ignored the announcement and closed his eyes.

When the second call came, he didn't move. His coach did. "Ben, you better warm up soon," urged Francis, often made anxious by his sprinter's race-day snoozes.

Johnson looked at his watch. "I still got time," he said, tucking an arm under his head for "a power nap" as Francis paced.

4

When the third and final call came, Johnson sat up, swung his legs off the table, grabbed his gear—spikes and a water bottle in a small kit bag—and began walking with Francis through the tunnel to the main stadium.

Francis took the opportunity to remind Johnson to leap from the blocks—his unique advantage since no one reacted faster to the gun—then accelerate smoothly over the balance of the race. He was shocked to hear the sprinter say no; he was going to fly out of the blocks as usual and then accelerate at the forty-meter mark.

Francis stared in disbelief. Twelve years of training for this one race—all that work to perfect the mental, physical, and metabolic elements in a human body to run 100 meters faster than anyone in history—and now coach and athlete were out of sync.

"I have two styles of running. One, I get out of the blocks and just keep running. That one style you saw in Rome," Johnson said of his world-record romp a year earlier.

"The second style is I shift gears at forty meters and just keep running. I said to Charlie, 'I'm going to shift gears very early in the race.'"

Francis blanched. "No, no, no. I want you to run nice and smooth."

"No, I'm going to shift gears and go."

Recognizing that stubborn look in the runner's eyes, Francis said nothing more, but Johnson knew exactly what his coach was thinking: "He was scared that if I tried to change gears, I might pull my muscles because of the power and speed I'm traveling with." A mid-race injury would be a nightmare, probably preventing him from finishing and killing the dream for them both.

While Francis stewed, Johnson was supremely confident. He'd planned his race week to near perfection with a combination of meditation, rest, treatment for his swollen Achilles, and light workouts. With the exception of one heart-stopping mistake in the heats, the plan was working.

The mistake had come in the second of two rounds of the heats the previous day. Johnson had breezed to a first-place finish in 10.36 seconds in the first race. He then outsmarted himself in a stacked second round against medal threats Linford Christie of Great Britain and American Dennis Mitchell. Johnson decelerated around the 60-meter mark, wrongly thinking he'd easily finish first or second to grab one of two automatic berths to the semifinals. Christie and Mitchell nipped him at the wire. Suddenly, Johnson was in peril. His time, 10.17 seconds, was very fast, but it still had to be one of the four fastest clockings [outside of the two automatic qualifiers from each heat] to move on to the sixteen-man semifinal round.

"I looked at the scoreboard and asked Charlie: 'How many more heats left?'" Johnson said.

Francis said, "Five."

"Which countries are they from?"

"Mostly African countries."

"I don't think they are going to run faster than me."

"You better hope not."

The tense pair watched the remaining race times flash across the scoreboard. Fans in the stands understood the trouble: Johnson's Olympics could end if his time was eclipsed. Fortunately, it stood as the swiftest of the final four semifinalist qualifiers.

Francis was relieved, but annoyed. "You were lucky to get in. Don't fool around anymore."

The runner, chastened, vowed to "put on all burners in the semifinal."

He did. On the morning of Saturday, September 24, he clocked 10.03 into a headwind to win his semi, a race delayed by two false starts, the second charged to Johnson, who was visibly angered (in 1988, sprinters were allowed one violation).

There is a side story regarding that false start. It involves Canadian International Olympic Committee member Richard "Dick" Pound, the man who two days later would play an even greater role in Johnson's life.

Pound was a fast-rising young IOC vice president who negotiated the games' television and sponsorship rights. He and his wife Julie watched the 100-meter semis from high up in the stadium stands. They were outraged when Johnson was charged with a false start. The crowd whistled in derision at the call. The sprinter was still upset. He'd have to play it safe when they lined up again. This was not an ideal situation in an Olympic semifinal.

Urged by his wife to intervene after Johnson was safely through to the medal final, Pound did something extraordinary. He strode down to the trackside statisticians' tent—his IOC accreditation allowed him to enter the restricted area. He confronted a Hungarian athletics official, Artur Takac, to complain about the on-track starter, "who doesn't understand the way Ben starts."

"This is not fair, you guys know Ben wins his races at the start and Carl wins them at the end . . . and this guy is trying to take away his start," Pound said, worried the same violation would be called on Johnson in the afternoon final.

Takac denied any miscue had occurred. The IOC technical consultant said the electronic sensors in all starting blocks recorded each athlete's movement as the gun fired, and therefore, the electronic reading would back the starter's contention that Johnson moved before the pistol fired.

"Can I see it?" Pound asked or, more accurately, demanded.

Takac huffed off. Five minutes went by. Then ten, fifteen, and longer. Averting Pound's steady gaze, the official returned without the printout and sheepishly hemmed and hawed that "well, ah, sometimes, these things are not quite as clear as you might expect."

Pound made himself clear.

"If this happens in the final, I'm going to describe the discussion we just had to the world."

The message was unmistakable. Pound was exerting his considerable influence over a race official on Johnson's behalf. The starter and the sport were on notice if Johnson was charged with another violation.

By comparison, Lewis's semifinal run was a bore. No drama, just speed. The American was faster than Johnson, winning his semi in 9.97 with a legal tailwind. Johnson, who usually ran heats just quickly enough to qualify for the next round before going all out in a final, believed Lewis ran a faster-than-required time as an intimidation ploy.

"He was showing off, but he was in good shape. He came to run."

As they came through the tunnel before the medal race, Francis's parting words to Johnson were, "Just run the way you're supposed to run."

"Don't worry, everything will be okay," Johnson assured him.

Francis smiled, patted him on the back, and then searched for a seat in the stands. Coaches were not permitted on the main track with their athletes. A security guard let Francis squeeze into a media section near the finish line, where photographers who had camped out overnight to claim a seat for the Olympics' most anticipated event would capture history on film.

* * *

Ben Johnson was true to one of his favorite sayings: "When the gun go off, the race be over."

It was over less than a second after the pistol fired. A clean start. Johnson leapt from the blocks the fastest, both feet off the ground, arms flung unnaturally high behind his shoulders, and fingers spread wide on each hand. Airborne. Carl Lewis could only play catch-up.

Johnson's peripheral vision confirmed in that instant that he was flying toward gold.

"When the gun goes and I move, even though I was looking straight ahead, my side eyes showed no one was out [of the blocks] yet," he said.

"In my mind, I said to myself: 'Shit, this is fast.'"

Seventy-thousand screaming people thought so, too. Johnson heard nothing but his rapid breathing as his arms sliced high, his legs pumped, and he gained speed.

He widened the gap on the field and, at about forty meters, "just pumped it." His surge made broadcasters gasp.

"They're away cleanly, Ben Johnson flying out of the blocks," began Don Wittman's trackside call for Canada's public television network, the CBC. "Can Carl Lewis make up the deficit? Ben Johnson is in the lead—can . . . he . . . hang . . . on?"

The surge continued through the seventy-meter mark, where Johnson began to wonder how far he was from the finish. On pace to break his own world record, he sensed that his historic effort was emptying his tank. Uh oh.

"I didn't plan to fail, I planned to be successful," he said. "So I just kept my focus, kept pumping my arms, kept breathing and as I reached ninety meters, I could see the [electronic scoreboard] right in front of me, because the numbers were pretty big."

"The number said 9 seconds flat."

A longtime clubmate and friend of Johnson's, Canadian Olympic sprinter Angella Issajenko, was watching. She knew he was racing into the record books.

"He just had everything together, it was just complete. No weaknesses at all," she said.

World-class athletes, regardless of the sport, possess a competition awareness exclusive to only a few at the top: Serena Williams in tennis, Lionel Messi in football, Simone Biles in gymnastics, Wayne Gretzky in ice hockey, and Kobe Bryant in basketball. That heightened awareness can strike like a lightning bolt, flooding an athlete with certitude. Johnson experienced it a few strides from the finish line in Seoul. He knew that no one, not even an exceptional closer like Lewis, could pass him.

"It's impossible for someone to be there [with me] at ninety meters," Johnson told himself.

"If anyone *was* there," he said later, "I was going to panic because you're not supposed to be there. It was too fast for someone to be right beside me."

Lewis stole three fretful glances at Johnson while desperately trying to close the gap. He also stepped out of his lane. Costly mistakes. He wrote in his 1990 memoir that even in mid-sprint, he knew Johnson had an insurmountable lead.

"[About] eighty meters down the track—with the finish line flying toward us—I looked at Ben again and he was not coming back any. He still had those five feet on me. Ben had pretty much the same lead all the way through and I knew I couldn't get him. Damn, I thought, Ben did it again. The bastard got away with it again."

The cocksure Johnson then did something he'd long plotted to humiliate Lewis. Two steps before crossing the finish line, he slowed slightly, turned his head left to look at the distressed American, and raised his right hand to the sky, his index finger indicating No. 1.

"Every time Carl Lewis beat me, he said, 'This was the most perfect race I've ever run.' Every time he lost, he said, 'I don't think I ran the best race of my life,'" Johnson said. "So, too bad. You lost. Plain and simple."

Johnson demolished the Olympic and world records in forty-six strides, with a time on the scoreboard as 9.79 seconds. It was a mammoth slice off his Rome mark of 9.83. Johnson later said he would have run closer to 9.72 had he not slowed to stare down Lewis.

In all, four men ran under ten seconds in Seoul, making it the fastest 100 meters ever. Lewis was second in 9.92, Christie third in 9.97, and Smith fourth in 9.99. The stadium crowd roared its approval—for the winner, for Lewis, for the entire field in delivering a race for the ages.

Johnson's mother, Gloria, was ecstatic, even though she'd missed seeing part of the race. She'd been praying, her eyes shut, when her son was in the blocks. Beside her were her daughter, Jean, and the sprinter's club team doctor, Jamie Astaphan. They hugged, jumping up and down in celebration, their joy broadcast across the planet by network cameras zooming in on them. (The runner's father, Ben Sr., could not be in Seoul. He was stranded in Jamaica after Hurricane Gilbert decimated the island in mid-September, grounding all air travel.)

Lewis jogged after Johnson and tapped his shoulder, stopping him to shake his hand. The Canadian reluctantly obliged in an awkward exchange. Johnson then ran half a lap holding aloft a large Canadian flag he was given by a fan, saluting an adoring crowd with Desai Williams, who finished seventh, at his side.

In that moment, with the red maple leaf billowing behind him, the son silently praised his mother. He'd just honored her the best way he knew how.

"In the Olympic Games you have to run for a country, and I was running for Canada, but in Seoul, that race was for my mother."

Johnson's performance buoyed the spirits of other Canadian Olympians in Seoul, who were glued to the race at their various sporting venues. It was an inspiration for fellow athletes who had yet to compete. He was the first Canadian to win an Olympic 100-meter race since Percy Williams clinched gold at the 1928 Olympics in Amsterdam.

Back in Canada, it was a seismic moment. Johnson was a hero, galvanizing the nation. The dramatic victory was imprinted on jubilant Canadians, who would long remember exactly where they were and who they were with when they watched Johnson win. They had lapped up the Johnson-Lewis feud over the past year and transformed it into something more patriotic: a Canada versus USA smackdown. Intoxicated by Johnson's cheeky and decisive achievement, Canada, living in the shadow of the alpha male to the south, had the rare chance to tweak the nose of Uncle Sam. It felt good.

"Ben's Pure Gold" screamed the banner headline across the *Toronto's Star*'s front page.

"Johnson Brings Home the Gold," cheered Toronto's *Globe & Mail*.

"Johnson Sets World Mark and Tops Lewis in the 100," reported the *New York Times*.

My sidebar ended up being on Lewis, who did a mic check—something like, "Can you hear me?"—before he addressed the assembled world media. He was not happy. He did not refer to Johnson by name during the entire post-race press conference.

Back at track level, Francis couldn't immediately reach his sprinter, who was thronged by reporters, photographers, security guards, and track officials. He caught up with him about half an hour later under the stands, when the three top finishers gathered to walk into the stadium again for the medal ceremony. Johnson received his medal from Primo Nebiolo, president of the International Amateur Athletic Federation. The Canadian flag was raised, and "O Canada" was played. Johnson was stoic—no tears, no emotion.

He was again mobbed as he was escorted to the stands by a Royal Canadian Mounted Police officer to take a congratulatory phone call from Canadian Prime Minister Brian Mulroney. The Mountie stayed with him as security when he headed to the doping control center to provide his post-race urine sample. The center, beneath the stadium stands, contained a small office area for athletes to provide samples under the watchful eyes of certified anti-doping officials. Those officials also oversaw the paperwork that accompanied the coded, labeled urine specimens sent to the main testing lab in another building across town.

In addition to the officials' office, which contained the only toilet, there were small holding areas for athletes to wait for their turn to pee, plus an outer waiting room. Entry to the doping control area was supposed to be heavily restricted. A special access pass was required for nonathletes, and each visitor's name was written into a logbook at reception. An athlete reporting to doping control could bring one "accompanying person" with them. Johnson chose his massage therapist, Waldemar Matuszewski, because his aching Achilles tendon needed treatment before the 4×100-meter relay later in the week. Francis was not admitted. The Mountie was permitted to stay in the outermost waiting area as Johnson's security detail.

Johnson recalled that the doping control center was like a party room. He said people were cheering for him, taking photographs, and asking for his autograph. Other competitors were in and out. Swedish IOC medical commission member Arne Ljungqvist was on the scene and would later be confronted with alleged security breaches.

When Johnson entered the area designated for him, it contained a massage bench and, inexplicably, an American man sitting splay-legged on the floor beside a tiny fridge. The man had a security pass around his neck, a camera, and a zippered fanny pack fastened to his waist. The sprinter said this same man had hovered around him the day before at the warm-up track, saying "hi" once or twice between the heats. Johnson didn't know his name, didn't recognize him either, even though they'd hit a nightclub together two years earlier. Nor did Johnson know the man was a close friend of Carl Lewis's— so close, in fact, that while in Seoul, the man lived with the Lewis entourage in a rented home away from the distractions of the Olympic Village.

But Johnson was beginning to let the elation of his run sink in. He was exuberant. He didn't pose many questions while on the massage table, other than to happily ask the unnamed man to pass him cans of beer from the fridge. Dehydrated, the Canadian needed about six to eight beers before he could provide anti-doping officials with a urine sample.

He left doping control at 3:45 p.m., a little more than an hour after entering. He arrived at the news conference a bit tipsy, giggling with Francis before describing the greatest achievement of his career.

"I'd like to say my name is Benjamin Sinclair Johnson Jr. and this world record will last 50 years, maybe 100," Johnson said, more making a statement than answering a reporter's question.

Then Johnson told his burning truth. "The important thing was to beat Carl."

The American with the zippered fanny pack was forgotten. Briefly. Forty-eight hours later, the fuse on the most scandalous episode in Olympic history was lit, and a frantic hunt for the "mystery man" would begin.

It would take many months for the public, and Johnson, to learn the man's name was Andre Jackson. And over the decades, Jackson would play a game of cat-and-mouse with the Canadian runner about how his positive test came to be.

CHAPTER TWO

THE CATCH

The Monday morning of September 26, 1988, dawned fresh and cool in Seoul. At the Hilton hotel, clattering breakfast trays were being wheeled along halls by room service staff when Charlie Francis banged on the Olympic sprint champion's door.

Ben Johnson opened it. He froze when he saw his coach's stricken face.

"You tested positive."

Johnson stared in disbelief. Waves of icy dread gripped his insides, alarm and gorge rising. Staggered, he backed into his room, sat on the edge of a sofa, and buried his head in his hands.

"No, no," he moaned softly, shaking his head. "They finally got me."

Not quite yet, but the process was rapidly unfolding.

The previous night, a preliminary "A sample" screening of Johnson's urine sample was red-flagged for a performance-enhancing drug. It was the first of two anti-doping tests to be conducted on the seventy-five-milliliter specimen he had provided after the Saturday race. Neither Johnson nor Francis were told about the nature of the illicit substance, but they had a good idea: an anabolic steroid.

They were genuinely shocked. They believed they'd perfected steroid clearance times and, as an added precaution, left a roomy margin of error before race days. Based on their years of experience,

Johnson's system should have been flushed clean nearly a week before he won the gold medal.

"There has to be some mistake," Johnson said, bewildered.

His reaction was understandable. Weightlifters and shot-putters were the type of athletes who failed steroid tests, not world-class sprinters, even though Johnson believed many of his rivals secretly doped.

Anabolic steroids, synthesized versions of the naturally occurring male hormone testosterone, were lab-developed in the 1950s, two decades after German scientists first isolated testosterone. They were designed for medical uses such as rebuilding weakened tissue in severely ill or injured patients. As word spread about the drug's muscle-growth ability, competitive athletes began taking it. They discovered that steroids indeed produced larger muscles and that those muscles recovered more quickly after heavy exercise. That meant athletes had the potential to get stronger and, in the case of sprinters, faster. Some felt more aggressive on the drug, a psychological bonus in competitive situations.

Athletes who doped achieved desired results that they couldn't reach drug-free. That was (and is) the irresistible lure of anabolic steroids: they work. In the 1970s, this artificial sporting enhancement was deemed cheating by in-house scientists, who drew up lists of banned substances for amateur sports federations. The International Olympic Committee added anabolic steroids to its doping list in 1975. The Montreal Summer Games in 1976 were the first Olympics to test for steroids. But the new anti-doping rules weren't much of a deterrent.

By the 1980s, steroid use was pervasive at the elite level across many amateur sports, including weightlifting and track and field. A former sprinter described that era as "the Wild West" of doping in track. Drug testing in the 1980s was limited largely to the amateur sports world (professional sports testing would come later) and almost always conducted during competitions, meaning users could load up on steroids worry-free during the off-season when the heaviest training workouts occurred. This practice gave dopers the exact dates on which they were likely to be tested. All they had to do to beat the system was stop using the banned drugs early enough to excrete all chemical traces by competition day, a period called the clearance time. Positive tests were relatively few, and due to clearance times too short for the dosage taken.

Johnson had passed every anti-doping test he'd taken, dozens of them, since starting his steroid program in late 1981. As far as he and Francis knew, the steroid they'd most relied on in recent years, known generically as "furazabol," was undetectable in sports labs. They believed they were doubly safe going into Seoul: Johnson had plenty of clearance time—more than three weeks before race day—for a steroid invisible to testers.

In addition, Johnson had benefited from a free pass or two along the way, knowing some meet directors would deliberately choose other runners for testing or somehow bypass him in random post-race selections. He had not been selected to provide a urine sample after winning the 100 meters at the 1988 Canadian Olympic trials. After capturing the 1987 world championship in Rome, he'd been removed from the Olympic stadium's doping control center by Primo Nebiolo's bodyguard and taken by limousine to a thoroughbred track where Nebiolo waited. The Italian president of the IAAF wanted the world-record-holding Canadian to pose for photos with his wealthy horse-racing friends and their champion steed. Afterward, Johnson was chauffeured back to his Rome hotel. No official ever asked him to provide a urine sample.

"I think [Nebiolo] was just thrilled by what happened," Johnson said. "I was the fastest man in the world, taking pictures with the fastest horse in the world, worth lots of money, publicity, and sponsors. And they had me take pictures with this lady, this horse, the jockey, and everything . . . I think he just wanted to brush [the drug test] under the rug."

Johnson received similar treatment on the track-and-field circuit, where top runners were paid appearance fees by meet directors to boost ticket sales. He could command $40,000 (US) just to show up and run. Francis had told him that at one indoor competition, he was paid a smaller appearance fee by a meet director who quietly ensured that Johnson would not be selected to provide a testing sample after his race.

Incidents like these bolstered Johnson's confidence that the sport's power brokers, besotted by his escalating rivalry with Carl Lewis and the profits it generated, would protect him.

So, in 1988, a Johnson bust was unimaginable. No champion of his stature had ever failed a steroid test.

"In our sport, a positive drug test was the ultimate horror," Francis wrote in his 1990 memoir, *Speed Trap*. "It was like a fatal car crash: You knew it could happen at any time, to almost anyone, but you never believed it could happen to you."

Back at the Seoul Hilton, just after 7:30 a.m., Francis was about to leave Johnson's hotel room for an emergency meeting in the Canadian Olympic Association office with Team Canada *chef de mission* Carol Anne Letheren. She'd had a hand-delivered letter from IOC medical commission head, Belgium's Prince Alexandre de Merode, slipped under her hotel door around 1:45 a.m., informing her of Johnson's A sample result. Stunned, she wandered around the Olympic Village alone. When the sun rose, she broke the news to key personnel. One was track-and-field team manager Dave Lyon, who had alerted Francis around 7 a.m. It was going to be an agonizing day for all involved.

Johnson glanced at a small black bag that held a box containing his gold medal. His name was engraved on it, as was the event he won and his world record time of 9.79 seconds. He'd owned the medal and been feted for it for less than forty-eight hours. Such a short span of glory. Going forward, time would seem to tick unnaturally fast; before lunch, he and Francis would face Olympic officials, including two from the IOC's all-powerful medical commission, whose members were tasked with testing, prosecuting, and passing judgment on athletes.

Johnson had a chance, a slim one, to avoid a life-altering crisis. His trouble was detected in the A sample portion of his post-race urine specimen. In Seoul, all urine samples provided by athletes at doping control centers were subsequently split into two rubber-stoppered bottles, labeled A and B, for analysis at the IOC's state-of-the-art lab. The two bottle labels had identical numerical codes assigned to the athlete. Those codes could be cross-referenced to a corresponding name list when a doping infraction surfaced. Alexandre de Merode kept the confidential coded names list in a hotel safe until a sample was flagged by the lab and that athlete had to be informed.

If an A sample was negative for banned substances, no further analysis was required. The athlete passed as clean, and there was no need to ever identify an athlete linked to a clean A sample.

However, if the A sample yielded a positive for any substance on a long IOC list of banned performance enhancers, from steroids to stimulants to masking agents like diuretics, the athlete was identified and alerted. Then, the urine in the twin-B specimen was tested. A doping violation became official when the A and B samples were positive for the same substance. Disqualification was likely to follow.

If the B portion was found to be negative after an athlete's A sample produced a positive finding, it was considered a false positive, and the athlete was cleared. Johnson's B sample had not yet been analyzed. Hope rested on the rarest of scenarios—a clean B sample.

"Don't say a word to anyone," Francis cautioned before he departed for his meeting.

Francis met with a subdued group of Canadian officials at the Olympic Village. He and some of the group, including Canadian chief medical officer Dr. William Stanish, drove to the anti-doping lab for a 10 a.m. appointment with IOC medical commission members. In a large room, three major players who would determine Johnson's fate not just that day but for decades to come were already seated at a conference table: commissioners Arnold Beckett of Great Britain and Manfred Donike of Germany, and Seoul lab director Jong-sei Park, who was acting under the authority of the local Olympic organizing committee.

The session began with Beckett asking Francis a question. Could he think of anything that may have produced a positive result in Johnson's A sample? The Brit did not reveal the offending substance. Beckett didn't want to give Francis any edge to offer exculpatory answers that could be false.

When Francis didn't offer an explanation, Beckett gave him the news: Johnson tested positive for the anabolic steroid stanozolol. The chemical "fingerprint" of stanozolol, called a metabolite, had been detected in Johnson's urine sample. Metabolites are the identifiable products of the drugs after they are broken down in the body.

Francis was speechless. He knew his athletes (members of the Toronto-based Mazda Optimist track and field club, including Johnson) rarely used stanozolol because it stiffened their muscles, and that drug was in the anti-doping movement's crosshairs with testing development. In fact, in late 1985, Francis's sprinters switched to another steroid, furazabol, at the insistence of club doctor Jamie Astaphan. The doctor advised it would be easier on their muscles, and, again, furazabol was undetectable.

With Beckett intently studying his face for a reaction, Francis could do little but vehemently deny Johnson had taken stanozolol. And as far as the visibly shaken coach knew, that was the truth.

According to Stanish, Francis was a distraction to the proceedings. "In that circumstance where cool heads clearly must prevail, it was disturbing in terms of his agitation," the orthopedic surgeon would later tell a public inquiry. "He was commenting, 'I'm out' . . . meaning that 'I'm leaving track and field, there's got to be some mistake,' and so on. So it was difficult for the [IOC] medical commissioners to carry on with the business at hand in that sort of atmosphere."

Around 11 a.m., Johnson arrived. If Francis was near hysteria, Johnson was as cool as a marble slab. He'd gathered the medications he had in Seoul, as he'd been asked, and wordlessly gave them to Beckett. The Brit read the accompanying handwritten note from Astaphan listing the items, which were mostly vitamins and deemed them harmless. When Beckett asked Johnson if he was "taking anything" like a performance-enhancing drug in Seoul, he denied it.

"This was the biggest race of my life," Johnson told Beckett. "Why would I take something to [harm] myself? It doesn't make any sense."

It was the truth. He wasn't using steroids *in* Seoul, which was what Beckett asked. "No one asked me about using steroids before I came to Seoul," the sprinter said, splitting a hair. Plus, Johnson knew using steroids on or close to a race day would not boost his speed; they were for training periods.

Next, Stanish stepped up to confirm that the B sample was indeed the sprinter's. The doctor witnessed lab technicians open the specimen bottle and then begin the process of analyzing the urine under Park's supervision. The test would take about eight hours on the gas chromatography/mass spectrometry machinery before spitting out results. Johnson declined to participate in or watch any of these steps.

Prior to Seoul, rumors had circulated for years that well-connected amateur athletes had their doping violations disappear when the bottles containing their B samples were "accidentally" dropped to shatter on the floor, spilling the urine contents. Or stomped on by a quick-thinking entourage member who grabbed it off a table. Or flung hard to break against a wall before lab workers could react. When there was no intact B specimen to test, there was no way to confirm a positive A finding. Sometimes, money changed hands to make a doping matter go away, or so the rumors go.

At the 1984 Los Angeles Olympics, the lab detected nine positive A samples over the final two days of competition. However, those results could not be matched to the athletes who provided the flagged specimens because the coded list of names was stolen, lost, or fed into a shredder shortly after the games ended and before lab staff realized it was gone. Nine suspected doping athletes walked free.

In Seoul, no one intervened for Johnson. No thieves, no shredders, no smashed bottles, no cash pressed discreetly into palms. The only notable moment in his process arose when the sprinter volunteered the sabotage theory.

"I knew there was something funny going on with that guy in doping control," Johnson said. "He shouldn't have been in there."

Beckett asked to hear more. Johnson told him about a tall, dark-skinned American man in the doping control center who must have spiked his beer with stanozolol pills. He recalled that this same man had been hanging around the warm-up track the day before Friday's 100-meter heats, speaking to Johnson briefly at the Canadian tent but only when Francis wasn't around. Nor was this guy a competitor. Johnson now wondered how the stranger could wander freely through restricted areas at the track venue and breeze through doping control center security when his coach, Francis, wasn't even allowed in.

Francis jumped on the mystery man theory, also noting correctly that IOC anti-doping security rules were breached by this man's presence.

Johnson's explanation was shaping up to blame lax security that permitted an American to spike his beer with a steroid, an act that ultimately promoted Carl Lewis to Olympic champion, Brit Linford Christie to silver, and American Calvin Smith to bronze.

This pill-in-the-suds scenario would be a tough sell. It would be even tougher without the American's name, which left officials with no way to find him and question him. Yet it would serve as the only life raft Johnson could cling to when, by that evening, Park's analysis of the B sample also showed the sprinter's urine contained stanozolol metabolites.

Again, time galloped. The IOC Medical Commission convened a hearing for Johnson at 10:00 that evening. The committee would hear Johnson's defense and make a recommendation on whether to disqualify him from the games. That recommendation would go to the IOC's executive board the next morning, Tuesday, September 27, where members would vote with a show of hands to accept or reject the commission's decision.

Now, the race was on for Canadian officials to find a suitable Canadian lawyer with an experienced sports background to represent Johnson. The only one in town, literally, was Montreal's Richard Pound, a former Olympic swimmer and international tax lawyer. He was intelligent, quick-witted, and widely considered the successor to the IOC's Spanish president, Juan Antonio Samaranch.

Pound had many areas of expertise in sport and law, but forensic toxicology was not one of them. His IOC colleagues would exploit that.

* * *

It was around noon on Monday, September 26, when Juan Antonio Samaranch spotted Richard Pound entering the Spaniard's sprawling Shilla hotel suite. Well-heeled games sponsors were milling about the luncheon tables, ready to tuck in and rub shoulders with Olympic officials. Moving nimbly through the crowd of suits, Samaranch intercepted Pound and steered him into the suite's empty bedroom.

Pound wondered what was so urgent that they had to hide from their guests. Samaranch told him: An unthinkable drug scandal was about to explode, and it involved Ben Johnson.

"Oh shit!" said Pound.

He instantly understood the magnitude of Johnson's trouble. If the A sample was positive, the B sample would be too.

Worse, whispers that Johnson was in trouble were circulating. He'd been seen at the main testing lab, and there was only one reason an athlete would be there: to open a B sample. Samaranch knew word was spilling out and that the media would be calling.

Mind racing, Pound returned to the luncheon for the games' best clients, many of whom he knew well. He was the IOC's top money man, whose skill in selling the Olympics to media and corporations accounted for most of the IOC's revenue in those days. He'd sat across negotiating tables with these luncheon guests, coaxing fortunes from them. He hoped his poker face held no tells.

"I remember sitting beside the wife of one of the Coca-Cola directors, and she said, 'I'm so glad your nice Ben Johnson beat that dreadful Carl Lewis, and I said, 'thank you very much,'" Pound said of forcing small talk while the disastrous doping news preoccupied him.

As soon as the meal ended, he hustled to his Shilla suite to call Carol Anne Letheren. They arranged an urgent meeting in his room with other officials, including Dr. William Stanish and Canadian Olympic Association president Roger Jackson.

As this meeting was being called, Francis and Johnson were being driven separately to the Shilla from the main testing lab. Francis arrived first and asked Pound for legal assistance, but the lawyer's help would not be automatic. Pound recognized his obvious conflicts of interest if he advocated for Johnson in a formal IOC setting. He'd already leveraged his position to make Olympic track officials squirm when he complained about Johnson's false start in the semifinals. Trying to overturn a doping violation for a fellow Canadian was a much different matter.

"I said, 'I'm conflicted up the yin-yang here,'" he told Francis.

Pound also noted a bizarre situation could occur: as an IOC executive, he would participate in the final vote to strip Johnson of his gold medal should the lawyer fail to convince the medical commission the sprinter had not doped.

"I'm vice president of the IOC, and if this [doping positive] does not go away tomorrow morning at the executive board meeting, I'm going to be part of the decision of whether he's disqualified or not."

Pound wanted to interview Johnson before committing to his cause. His wife, Julie, went to the Shilla lobby to escort Johnson up to the suite. She tried to make the sprinter's presence in the IOC's hotel look casual to the curious onlookers staring at the pair. Johnson said Pound stopped him as soon as he entered the suite.

"Charlie was already inside the room, and Pound held me back by my hand and said, 'Tell me what you did. Are you taking anything?'" Johnson recalled as Pound looked directly into his eyes.

"I looked at [Pound] and said, 'No, I'm not taking anything.' He said, 'Are you sure?' I said, 'Yes.'"

It would be the same response all day: deny, deny, deny.

That denial may have been partly based on fear that he'd end up without legal help. Pound had warned Johnson that he would not represent him if he believed the sprinter was guilty. Francis had made him suspicious. In the suite, the coach blurted out that he didn't want his athletes on stanozolol because it made their muscles tight, a statement Pound found troubling. He thought this may be a case of *what* type of steroid Johnson was using, not *how* it got into his system.

Though he was wary of Francis, Johnson had professed innocence, and this was about the athlete. "I told him I'd see what I could do because it's going to be an uphill struggle," Pound said. "In those early-ish days in the analysis business, [testers] were far more likely to *miss* that something was there than to *find* something that was not there."

After Pound finished his private chat with the sprinter, they joined the group meeting. Francis urged Pound to deploy his IOC authority to find an excuse to quash the test results. Pound's response was like a dagger to Johnson's heart.

"Charlie was asking, 'How can we make this thing go away?' and Dick said, 'We can't do anything about it now because it's been leaked to the media,'" Johnson said.

If Pound, one of the IOC's most powerful men, had no pull, he would be dead. He wondered if the lawyer was protecting his own reputation by not calling in favors. "I said in my mind: 'This guy's not really helping me. He's running for IOC president . . . how's this guy going to defend me?'"

Yet Johnson didn't object to Pound's representation at the time. He didn't say much at all. Some in the room thought he looked disinterested, but that was not the case. Johnson said he was traumatized, emotionally numb and nearly paralyzed with fear, although outwardly calm. Not even Francis, normally rock steady but now panicked, recognized his sprinter's fraught psychological state.

Pound hurried down the hall to ask Samaranch to waive any conflict-of-interest concerns in defending Johnson. The IOC president signed off on the request but warned the younger man he was courting a damaging fallout to his Olympic career through this action. Pound understood.

He hustled to build a "reasonable doubt" defense. It would be two-pronged, anchored by Johnson's denial that he'd taken stanozolol. On top of that, Pound would claim doping control security was breached by unauthorized people in the room, which would introduce the mystery man's presence and the sabotage theory.

As for the mystery man, Johnson couldn't summon his name, not even when Francis begged him to try. Francis had not been in doping control. Had he been there, Johnson said his coach would have recognized Andre Jackson as a friend of Carl Lewis.

Pound believed it was better not to find the stranger because he may have had a legitimate reason for being in doping control, and then the sabotage theory, shaky as it was, would be sunk.

Johnson did not attend his own hearing. He said he was told to stay away; Pound recalled that the sprinter didn't want to be there.

"The Canadian collective view was that it was probably better that Ben was not there because Ben had nothing to say, and we were afraid Ben might say something to make things worse," Pound said.

At the time, still in shock, Johnson didn't argue about being sent back to his hotel room to wait it out. He told his mother, Gloria, what had happened and what could happen. She didn't judge or blame. Gloria sat by his bed, gently stroking his forehead as he lay staring at the ceiling, hands clasped behind his head. She told him everything was going to be okay.

Francis would wait it out too, pacing the Shilla hotel lobby, a throbbing toothache adding to his misery. The collective view deemed it best that the coach shouldn't attend the hearing either.

It would be all over shortly after midnight.

CHAPTER THREE

THE TROPHY

Ben Johnson's heart raced as he lay on his hotel room bed. How could he have failed a doping test? And how could it have been stanozolol? He feverishly rehashed his doping history.

The anabolic steroid program Charlie Francis and his team doctor, Jamie Astaphan, devised three years earlier had seemed foolproof: they'd steered their athletes away from muscle-stiffening stanozolol and to furazabol, an injectable steroid that was undetectable in anti-doping labs. Sabotage was the only act that made sense.

But was it also possible that the state-of-the-art Olympic lab machinery produced a false positive? Or had Astaphan somehow screwed up? The doctor turned to the black market on occasion to buy drugs; did he really know what was in those vials? In May 1988, Johnson injured his hamstring and flew to St. Kitts to work with Astaphan during a brief feud with Francis. The doctor, who had a practice on the island where he was born, gave the sprinter a few stanozolol pills to speed muscle healing during rehab sessions. But surely, five months later, that oral dose was long gone from his system.

Different scenarios looped endlessly, hopelessly, through his mind. Johnson retraced the critical weeks leading up to the Seoul Olympics. He believed a key place to start was after his St. Kitts escape, after he'd buried the hatchet with Francis and returned to competition in early August.

He'd romped to victory in the Canadian Olympic team trials in Ottawa, Canada's capital, on August 6, with a wind-aided 9.90, a strong showing, even with a gentle tailwind. His hamstring appeared to be healed. Then he, Francis, and teammates from the Mazda Optimist club, several of them Olympians, headed off on a short pre-Seoul European tour.

In Italy, Johnson won an event in Sestriere with a time of 9.98 on August 10. Slower than in Ottawa, but good. Three days later, he ran a relay leg at a meet in Cesenatico; his hamstring was not feeling right and his stride was a bit off, but under Astaphan's advice, Johnson and Francis agreed it was safe to race in Zurich's high-profile Weltklasse meet on August 17.

The Zurich commitment was no casual decision. Johnson and Carl Lewis would meet outdoors for the first time that year after each had accused the other of dodging head-to-head races. The Canadian held the Weltklasse edge, beating Lewis three straight years from 1985 to 1987 in tough international fields.

The 1988 event was hyped as a Johnson–Lewis pre-Olympic show-down, the final race before Seoul. This time, Lewis was triumphant with a time of 9.93. Compatriot Calvin Smith was second at 9.97. Johnson finished in 10 flat. Lewis exulted in the win, saying he was ready to take gold in Seoul. Johnson was nonplussed, vowing he'd be in peak form by the Olympics.

Francis didn't agree with his star's bravado. He saw deterioration, a concern that was heightened after their next stop in the German city of Cologne, where Johnson was even slower; he ran third in 10.26 seconds. His times were moving the wrong way.

Francis canceled Johnson's final European race. He had concerns about his other Mazda Optimist Olympians, too: sprinter Angella Issajenko and hurdler Mark McKoy were struggling. Whether those struggles were linked to racing conditions in Europe or general fatigue from traveling, an emergency course of action was needed. The solution was a few days of rest and a mini-cycle of restorative steroids.

It should be noted here that doses were usually guesswork, among not just the Optimist group but all steroid users. Amounts were often decided by trial and error. Did it make an athlete's muscles too stiff to train? If yes, then lower the dose or change drugs. Sometimes, doses were based on information from other users, so-called experts in the field (i.e., bodybuilders or underground steroid manuals). Even Astaphan made assumptions when determining the dose and days the drugs should be taken, also known as the cycle. It follows that clearance times were also guesswork.

Between August 24 and 28, Johnson was to receive three injections of furazabol and three of another banned substance called human growth hormone (HGH was perceived to have anabolic effects and was undetectable at that time). Drug stacking like this was not unusual for the group. That mini-cycle gave Johnson thirteen days of clearance time before a pre-Olympic meet near Tokyo, where there was a possibility of being drug tested, and twenty-six days before the 100-meter final in Seoul. The team's preferred clearance time was twenty-eight days, but sometimes it was half that if a racing opportunity like the Tokyo meet came up.

In a departure from his typical doping oversight, Astaphan arranged for the runners to receive diapulse treatments at a Toronto clinic. These used electromagnetic waves to increase blood flow deep within tissue. The group members assumed Astaphan wanted extra insurance to excrete traces of steroid metabolites from their systems before the Tokyo meet.

Johnson says he skipped two or three injections in Toronto and that his clearance time before the gold medal race was twenty-eight days, not twenty-six as later calculated at a public inquiry. He only wanted a quickie steroid top-up in Toronto as insurance for his injured hamstring. Hastening muscle and tissue healing was another steroid use for the Optimist group.

"I needed just enough for recovery, to get me back on my feet for the Games, and that's what I did," Johnson said.

This "harmless low-dose" mindset was scoffed at by medical experts, who would later testify at an inquiry that no steroid dose is safe for a healthy person not in clinical need of the drug. However, in Johnson's world, low-dose steroid cycles were seen as just one of many elements required to create a perfect race, no different from proper coaching, good nutrition, weightlifting sessions, vitamins, hydration, sleep, and massage therapy.

Like his coach, Johnson reasoned that moralizing about cheating was a waste of time since he suspected others of doping, too. He also believed that a short series of steroid injections was useless without putting in hundreds of hours of tough training and competition. "With my natural ability, I was able to do the rest on my own," is how he put the drug into context.

The reality is that doping gave him an edge to build speed and endurance and hoist greater loads in the weight room—he maxed out his bench press at 425 pounds (any heavier would adversely affect his track performance). The drugs and the training strengthened his muscles and permitted them to recover more quickly. It all made him faster. According to Francis, when Johnson ran drug-free, he automatically gave up a stride length over 100 meters to cheating rivals whose steroid use went undetected. When Johnson turned to steroids at Francis's suggestion to level the playing field, his increased power and speed closed that stride-length gap, and then some.

Johnson's final few days on the track in Toronto before jetting to Seoul seemed to support his steroid philosophy that less is more. He said his speed over 200-meter endurance drills was 20 seconds flat, the best he'd ever run. Johnson figured that rate meant he could hit 9.79, 9.78, or lower by the Olympic final, far faster than his world record of 9.83 in Rome. When Johnson discussed those times publicly, track aficionados laughed. No one could possibly run that fast, not even the man who put 9.83 in the record book.

Canada's Olympic contingent, nearly four hundred athletes from all sports, was to depart for Seoul from Vancouver in stages in early September. Track-and-field athletes, including Francis's sprinters, flew first to Japan for a final training camp in Narita, about sixty kilometers from Tokyo, where a pre-games meet was scheduled.

In Narita, Astaphan gave Johnson diuretic pills. This was also unusual. At first, Johnson didn't ask what pills he was taking or why. He complied, but complained after a few sleepless nights. "I started receiving these pills from Jamie, and he said, 'Take this, drink glasses of water for hydration,'" said Johnson, whose Narita training consisted of lifting light weights, easy running drills, and soaking in baths of hot and cold water. "I couldn't sleep. I was going to the washroom seven times a night. Now, I'm getting tired because I can't sleep, and I need my rest."

When Johnson finally asked about the medication, the doctor explained they were diuretics to eliminate excess water. "We were drinking lots of water, and he [Astaphan] wanted to get rid of that water weight," said Johnson, who lost a few pounds but stopped taking the pills. "If you have 10 pounds of water on you, that's a lot of weight to carry [into competition]."

Diuretics are on the IOC's banned substance list. They can mask the presence of other banned drugs, like steroids, and hasten their elimination from the body. Even though furazabol was not something testers could yet detect, the group still operated by better-safe-than-sorry guidelines.

At the Tokyo meet, Johnson skipped the 100 meters but ran a relay leg. He was not selected for drug testing but wasn't worried if he had been. He believed his system was already flushed clean. He was also pleased his speed endurance was back, his hamstring was trouble-free and, more importantly, he and Francis were a team once more.

"One mind," Johnson said of their unspoken connection.

Like his mother, Gloria, Johnson believes in a higher spiritual power. Before leaving Japan for the Korean peninsula, Johnson heard about a beautiful local Buddhist temple. Intrigued, he arranged a visit to "give praise" to God.

There, Johnson requested a personal blessing. A Buddhist priest recognized him and obliged. The holy man prayed intently over him while wispy incense smoke curled around Johnson's face and body. It turns out the priest must have been a sports fan, too.

"He said, 'You will do good, you will win the gold medal.' And I said, 'I certainly hope so because I'm here to do everything good,'" Johnson recalled.

That temple visit was one of the last items on the Narita leg of the Olympic journey. The Francis-led group left Japan and arrived in Seoul on September 16. Johnson and his coach were mobbed in Kimpo Airport by fans and media clamoring to meet the fastest man on Earth. Annoyed there was no security for them, they pushed through the aggressive crowd—Korean media described Johnson as rude and foulmouthed—which followed to their awaiting vehicles. The pair sped off to the athletes' village.

Johnson lasted one night in the Olympic dorms. The next day, he quietly checked into the Hilton Hotel, under his mother's name, to escape the noisy village and snooping media. He'd learned from his 1984 games experience that the athletes' village was not an optimal place to reside before the biggest competition of one's life. Besides, he could afford a hotel room as well as a second suite for his mother Gloria and sister Jean; Johnson was already a multi-millionaire, pulling in nearly $450,000 (US) a month in sponsorships and endorsements.

"I didn't want to be around a lot of people screaming and coming in late at night or bothering me for photographs," he said. "I just wanted to be alone so I could focus on the race."

He and Lewis still managed to make time for pre-race chest pounding. At the end of a training session in Seoul, Lewis answered questions from the milling media about his 100-meter prospects. "The gold medal is mine," he said. "I'll never lose to Ben Johnson again."

Johnson was slightly more expansive at a news conference for Canadian media two days later. "This time, Carl Lewis is going to have to run my race. He's going to have to catch me if he wants to beat me. That's the way it's going to be. I'm No. One and I'm not going to lose."

Johnson also had to answer media questions about skipping out on the opening ceremonies, where he was expected to be Canada's flag bearer. Lewis had happily attended the event with the US contingent, so why couldn't he?

Johnson chose to watch the parade of nations on television in his air-conditioned hotel room, with Francis's blessing. Canadian synchronized swimming world champion, Carolyn Waldo, replaced him as flag bearer. Accusations of being selfish or unpatriotic didn't bother him; he excelled at blocking out distraction when a race was pending.

"Two and a half, three hours, standing out there in a field, under the sun, to hear somebody talk? No thanks," Johnson said.

There was also a therapeutic reason behind his no-show. A sudden bout of bursitis in his left heel had inflamed his Achilles tendon and made it painful to touch. He couldn't walk on his left leg properly, never mind run full-out. He'd hoped to keep this under wraps, but a *Toronto Star* article broke the story.

"New injury hits Big Ben as the Seoul Games begin" was the headline on September 17, 1988. Francis downplayed the story as inaccurate and claimed Johnson was fit, which was not the case. He was laid up, hurt.

Astaphan visited Johnson's hotel room on the Monday of that week, six days before the gold medal final, with another type of corticosteroid to treat the bursitis. (A corticosteroid is an anti-inflammatory drug and is in a different steroid class from banned anabolic steroids.) The therapeutic corticosteroid shot was a common, permissible treatment for the ailment. Johnson remembers gritting his teeth and trying not to squirm when the needle plunged in deeply and uncomfortably.

As he awaited his fate in his Seoul hotel room, Johnson wondered if this injection had been something other than a corticosteroid. The doctor and the sprinter had been butting heads over money. Shortly after arriving in Seoul, Astaphan demanded $1 million (US) from Johnson to pay for the doctor's exclusive attention and, obviously, ensure his silence. Johnson was shocked at the bold request and the amount, so close to race day. The sprinter was also dumbfounded when two Australian athletes asked the doctor—in front of him—if he could fix them up with steroids, and Astaphan assured the pair he could. Johnson realized his drug secrets were being spread by his braggart doctor. If anyone suspected the Toronto sprinter was doping, Astaphan had just confirmed it to the Aussies.

"I was so angry, I said I was firing him after the games," Johnson said. "Jamie had a big mouth."

The two argued but cooled down quickly enough to save their working relationship for the balance of the Olympics. To keep the peace and prevent more careless chatter, Johnson assured Astaphan he'd get his payday when the gold medal was around his neck.

Despite Astaphan's indiscretions, it's improbable he'd jeopardize a cash windfall by deliberately injecting the sprinter with stanozolol days before the race. It made no sense. Johnson was his golden goose. Johnson was everybody's golden goose: the Canadian Track and Field Association made about $1 million in revenue off him leading up to Seoul. A disqualification meant no one got money. Additionally, Astaphan's license to practice medicine could be yanked if he was linked to a drug scandal or the extortion of a patient.

Besides, the cortisone injection had worked. The pain and swelling in Johnson's Achilles subsided quickly. He took additional measures to accelerate the repairs; he didn't leave his hotel room for three days to keep weight off his feet.

"I put a 'do not disturb' sign on my door, and even though I loved my mother to death, my mum kept away and just let me be," he said, recalling that he filled in room service menus each morning for all meals and snacks to be delivered and watched a lot of movies.

"I just started to meditate about the race. Everything had to be precise. How I am going to warm up, what I'm going to do in each segment of the race, and precisely the time I want to run in each round. Then I locked it in my mind."

By Thursday, September 22, Johnson felt good enough to try a light afternoon workout at the warm-up track beside the main Olympic stadium. He was pleased with how he felt. So pleased, he decided to reward himself with a trip to a dance club and a glass of champagne that night.

Johnson had a crush on American runner Sherri Howard and invited her to join him. She agreed. Johnson was sipping bubbly with his 100-meter heats the next morning and enjoying her company.

He left Howard's side briefly to accommodate an autograph seeker, then hustled back to finish his drink. "You can't leave a girl like that alone too long," he said, chuckling. Around midnight, Johnson bid Howard a friendly good night and headed back to the Hilton.

Now, having tested positive, he worried about leaving his champagne unattended. Had someone slipped pills into his drink? Even if that were the case, Pound had reminded Johnson that an athlete was solely responsible for all food and drink consumed before a competition. If a potential sabotage scenario occurred after his race, Johnson might have a shot at clearing himself.

Yet another sabotage possibility that occurred to the brooding sprinter dated from the day of the men's 100-meter heats. He drank from his water bottle after racing in his two heats and swore something was amiss.

Before a race, runners put their belongings—sweats, flat running shoes, a water bottle—in a basket assigned to their lane. In Seoul,

Olympic volunteers removed the numbered baskets and carried them down to the finish lane area, where they were lined up in lane order. The items were watched by the volunteers until the runners reclaimed them. For the fifteen or so minutes the baskets were out of their sight, runners would have no way of knowing if their belongings had been tampered with.

Johnson said he drank from his water bottle after each Friday heat. That night, he felt dizzy and sick to his stomach. His insides were cramping violently, but he could not vomit. He complained to his mother about how ill he was, but she doubted it was anything but temporary discomfort. Johnson chugged tap water to ease the symptoms, took some vitamins, and had Waldemar Matuszewski massage his leg muscles, which felt stiff. He went to bed early, slept soundly, and awoke with the stomach cramps mercifully resolved.

* * *

Nearly two dozen members of the IOC medical commission's subcommittee on doping, a specialized group of drug detection experts, filled one end of the conference room at the Shilla Hotel on the night of Monday, September 26. Ben Johnson's 10 p.m. hearing was underway, with a small Canadian delegation facing the IOC panel. The atmosphere was tense.

German chemist Manfred Donike chaired the hearing. Swedish commission member Arne Ljungqvist was also present, sitting near American Don Catlin and Australian Kenneth Fitch. Ljungqvist was surprised when he noticed Johnson's absence.

"I remember talking to Don or Ken and saying, 'Ben is not here,'" the Swede said. "It was supposed to be a hearing with him."

A country's delegation had the right to choose how to proceed, and excluding Johnson from the proceedings was permitted. However, seeing Pound lead the sprinter's defense troubled panelists, who perceived it as a form of intimidation. The Canadian was an IOC executive superstar, not a run-of-the-mill glad-hander. The IOC's financial health was reliant on Pound, and in the 1980s, Samaranch valued him for going nose-to-nose with equally tough American television network executives in their bids for broadcast rights.

When later asked if it was a conflict of interest to have a high-ranking IOC executive advocating for a Canadian gold medalist accused of doping, Ljungqvist replied: "My answer to that is yes. Normally it would be the head of the [country's] Olympic delegation, and we were expecting Carol Anne Letheren [Canadian *chef de mission*] to be there, leading the delegation." Medical commission members were so annoyed at Pound's dramatic appearance to defend a doping case that they soon voted unanimously to demand Samaranch ban any other IOC vice president from doing the same.

Early in the hearing, the Canadians, including Letheren, Roger Jackson, and chief medical officer Dr. William Stanish, were given deflating news: lab director Jong-sei Park had analyzed aliquots (small portions) from Johnson's B sample vial at least twice, and each time the result was positive for stanozolol. The lab detected 80 nanograms per milliliter of stanozolol metabolites in Johnson's urine, a relatively large amount to be found on a race day after weeks of clearance time. When it came to doping violations involving anabolic steroids, the metabolite amount in the urine didn't matter. Their mere presence was an automatic positive. Unless a credible explanation was forthcoming, Johnson faced certain disqualification.

It was left to Pound to persuade an expert panel that Johnson's positive was the result of a cloak-and-dagger scheme that sounded like it was ripped from the pages of a spy novel. Jackson knew from the look on the panelists' faces that they weren't buying it.

"You can imagine him telling that story in front of twenty skeptical doping experts, but that was the only explanation Dick could offer, saying it had come from Ben," he said.

Still, Jackson said Pound delivered as many punches as he could while "walking a very fine line" in front of his colleagues. The IOC vice president told panelists that the sprinter was "a slow learner" and that after drinking several beers, Johnson was "less than his normal self" at the post-race press conference.

"Whether he believed [the sabotage explanation] or not, he was trying to protect Ben in the sense that he wanted to present the story Ben told him," Jackson said.

Pound's attempt to raise security breaches at the doping control center was shot down by Ljungqvist, who was at the facility on the day of the men's 100-meter final.

Ljungqvist assured Pound that no interloper had gained access to the restricted area (the small office containing a toilet) or the larger waiting room beyond. A special pass authorizing entry was required. It was later determined that Carl Lewis's friend, Andre Jackson, had one of those passes, even though he wasn't an athlete, coach, or one of those official "accompanying persons" chosen by a medalist to be there on September 24. The Swede would not remember seeing Jackson.

Ljungqvist recalled that Johnson took "some time" to provide his specimen, and the doctor, Johnson, and Waldemar Matuszewski idly chatted as the doping control room emptied. On that day, athletes from other events were also tested.

"In the end, it was just us three, as far as I can remember, who were staying the longest. Then I was free to leave, also," Ljungqvist said.

Regarding the porous security claim, Johnson had a paperwork problem.

After providing his sample, Johnson signed an official form (required of all athletes) agreeing that he was satisfied with the doping control process. He had not reported anything amiss, such as an unauthorized person near him. This sign-off didn't help, although no one thought to mention Johnson's quick consumption of six to eight beers, which may have impaired his judgment before signing the form.

Pound tossed all the exculpatory scenarios he could at the panel, from a doctored water bottle used after the heats, another water bottle contamination opportunity during the post-race chaos around Johnson at the finish line, to a beer saboteur. He asked that "the Olympic champion be given the benefit of the doubt," which was Pound's way of hoping the all-powerful anti-doping fraternity would let the Olympics' biggest hero off the hook.

"You get to the point where you have to throw yourself on the mercy of the court," he said.

As for the assertion that Johnson's name had been improperly leaked after his A sample turned up positive, that, too, was swatted down by commission panelists, although insiders were indeed talking about the impending scandal. Over a late-night dinner between two IOC medical commission members working with the Seoul lab, shortly after Johnson's preliminary A sample was red-flagged, Canadian Robert Dugal told American Don Catlin that the United States had won another gold medal because Johnson's A sample was positive. This is not to suggest either man further shared this confidential information, but people were gossiping about Johnson's doping trouble the day before the sprinter was informed his A sample was positive.

At this point in the hearing, the German chair, Donike, dropped a bombshell.

An Olympic cyclist-turned-pioneering chemist, he had heard quite enough from Pound. He was peeved at the allegations of lax security and decided to highjack the proceedings.

"He said, 'Mr. Pound, would you be interested in hearing about the scientific results of the tests'?" Pound recalled, imitating a German accent.

The IOC vice president sensed Donike was about to ambush him. He was right. Donike explained that in addition to stanozolol metabolites in Johnson's urine, a second screening test being

40

developed by the chemist, called endocrine profiling, revealed that Johnson was, in fact, a longtime steroid user.

The Canadians gasped. They didn't immediately understand the science behind Donike's newfangled test, but they knew that the German had a reputation for testing innovations and that Johnson's predicament had gone from bad to worse.

"We had no idea," said Jackson of the news Johnson had been doping all along.

It was explained to the shocked Canadians that endocrine profiling is a way to measure natural testosterone levels produced by the body. Donike told the gathering that Johnson's renal cortex function was suppressed, an indicator he'd been doping for some time, and that the endocrine profiling reading was not the result of a single recent dose, sabotage or not.

Pound had no rebuttal to the Donike blindside. The defense rested rather meekly. No one in the Canadian group complained about the lack of disclosure or challenged the validity of this new test.

The IOC medical commission panelists retired to discuss the case in camera. A fast decision was expected.

An hour ticked by. Then ninety minutes. Pound, who'd been sent to a separate room to wait with the Canadian group, including Francis, was hopeful. Jackson was not.

"We were in that room for an hour and a half to two hours. It was ridiculous. I said to Dick, 'How can you think this is going to be anything other than a guilty verdict? From the evidence of the A and B samples and from the history of the [long-term] use, it looks like he got caught,'" Jackson said.

"And Dick said: 'You never know what a jury will do. The longer they take, the better it is. They are trying to figure out whether this really was a violation or not.'"

Pound's optimism was soon dashed. The Canadians were recalled close to 1 a.m. on Tuesday, September 27. The medical commissioners would recommend to the IOC executive committee that Johnson be disqualified, his world record annulled, and his medal forfeited immediately.

IOC justice was speedy. It took about twenty-four hours from the time Letheren received de Merode's letter to the recommendation that Johnson be stripped of his gold medal. The IOC executive committee, including Pound, voted unanimously at 9 a.m. on Tuesday to accept the medical commission's recommendation. In 1988, there was no sports-related avenue to appeal an IOC doping disqualification decision, or so Johnson was led to believe.

Jackson remembers talking to Francis after he was told of the decision. The coach's reaction startled him.

"Charlie's only question to me, after just absorbing this information, was: 'Do they think it was injected or taken orally?' I said I have no idea . . . but it had an impact on Charlie because whatever the answer was, [Francis and Johnson] might have used the wrong process to juice him up, right?" Jackson said.

"So that confirmed in my mind that he knew they had been using."

* * *

It remained to tell Ben Johnson. Charlie Francis drove to the Hilton with Carol Anne Letheren and Dr. William Stanish. Francis asked for half an hour alone with Johnson to break the disqualification news to him. They agreed.

While in Johnson's room, Francis reassured him that the conspiracy of silence would remain intact. They'd meet back in Toronto and quickly get a united message of innocence out to the public.

"Charlie said, 'Do not talk to anybody. Go home. We're all going to go home, and we're going to sit down and figure things out, what to say to the media,'" Johnson said.

Around 3:30 a.m., Letheren knocked on Johnson's hotel room door. She was accompanied by Ottawa-based RCMP inspector Larry Comeau, who supervised Canada's security detail in Seoul with the assistance of Korean law enforcement.

Gloria was now at her son's side, as was his sister, Jean. They'd been crying. Johnson's agent, Larry Heidebrecht, was in the room, too, along with Dr. Jamie Astaphan.

"Carol Anne came in and said, 'Ben, this is a hard thing I have to say, but I need for you to give me the gold medal back,'" Johnson recalled, noting she was crying.

"I reached down to get it. I had tears in my eyes. She said, 'I'm sorry I have to do this.' I looked up and gave it to her."

Gloria sobbed. Johnson hugged her, told her not to worry and that "nobody died."

He'd never told his mother he was using steroids, but he sensed she'd known. Two years earlier, Gloria Johnson began warning of potential danger when he became the world's top-ranked sprinter. She would tell him, "Son, they can't beat you on the track, they can only beat you in the doping room." She'd remind him not to eat or drink anything given to him by strangers. "I kept that in my head all the time, all the time, all the time, try to stay away from jealous people."

Next, Comeau took command. His priority was to get Johnson and his family swiftly and safely out of Korea.

As a law enforcement guest in Korea, Comeau had to liaise with the Seoul police force to protect Canadian Olympians, whatever the daily need might be. This need was a big one. Comeau instructed the Johnson family to pack immediately. The Mountie had requested help from the Seoul police to ensure "safe passage" for the Johnsons to Kimpo airport to catch the first Korean Airlines flight to New York City. By now, it was around 4 a.m. The airport should be empty at this hour, Comeau thought as he climbed into a police vehicle with the sprinter.

Kimpo wasn't empty. It was a media circus. Johnson's bust was already moving on international news wires.

"Somehow, it leaked out that we were going to the airport," Comeau said. "When we got there, it was clear that the media knew Ben would be there and at what time he'd be there. It was madness."

The plan had been to protect Johnson, not expose him to a mob. The Johnsons had to be ringed by police, including Comeau, who shouldered their way through the surging airport crowd. Reporters and photographers rushed the sprinter, yelling questions and waving cameras. Others stood on chairs, benches, and stairs, jostling for the best view. The besieged runner held his briefcase up to his face, trying to avoid photographers.

Once the family was in the departure area, the trick was getting the sprinter and his entourage—Astaphan was there, too—onto a plane not filled with reporters who were wildly buying plane tickets on spec. Not many suspected he'd fly to New York City. Vancouver was the odds-on bet.

By coincidence, longtime Ottawa high jump coach Pat Reid was on the New York-bound jet pushing back from the gate. Reid was a national junior team coach who'd made a four-day trip to Seoul to watch one of his jumpers compete. When the jet suddenly stopped on the tarmac, Reid looked out his window. He saw a small vehicle carrying a group of people and another vehicle with a set of portable stairs driving to the plane. The jet's forward door opened, the stairs were secured, and the Johnsons boarded, carrying all their luggage.

Reid knew of Johnson's disqualification. The news was everywhere. In the airport, the media asked Reid, who was wearing a junior national team track suit, if he was Charlie Francis.

Reid walked to the front of the plane after takeoff and saw the sprinter sitting in a jump seat. The family's luggage was strapped into empty passenger seats. Reid was also the director of the Ottawa indoor meet that Johnson competed in for years, and they knew each other. They spoke for about thirty minutes.

"He said, 'Somebody put something in my water,'" said Reid, recalling that Astaphan came over to listen to their conversation, said nothing, and didn't introduce himself. Johnson was glad to see a friendly face and told Reid they'd reconnect on the ground in New York, then catch a connecting flight to Toronto together.

* * *

In the Olympic media village, a phone call from *Toronto Star* sports editor Gerry Hall woke me around 4:30 a.m. Hall barked that Johnson had tested positive and was disqualified from the games, so go find him. The news was moving across wire services.

Colleague Al Sokol had received a similar call in his room. We dashed out of the media village together to find a taxi in the pre-dawn. Could we get the Olympic scoop of the century—find Johnson and have him tell all? Alas, we noticed a trickle of reporters quietly running behind us to the cab stands. Lights began to flick on across darkened media dorms. Photographers were also hustling out, cameras roped around their necks and slapping against their canvas vests, their many pockets stuffed with film.

There would be no scoop. The whole world seemed to know the news before the sun rose on the Korean peninsula on Tuesday. I'd guessed wrong and went to the Hilton Hotel to find Johnson. He was long gone.

* * *

There was pandemonium at JFK Airport. Reporters flooded the terminal. Making matters worse, the Johnson group had to transfer from JFK and get to La Guardia to catch the Toronto flight. Jamie

Astaphan secured a driver who waited curbside. Pat Reid helped ferry a mountain of luggage to the vehicle, and once Johnson's mother and sister were safely buckled in, the sprinter ran out and dove into a back seat. The media chased him, breaking a glass terminal door with a mighty crash, Reid said.

The party sped to La Guardia, where, again, reporters and photographers were buying fistfuls of tickets for Toronto-bound flights. They tried to buy VIP lounge memberships for various airlines on the chance of snagging an interview with Johnson while he waited to depart.

The RCMP's Larry Comeau had already arranged for additional FBI security in New York for Johnson through an FBI colleague in Seoul. The FBI agents hustled the Johnson group through a backdoor to clear US customs, then tucked the travelers into a private room until takeoff. Their Air Canada flight was almost full and could take all but one: Johnson volunteered to wait for the next northbound jet. No way, said the American agents. They contacted the pilots, who said Johnson could sit in the cockpit with them.

FBI agents directed the plane to pull away from the gate, then stop so the Johnsons and Astaphan could board via mobile stairs. Loads of unhappy reporters watched from the departure lounge while Johnson made his cockpit escape.

More bedlam awaited the sprinter at Toronto's Pearson International. Hundreds of media stood by. The ever-vigilant Comeau had arranged via RCMP headquarters in Ottawa to have officers escort the Johnsons to a waiting limousine.

At home, Johnson muscled through a final media gauntlet of reporters and camera crews staked out at the east-end Toronto home he'd bought for his mother three years earlier. Once safe inside the tidy Scarborough bungalow, he waited to hear from Francis to strategize a public defense. He was counting on it. He needed direction, answers, and comfort. His world had collapsed.

Before his plane touched down at Pearson, Johnson had been declared an athletic outcast by the same government that had hailed him as a Canadian hero three days earlier.

Federal Sports Minister Jean Charest banned him from the national team program for life and strongly suggested Johnson hadn't acted alone, which in turn prompted terrified friends and teammates to lie low or lawyer up.

There would be no high-profile visitors to the bungalow.

"I was waiting for days and days and days in Scarborough," he said. "But no one came."

Not Francis. Not Astaphan. No one from the Canadian Track and Field Association.

At the most vulnerable moment of his athletic career, Johnson was entirely alone.

CHAPTER FOUR

CANADIAN TO JAMAICAN

The IOC had landed a trophy catch. Nobody bigger had ever fallen like this. The formal announcement of Ben Johnson's disqualification from the Olympics and the forfeiture of his gold medal was a somber, righteous news conference at the Shilla. Officials boasted that their crack anti-doping squad would spare no one—not even a colossal track star—to rid sport of drugs. People believed it. Purportedly, a new, clean era was underway.

Next, the International Amateur Athletic Federation held its own news conference at a nearby hotel. As soon as the IOC expelled Johnson, his case became the responsibility of his international sports federation. Arne Ljungqvist, who was also an IAAF vice president and chairman of the federation's own medical commission, recalled a curious moment during his drive to the news conference with federation president Primo Nebiolo. The Italian, usually a hog for the limelight, bailed out on this historic moment.

"He was quite keen on appearing in front of the world media, but he took me on the ride from the IOC hotel and in the car told me, 'Arnold, this conference, you take.'"

Ljungqvist obliged. He remembered getting the same question repeatedly from reporters about Johnson's doping failure: Is this the death of competitive Olympic sport?

"I said it's exactly the opposite," Ljungqvist recalled. "I think this is a great chance for the world sports leader(s) and for the public at large to understand that something needs to be done [about doping] and this cannot go on."

While the press conference was underway in Seoul, most of Johnson's sponsors were dropping him with scalded hands, including Mazda, which had generously underwritten Francis's cherished Optimist sprint club. The tens of millions of dollars Johnson had been expecting from new and existing sponsorship deals vaporized. Even work on a set of commissioned, life-sized sculptures was halted; the artist's depictions of Johnson's flying out of the starting blocks to full stride would wind up in storage.

More than a few international athletes in Seoul buckled. Events were skipped, injuries flared, and some off-the-podium finishes by medal hopes were head-scratchers. Johnson's Toronto teammates felt the pressure. Mark McKoy, a contending hurdler, flew home, despondent, after finishing seventh and skipped the men's relay. Angella Issajenko passed on the 200-meter sprint but remained to run a relay leg. She recalled hearing other Canadian Olympians taunt her and seeing a banner reading "From hero to zero in 24 hours" in the athletes' village courtyard.

At home, the federal government moved aggressively to punish Johnson. Sports Minister Jean Charest was not much older than the twenty-six-year-old sprinter. COA President Roger Jackson made an urgent phone call to Ottawa and tracked down Charest on the House of Commons floor. It was pre-dawn on Tuesday, September 27, for Jackson in Seoul, and it was midafternoon on Monday, September 26, for Charest in Ottawa. Jackson gave Charest a heads-up on the Johnson news, and the minister acted quickly. Without waiting to speak to

Johnson, Charest announced on Monday, while the sprinter was still in transit, that he was banned for life in Canada from competing or receiving government funding.

"I feel disappointed. I feel bad for Ben Johnson. It's obviously a great personal tragedy," Charest told a hastily called news conference in Ottawa. "[The gold medal final] was a moment of great national pride, and in a very short time we have gone from there to now sharing a moment of national disappointment."

Johnson was not the first Canadian athlete to receive a lifetime ban for failing a drug test. But his fame made him the first to command massive national attention for the swift, severe, and very public government sanction.

For days, Johnson's disqualification was the biggest news story in the world. He was also the only track and field Olympian to fail a drug test in Seoul.

Network television and radio kept pace with emerging details faster than newspapers could run their printing presses. Outrage and disappointment were common takes from commentators. Blame flew, too. The first question Jackson faced at the IOC news conference came from a Spanish reporter who demanded to know if he was prepared to resign over the matter.

Canada's life ban contributed to an unprecedented media attack on an amateur athlete. Trigger words and racialized tropes rolled off keyboards and out of microphones with alarming ease. References to Johnson as a Jamaican immigrant were frequent, part of an attack arsenal that today would properly be called out as racist. Some reporters argued for compassion and context commensurate with Johnson's offense—he had not committed a crime—but they were swamped by rolling waves of shaming journalism.

"Thanks Ben. You bastard," wrote Canadian sports columnist Earl McRae in one infamous screed in the *Ottawa Citizen*.

"Why Ben?" asked the tabloid *Toronto Sun*.

The *Toronto Star*'s John Robertson wrote in a somewhat sympathetic column that nothing since the Kennedy assassinations "seems to have affected so many people so profoundly or generated such an overwhelming sadness."

It was even suggested that the sprinter could have an impact on the upcoming federal vote in Canada. "Johnson's Olympic disgrace casts pall over Canadian election," read a headline over a wire story just weeks before voters cast ballots. (Prime Minister Mulroney, who'd called to congratulate Johnson in Seoul after his win, would retain a majority government.)

A cartoon in the *Kingston Whig-Standard* newspaper showed the same image of Johnson in the starting blocks over three frames, but with three different captions. The first stated he was a Canadian. In the second, he was a Jamaican-Canadian, and by the third, he was a Jamaican.

One of the more stunning written reports appeared in *Sports Illustrated* magazine just days after Johnson's disqualification. It was headlined "The Loser." The article accurately reported that Astaphan had given Johnson a cycle of steroids with the sprinter's full knowledge during a six-week stay in St. Kitts during a short split with Francis. It was an explosive revelation—no one but a few insiders would have known this; the piece relied on anonymous sources.

The article also claimed Astaphan had long idolized the Bulgarian team doctors, who were "expert" at evading drug detection. But not in Seoul, apparently. Two Bulgarian weight-lifting gold medalists tested positive early in the games, and the entire weight-lifting team left South Korea. If Astaphan had been following a Bulgarian steroid methodology, as the article suggested, Johnson was ripe for detection.

While the *Sports Illustrated* reporting was sound, the writing characterized Johnson in harsh terms. It claimed he fled Seoul "like a criminal" and that in the starting blocks, he had stared down the track "with a murderous expression." It concluded that his once-bright future had crashed, and he was now "a man with nothing to look forward to but days of shame." The magazine article also praised a few track-and-field Olympians in Seoul, including Carl Lewis, who "are acknowledged to be winners without dope." In fact, Lewis had failed three doping tests earlier that summer but was absolved of the infractions behind closed doors by US Olympic officials, news kept secret for more than a decade.

In time, six of the eight finalists in that 100-meter final in Seoul would be linked directly or indirectly to anti-doping violations.

CHAPTER FIVE
JAMAICA TO CANADA

The Toronto-bound airplane arced gracefully above Montego Bay as it gained altitude, leaving behind a sun-soaked Caribbean island, turquoise waters, and an unhurried way of life. On board, amid sunburnt Canadian tourists wishing their vacations had been longer, were four young Jamaican siblings, jetting to the place their parents had chosen for their futures. A place they had never visited but would now call home.

It was April 29, 1976, a time when Canada was governed by the charming and controversial Pierre Elliott Trudeau. The country's immigration pipeline was frequently filled with arrivals from fellow Commonwealth countries, including Jamaica, and they often chose to settle in Toronto, the growing financial heart of English-speaking Canada.

Gloria Johnson fell for Toronto during a 1972 visit to a friend who'd once been a neighbor in Falmouth, a centuries-old northern Jamaican port town. Gloria absorbed all that the Canadian city offered and envisioned a wider potential for her children. She would have the support of her husband, Ben Sr., to immigrate in 1974, then send for their six children when she'd secured housing and, for the first time in her life, a job outside the home.

It was not a decision made lightly. Life in Falmouth was happy, and the Johnsons were comfortable in their four-bedroom home on the town's main strip, Market Street. They had a personal car in addition to the Jamaica Telephone Company truck Ben Sr. used for work as a repairman. The family was active and social: school, sports, visiting friends, picnics, weekend movies, beach swimming, and Sunday church attendance were part of the routine. But Gloria and Ben Sr. realized Falmouth, the capital town of Trelawny, one of the island's fourteen "parish" regions, was in economic decline, and that meant limited prospects for young people. They wanted more for their four daughters and two sons.

"To be honest, whether in Canada or the United States, it is much easier for a Jamaican to make a living abroad," Ben Sr. told author James Christie.

"A lot have chosen to get out. But if they have a lot of ambition and can get ahead, they can stay right here and do it. It's a lovely country, lovely sunshine and everything, but it's not easy. Not here."

For generations, both branches of Ben Jr.'s family called Jamaica home. They'd lived largely in the Trelawny area, where baking hot days are tempered with breezes rolling off the Caribbean Sea. It's a place of striking beauty with white sandy shorelines, the winding Martha Brae River, and tropical groves in every shade of green. Food hangs from trees, free to pluck. Ben Sr. used to say only an "idiot" would starve in Jamaica since mango and papaya grew wild and teeming fish bit any hook cast in the warm coastal shallows.

The family also has a history that dates back to colonial brutality and enslavement.

In the 1600s, invaders from Spain, then Britain, captured people from African nations and shipped them to Jamaica to work as forced labor, often on British sugar estates. Trelawny would house the most sugarcane plantations in Jamaica: crops grew tall and thick in its fertile soil, and easy access to deep-harbored ports pleased merchants, eager to export their harvests across the Atlantic for cash.

Evidence of Falmouth's colonial past is imprinted on the town in surviving structures, fortress ruins, signage, and historical names that have endured over hundreds of years. Market Street, for instance, was named for the weekly Sunday markets held in the town square. At those gatherings, enslaved Africans (and later "peasants") would gather to sell or trade provisions they'd made, grown, or fished. The William Knibb Memorial Baptist Church is a few minutes' walk from the Johnson home. Knibb was an English missionary and abolitionist who settled in the Falmouth area in 1825. He fearlessly spoke out against slavery, so much so that the British arrested Knibb and other abolitionist ministers in the early days of the Emancipation War of 1831–1832.

The Johnson family's oral history tracks back two centuries, maybe longer, with Ghana being one of the likeliest countries where ancestors were captured by the British. The Jamaican government's genealogical branch traced official family birth, death, and marriage records (with Ben Jr. as the subject applicant) back to the early 1800s.

Ben Jr. learned from his grandmother, Angelina, that the Johnson family survived slavery and that harsh times didn't necessarily end with emancipation. Born in 1895, Angelina passed on the family history when she babysat her grandchildren. "She would tell us stories of when she was a little girl; she would read books at night with her family," Ben Jr. recalled. "But when they heard someone coming near their home, they'd rush to hide the books in a hole in the floor under the kitchen table and turn off the lights." His takeaway from that memory: the local white authorities didn't support education for Black children.

As for the maternal branch, Johnson's aunt, Laura Case, doesn't believe her family descended from enslaved people. She said she's seen no evidence of it, and as a career trade union negotiator who studied labor law, she believes in facts.

When it was time for Ben Johnson Sr. to find a wife in the early 1950s, he traveled to the countryside because, as he told his son, that's where the most beautiful women lived.

Clark's Town, about fourteen miles from Falmouth, is nestled on higher ground, away from the water. Driving into it off the main highway means navigating narrow roads built into the rolling terrain, motoring past a sprawling sugar refinery, then tackling a few blind hairpin turns. Stray dogs and meandering goats share the road, which is peppered with potholes. In Clark's Town, Ben Sr. met Gloria Melrose Case. She was just seventeen years old, a petite woman with a winning smile, bright brown eyes, and a sweet disposition.

"Gloria was a pretty girl, with two dimples right here," said her sister, Laura, pointing to both cheeks. She was so pretty that when Gloria was little, a man tried to kidnap her off the street, but she managed to run away. Laura, in her mid-eighties, confirmed this terrifying episode.

The Case children grew up in a strict but loving Baptist home supervised by parents Aubrey and Sarah Jane Case. Laura described her father as a reclusive man who didn't allow his children to play in other families' homes. Conversely, friends were not permitted in the Case home.

Tall, charming Ben Johnson Sr. offered Gloria a life away from the tightly run Case household. He was a decade older and worldly; he had done a stint in the military toward the end of World War II, deployed to Chicago to work in munitions as part of the Commonwealth's Allied efforts. Later, he secured a good job with the Jamaica Telephone Company. He was also a trained mechanic.

"She decided to marry him, but she needed my father to sign a form to give his permission because she was under eighteen," Laura recalled. "She was determined."

Surprisingly, the man who was so protective of his children agreed. Aubrey Case approved of Ben Sr. as a man who could provide for his daughter.

The couple married in Clark's Town but settled in the Falmouth home the groom had built. Ben Sr. had saved enough money after the war to buy a plot of swampy land on Market Street. He tipped runs of dirt-filled wheelbarrows onto the plot, choking off the water and solidifying the ground for construction. He hired a builder who erected a wide, sunlit residence. It had a covered driveway to one side and enough farmland behind it to house chickens, store salted pork, tend honeybees, and grow vegetables and fruit.

* * *

One of young Ben Jr.'s earliest passions in Falmouth was running. He'd dash off to the local store for his mother, hustling back with bread or vegetables so quickly that she wondered if she'd lost track of time. He'd join friends who liked to race around a neighborhood block, kicking up dust with bare feet and laughing as they sped through the streets. And they played make-believe at full throttle.

"We were always fighting about who got to be [Jamaican Olympic sprint star] Don Quarrie," said Johnson. "Don Quarrie was my hero growing up. He was everyone's hero."

Sometimes the boys placed bets on who could run around the block the fastest. A few pennies here and there, enough to pay for afternoon movies on the weekend if one had a particularly speedy few days. Johnson collected a lot of change and saw a lot of movies at the cinema.

"It was all just for fun," he said of the little boy wagers. "Life was good."

He also recalled sprinting toward trucks that regularly hauled cut sugarcane through Falmouth. He and his buddies would slip alongside the flatbed and not-so-covertly yank a syrupy reed from the neat stacks to chew on.

"The driver always had this big stick, trying to hit us with it while he was driving, to stop us from taking some sugarcane," Johnson said. "But we always got some."

As speedy as young Ben was, he was not as fast as his older brother

Eddie, who trained with a track club. Ben wanted to be like Eddie, hoping to run for his club, but did not make the cut.

School offered other opportunities. He played every sport and game available at the Falmouth All Age School, where students were taught in a spectacular setting on the site of an English garrison, Fort Balcarres, built circa 1811 to protect the Falmouth harbor from marauders. Abandoned army barracks were converted long ago into airy classrooms and offices. These days, the students play soccer on a sandy patch near a weathered stone building that once held gunpowder and weapons. An original cannon sits on rusted wheels, its barrel pointed out to sea. The kids can see the blue water and feel the salty breezes from anywhere in the playground. It is a beautiful place, filled with laughter, chatter, and shrieks of joy.

"The school and the playground haven't changed much," says Johnson. He played soccer on that same patch and ran in school track meets. "We were active all the time; we just ran and ran and ran when we were outside," he said, watching the kids from under an ancient, leafy almond tree, sipping hot pumpkin soup from a local diner.

"We were always playing sports, always running."

In the classroom, Johnson had a different energy as a student. In a 1987 *Toronto Star* article, one of his first teachers remembered him as subdued and well-behaved.

"He was quiet and unassuming, never one of those problem children," said Vida Foster, former principal of the Falmouth All Age School. "He was actually shy and withdrawn. Definitely not a talker."

His last few years in grade school were a difficult emotional period for young Ben. He missed his mother, who'd moved to Toronto. During the time she was away, Gloria Johnson was sending money back for her children to pay for medical checkups and passports in preparation for their move to Canada. Eventually, she'd saved enough to pay for their airfare.

Not everyone was thrilled to be leaving Falmouth. The decision to uproot the Johnson children was unsettling for the older siblings, who were more established with friends and schooling. This was to be a major reset of the family dynamic. Sister Jean Hanlan, then seventeen, recalled her mixed emotions during the flight from Montego Bay with brothers Eddie and Ben and their youngest sibling, Marcia: "It was bittersweet because it was good we were going to be with our mum, but at the same time we were going to leave the life that we knew. We left our friends. I remember that day on the plane. I remember crying and crying because we were leaving, and I didn't understand what or why."

In contrast, fourteen-year-old Ben, seated next to Jean, was thrilled. Two years earlier, he'd sat on his mother's bed, crying and bewildered, as he watched her pack a small suitcase. He begged her not to leave. She would dry his eyes and reassure him that they'd permanently reunite in Toronto. On that plane, young Ben's heart was full: "I was happy, I was going to see my mother again. No tears for me."

Gloria herself wept when she met her children at the airport. She'd been desperately lonely without them in Toronto. The two oldest daughters, Dezrine and Clare, were still in Falmouth but would later join them.

Ben Sr. made his own difficult decision to stay in Jamaica. He was eligible for landed immigrant status but was unable to find employment in Toronto similar to his position and pay at home. He valued his career and found his work meaningful. Just entering his fifties, he also felt it prudent to remain in Falmouth in order to earn a full pension upon retirement. Eventually, he'd be promoted to a supervisory position. With his children in Toronto, he maintained the family property to make it available for them on their returns to Jamaica. In turn, he flew to Canada once or twice a year, never acclimating to Canada's long, cold seasons.

The Johnson children experienced a unique parenting relationship with their mother and father in different countries, independently running their respective households. Johnson doesn't recall his father sending money to help his mother handle the bills, but he understood the responsibility his father shouldered in keeping the Falmouth home running smoothly, along with a few smaller packets of land he'd purchased nearby.

"I wouldn't say they were separated," Ben Jr. said. "They just chose to live here and there." The couple did not divorce.

His father's physical absence did not preclude Ben Jr. from maintaining a relationship with him. He'd spent enough time with his dad in Jamaica to cement that bond, whether it was pushing wheelbarrows of rich earth with him into the backyard gardens or accompanying him on drives to deliver home-jarred honey.

Ben Sr. approved of his children's immigration; however, it left him lonely. "Sometimes, a man has to suffer to make good," he said in a 1987 *Toronto Star* story. "Let's face facts. Six kids and a wife make eight, and trying not to get too complex, with that many, it's easier for them to have a better life over there."

Johnson said his father never made him feel guilty for remaining in Toronto.

"My dad said if you choose to live in Canada, I will support you, your wishes, and your dreams," he recalled.

* * *

Gloria was well prepared to receive her children in Toronto. She'd squirreled away enough money from her cafeteria cashier job at an airport strip hotel and by sewing custom clothing orders to rent a two-bedroom apartment at 2960 Keele Street in North York, close to the massive Downsview military base. She made and collected new clothes for her kids, too. It was April when they arrived, and spring weather in Toronto could be cold and rainy—for the first time in their lives, they needed coats, mitts, boots, and toques.

Gloria carried an enormous set of parental duties beyond paying bills and cooking meals. She was tireless in her efforts to raise her children, spiritually, socially, and through education. She enrolled them in local schools that offered student busing. She moved to afternoon shifts at the hotel to be home during the day when she'd grocery shop and cook.

Gloria could be a ferocious mama bear, insisting that her children maintain good habits. There were bedtime curfews. She would expect the kids to be asleep long before she returned from work, which was often after midnight. Young Ben loved sitting in front of the apartment television long into the evening, watching westerns, comedies, and, with a fresh love, NHL hockey. "I'd watch the late-night movies when mum was working. I used to time it so she wouldn't catch me up, and I'd turn the TV off just before she got home," he laughed. "But sometimes the TV had been running for so long, and it got hot. She'd come in and put her hands on the TV. If it was still hot, she'd give me shit in the morning for watching movies when I should be sleeping."

A few months after Johnson landed in Toronto, Montreal was hosting the 1976 Summer Games, the first Canadian city to do so. Olympic fever swept the nation. During the opening ceremonies, at that emotional moment when the torch was lit, so too was a spark in Ben Johnson's imagination: could he, one day, be as fast as the great Donald Quarrie, the man who would leave Montreal with two medals, including a gold?

This new country, Canada, would be the cradle of Ben Johnson's athletic stardom. But first, he'd have to fight his way out of a Toronto schoolyard.

He was placed in grade nine at Pierre Laporte Middle School. Being a shy, small-ish student joining class late in the 1976 school year was difficult enough on its own, but Johnson was also Black among mostly white students. He had a Jamaican accent and a periodic but well-pronounced stutter. He was a magnet for school bullies. Two in particular, whom we'll call Mark and Jack, one white and one Black, tormented him daily.

"Right away, they picked on the [new] black kid," Johnson said. "They called me N-word, said, 'Go back to Jamaica,' and they'd have their girlfriends beside them, laughing and giggling and supporting them."

"I'd go into the cafeteria to eat my lunch, and they'd pull my chair out from under me so I'd spill my meal all over the place. They'd corner me, push me around, and say, 'Get out of here, go back home.'"

This was not how Johnson had experienced school in Jamaica. There was no camaraderie on a sandy soccer pitch. No open-air classrooms refreshed by saltwater breezes. No friend groups to walk home with. He was miserable.

To Johnson's horror, Mark and Jack were in most of his classes. His solution became avoidance. Johnson had noticed a group of young guys working on cars and motorbikes across the street from Pierre Laporte. He'd take his chances with the car crowd.

"I couldn't go to class because they were there. I would just skip school, go over to see what these guys are doing and saying, and hang out until school was finished," he said. He played hooky on and off for weeks.

It was Johnson's first exposure to overt racism, and it shook him to his core. Yet he kept this bullied existence to himself, a practice common to schoolyard victims who hope their tormentors relent if they don't snitch. It didn't work.

"I didn't tell my mother; I didn't tell my sisters about it or my brother," he said, adding there "would have been problems" for the bullies if he'd alerted sister Jean. Three years his elder, she would have confronted them.

Jean doesn't remember her brother complaining or confiding in a family member about the bullying. "If Ben had come home and said something, then we would have taken care of it, but he didn't," she said, noting she, too, was targeted by racist school bullies. "I didn't understand it then; we weren't used to it. We weren't exposed to it. I went to a Catholic school in Jamaica, and at the Catholic school, you had every nationality there."

In one instance, when Jean was brazenly picked on at Toronto's Downsview Secondary School—a male classmate fired paper balls at her from the back of the room—she marched over to him, threw the projectiles back in his face, and reported the incident to the principal's office. She said her complaint was taken so seriously that a student-led anti-racism committee was formed. Jean was part of that committee.

Her little brother had a longer fuse, but eventually he acted. Johnson devised a simple plan to end the trouble. He'd attended enough school from April through June to be eligible to participate in sports, including track and field, where he'd whip past classmates on skinny legs or vault his bony frame over the high jump bar. Quiet but observant, Johnson knew his peers underestimated his athletic ability and courage. He'd deploy both.

One lunchtime, he walked up defiantly to Mark, the white guy.

"I was getting tired of being pushed around, and I challenged him to a race," Johnson recalled. "I said, 'If I beat you, will you stop bugging me?' and he said, 'You can't beat me.'"

"And I said: 'Let's go. 100 meters.'"

A crowd of students gathered, sensing the teenage tension. Johnson pointed out the course on the field, essentially from end zone to end zone across the football field. A student called a teacher over, shouting excitedly: "There's going to be a race between Ben and Mark!"

The teacher agreed to act as the official starter. Both boys were on the field, poised for a standing start, knees slightly bent. The teacher counted down "ready, set," then clapped his hands for "go!" The rivals sprinted across the uneven sod.

"We go. I beat him, but not by very much, and he was so embarrassed," Johnson said. "He'd done all this big talk with his girlfriend, saying that he was going to beat me and that he was 'the man' because he was the best in the school."

The public humbling created more room for Johnson at school. "It kind of stopped, a little bit," he said. At least, the worst of the aggression was over.

This schoolyard race remains a point of pride for Johnson. He was empowered by slaying his trash-talking dragon before a crowd expecting him to lose. In many ways, it was his first significant victory. It also illustrates the devastating impact of racism and bullying on children by other children. Johnson had to prove he was exceptional, faster than the swaggering Mark, faster than everyone else in his school, simply to be accepted by those who'd delighted in making him suffer.

* * *

Gloria almost lost her baby boy, Benjamin Sinclair Jr., during infancy. As family legend goes, a killer illness swept through Falmouth in 1962, possibly malaria, claiming a slew of young victims.

Her son, born December 30, 1961, was stricken with the mystery ailment at about eight months. He was fevered, weak, and unable to eat, crying endlessly. His mother held him constantly in her arms, nursing him with fluids, including natural lemonade, on doctor's orders. She'd place tiny dabs of soft food on his tongue to get nutrients into his body. And she'd pray. By his first birthday, baby Ben had rallied and was on a robust road to recovery. A devout Christian woman, Gloria fervently thanked God for sparing his life when other local families had not been as fortunate.

Gloria loved all her children unconditionally, but she and Ben Jr. forged a unique connection, likely during that agonizing months-long health crisis. Before becoming pregnant with Ben, Gloria had given birth to another son, Norman, who died the day he arrived. The death of a second child would have been unbearable. To Gloria, Ben was her miracle survivor, the one God permitted to live so he could do great things in life. To Ben, his mother was the loving center of his universe, and he was devoted to her.

"There are only two people in this world who would tell me what to do, and I would do it," Johnson said. "The first was my mother. The second was Charlie [Francis]."

Sister Jean said that the mother—son link was one of a kind, even in their closely knit family. "He had a deep bond that maybe only Ben can explain, but watching him over the years, you realized how deep his bond was with mum," she said. "He was very special to mum. I don't know if it was because he was sick in his early years . . . but there was a special connection. It was fantastic."

One of Gloria's great fears for her children was the sea. Three of her brothers drowned near Kingston Harbor in a single accident in April 1966—one brother was caught in a riptide, and his two brothers tried in vain to save him. She insisted that none of her kids play in the water without parental supervision. Young Ben ignored her and often stole away with friends to swim. He was always caught, the sea scent on his skin and hair, and got a whipping from his father for defying a house rule.

In Toronto, young Ben worried about his mother. He was upset that she had to work to pay the bills. Each day, after he'd get off the school bus and tuck into the food Gloria had prepared, she'd walk out of the apartment around 4:30 p.m. to start her work journey. He stood glumly at the window as she headed toward the bus stop, bags in hand, soon to be on her feet for hours at the busy hotel cafeteria.

"I'd see her walking down the street, and I'd be so sad that I couldn't help," he said. "I was so young, only fourteen years old. And it crossed my mind, you know what? Whenever I make it—and I didn't know what I was going to make it in—but when I become good at something, I'm going to make sure my mum is taken care of. Give something back to her."

Jean was also keenly aware of her mother's roles as a breadwinner and primary parent in Toronto. "Don't forget, Mum never worked in Jamaica, so she was a tough cookie—she had to make a big adjustment to go into the workforce. She worked [and] we were good; we never got into trouble or anything like that. We took care of each other, and taking care of each other was something that was embedded in us at a young age by our parents. We were to take care of each other, no matter what."

Gloria maintained a faithful Christian home, encouraging spiritual awareness and personal relationships with higher powers. She would read the Bible aloud to her youngest son at night, him snuggling into her side. Her older son, Eddie, would become an ordained minister in the United States. Ben and Jean described their mother as spiritually sensitive in ways that would guide her in life, sometimes through visions she shared.

"She had a deep spiritual background that she would sometimes tell us about. We call it a vision because she would tell us things and it would happen," Jean said.

Johnson attests to his mother's "gift," citing one memorable vision that arose in Seoul. The Saturday night after he'd won the Olympic 100 meters, his mother dreamed of a snake slithering near her son, menacing him. In her dream, she begged Johnson to kill the snake, his enemy, but he didn't. He and Gloria interpreted that vision as a warning he was in danger, which by Sunday night in Seoul, with his A sample already screened as positive for an anabolic steroid, he was.

But he couldn't have his mother by his side every waking moment, and he stumbled a few times trying to navigate his new Toronto environment.

In the summer of 1976, Johnson and a few of his neighborhood friends played along a creek near the Keele Street apartment building. They fished, picked wild berries, and, occasionally, hunted birds as they used to do in Jamaica.

One day, a friend killed a pigeon with his slingshot. The hungry boys decide to roast it for lunch. They built a tiny fire just as a police cruiser rolled up. A uniformed officer stepped out, demanding to know what they were doing. Johnson piped up that he and his friends were going to cook the bird and eat it. The cop told the boys they weren't supposed to be killing birds or lighting fires. Lunch was scuttled. The boys tossed the pigeon aside, stomped out the flames, and ran off.

Johnson said the police officer didn't chase them, but the encounter revealed his daunting Toronto learning curve. He was now living in a city of rules rooted in a stuffy English Protestant work ethic. Back then, one could not even shop at most stores or buy liquor on Sunday or roast pigeons in parks. His mother was his touchstone for guidance when he was confused. Her problem-solving abilities were fluid and intuitive, and they usually involved prayer. That suited her son, who trusted his mother's judgment in all matters, even about girlfriends, when he was old enough to squire them around.

Some of Johnson's strongest memories of his mother were of her ability to understand his athletic needs, especially when it came to feeding a growing body.

Gloria ruled the kitchen. There would be no junk food in her house. Johnson counted on her wholesome home cooking—fragrant meals based around chicken, fish, rice, and vegetables—to replace the thousands of calories he'd burn up at the track and in the weight room. Those meals were ready for him after training, no matter if Gloria was already in bed since she knew he didn't have the aptitude or patience to cook for himself.

"Rice and peas, chicken, steamed fish, yams, dumplings, and bananas. Those are good slow-releasing carbs, and my mum cooked them very well. When I came home, my food was always waiting for me. I never had to wait for my food. I'd just warm it up in the microwave, sit down on the couch, and just watch TV and eat."

Ben Johnson began high school at Yorkdale Secondary in the fall of 1976. He would again struggle academically. He failed some classes and called himself "a dumb ass" for doing so. Coach Charlie Francis later acidly described the vocational school environment as a learning wasteland that failed to support students equally. Yet, somehow, Johnson scraped by each grade to advance to the next.

His on-again, off-again stutter didn't disappear. The speech pattern he said he developed around age eleven by imitating his brother Eddie, who stuttered as a boy, became a negative factor in the classroom. It made him a silent pupil. He'd rather say nothing than risk getting laughed at for stumbling over words. His reticence was often mistaken for being aloof, slow, or disinterested when it was more of a form of self-protection in a group setting. As a result, he didn't ask teachers for help in front of classmates, which likely contributed to the "dumb assing" at exam time.

His school challenges might have been addressed if supportive programs for students, especially Black students, existed as they do now, told Canadian teacher-turned-politician Jean Augustine, the first African-Canadian woman elected as a member of Canada's parliament. She knew Johnson when he was an up-and-coming national junior team sprinter. "The system didn't spend a lot of time with Black kids at the time. We didn't have parents talking to school trustees. We didn't have trustees talking to school boards, and we didn't have community interaction . . . so the student supports weren't there." Today, she says, there are better programs to boost student success, some of which she helped pioneer. "Even with stuttering, there is help given. Ben didn't get that kind of help."

Johnson made many friends at Yorkdale, most of them were crazy like him. One was another Jamaican newcomer who loved boxing,

Tony Morrison. He would become a Canadian pro heavyweight champ and a walking trivia answer as the Canadian prize fighter who knocked out fading US star Leon Spinks thirty-three seconds into a match.

"We were athletes, and Ben was a funny guy, a nice guy," said Morrison, who said Johnson was often misunderstood by high schoolers who weren't patient when he spoke. His halting speech unfairly labeled him a slow learner, Morrison said. "Ben has a stutter and sometimes doesn't talk so well, doesn't communicate so well, and that held him back a bit. Plus, he's shy. He's got a circle of friends he sticks to once you get to know him. He's not going to go out of his way to meet you."

Johnson, Morrison, and their band of buddies played as many sports as they could: soccer, cricket, basketball, track, baseball, and even table tennis. No ice hockey, though. The gear was too expensive, so the game was never an option. Morrison and Johnson said that their sporting prowess worked in their favor in high school. Morrison was a Canadian boxing champ at fifteen, and Johnson was soon traveling the world as a junior sprinter. The racism Johnson had experienced in middle school abated.

Despite his skills across the sports spectrum—he excelled at soccer—Johnson knew track was his passion. He joined his high school track team. Eddie, four years older, attended a different school, Downsview Secondary, and was already turning heads as an elite sprinter. He'd been offered a scholarship to Lamar University in Beaumont, Texas. Eddie wanted additional preparation for an NCAA career and joined a track club he'd heard about, the Scarborough Optimists. Although Scarborough is in the east end of Toronto, the club was decentralized, using volunteer coaches and a slate of city high school tracks to attract local kids to the low-cost, low-barrier program.

The Optimist track-and-field club was the brainchild of Scarborough public school teacher Ross Earl, who recruited coaches for young runners, jumpers, and throwers. A tireless volunteer, Earl also ran a modest Scarborough bingo that provided revenue for the club's annual budget to defray training and travel costs for the kids. Earl was kind, generous, and, by 1988, had grown the Optimists to about fifteen hundred affiliated members across Canada. I was one of them in the early 1970s, a lead-footed kid training on Scarborough's Cedarbrae Collegiate's cinder track. My sprinting career was short-lived, but it was a fun club experience.

In the spring of 1977, Eddie Johnson noticed his little brother was bringing home ribbons won at high school meets. Impressed, he took Ben to an Optimist practice at nearby Lawrence Park Collegiate. Eddie introduced Ben to Charlie Francis.

Then a part-time volunteer coach with the club, Francis, a former Canadian 100-meter champion who competed in the 1972 Munich Games, knew Eddie Johnson could run. But he wondered about the little brother in clunky running shoes without enough stamina to jog one lap, Francis wrote in his memoir.

"I can't say Ben bowled me over. At fifteen, he was at the ideal age to begin training, but he looked more like twelve, a skinny, awkward kid of ninety-three pounds. He wore tattered, black high-top sneakers that seemed too heavy for his long, pipe-stem legs. He *looked* slow, and he ran even slower than he looked."

Francis wandered over to the new kid as he staggered off the track to sit in the stands, winded. The coach asked what was wrong. The shy boy with a stutter said his legs were weak and he had to rest, draping himself across a bench seat.

Francis was not stern or judgmental. He understood that structured training would be overwhelming for inexperienced runners. Patience was required. Young Ben skipped a few sessions after that day before he decided to return to the club. Then he was all in. His speed and form transformed rapidly with better footwear, and the thoughtful gift of hand-me-down spikes from an older sprinter.

From there, Johnson embarked on club circuit track meets. He began placing in age-group sprints, sometimes winning. Francis was pleased but not yet convinced the short runner, at five-foot-three, had a shot at a track career. The coach couldn't envision the seven-inch growth spurt and the substantial gain in lean muscle that would fill out his frame. Nor did Francis guess that "those big eyes of his were fixed on goals beyond my vision at the time."

* * *

In retrospect, it's fascinating how Johnson and Francis digested the previous year's Montreal Summer Games. Johnson was entranced by the majesty of human athletic achievement and found inspiration in Don Quarrie's performances. With typical frankness, Francis described the games as a Canadian "nightmare." It was the first summer games at which the host nation did not win a gold medal.

The one glimmer of hope Francis saw in Montreal was that the Canadian Track and Field Association's national sprint coach, Gerard Mach, recruited to Canada from Poland, where he had worked with that national team, greatly improved Canada's sprint relay teams since the 1972 games in Munich. At the 1976 Olympics, all four Canadian sprint relays made the medal rounds in Montreal, with two finishing fourth. In Mach, he saw a mentor.

When Francis was a national team sprinter, he antagonized federation officials by lobbying for better programs to bolster performances, such as warm-weather training camps during the winter, more access to expert athletic therapists for injuries and injury prevention, and cutting-edge coaching modeled on nations producing championship sprinters. He felt the sport's Canadian stewards were inflexible, narrow-minded, and unwilling to modernize a system that demanded competition excellence but did not properly invest to attain it. Mighty sporting nations like the United States, Great Britain, East Germany, and the Soviet Union poured money and resources into their athletes, while Canada counted its nickels and dimes.

Francis believed the administrative mindset that hampered his athletic development also compromised the next sprinting generation. Although Mach was doing solid work with the national team, Francis wanted more: victory, not just progress, in major international competitions.

Francis formed his own coaching methods by observing and questioning others. He'd quiz technically skilled Canadian coaches like Mach. He'd chat up international coaches who'd produced champions. Coaches from East Germany, as the country was called at the time, often obliged the friendly Canadian's curiosity by sharing tips on training and, eventually, steroid use.

Francis would find a perfect cache of sprinters to coach for his new athlete-centric program: the Scarborough Optimists. They were mostly immigrant teenagers from West Indian nations, all of whom had open minds, a hunger to work hard, athletic promise, and aspirations to be world-beaters. The core group would include Angella Taylor, who later married and used the surname Issajenko; Desai Williams; Tony Sharpe; hurdler Mark McKoy; and Ben Johnson. Eddie Johnson left the Optimists after he began university in Texas.

By the end of 1978, Francis had developed the dominant group of up-and-coming sprinters in the country. He'd done it on gritty high school tracks in the summer and on a small indoor track in a building the kids called the "Pig Palace," the grandly named Swine Pavilion on the Canadian National Exhibition grounds, in the winter. (Soon, the club's runners would move to the Canadian Track and Field Association's new high-performance center at York University in northwest Toronto.)

Through the course of 1978, Johnson grew close to his adult height of five-foot-ten and drew attention with an unusual leaping start from the blocks. And he was getting faster. He was sixteen when he finished fifth in a semifinal of the 1978 Commonwealth Games Canadian team trials in Edmonton. Crushed because he didn't advance to the final, he picked up his gear, slipped away from his teammates, and cried in frustration. He'd be more upset later that year when he was not approved for financial assistance from Sport Canada, the federal agency that provides a slate of support for national-level amateur sports and athletes. The government's money enables elite athletes to train and travel full-time, free of the need to hold down jobs.

Financial assistance for top amateur athletes in Canada is commonly called "carding," and it exists to defray training and living costs. There are different levels of Sport Canada carding, meaning more money for athletes at the world-class level and less for up-and-comers like juniors. With the backing of their national sports federation, athletes apply for Sport Canada funding based on meeting certain metrics. For runners, carding payouts were largely based on performance times at high-level competitions. The richest carding money was tied to world-class results. Those results, Francis and others would later argue, were likely achieved by doping athletes, and therefore, almost impossible to match if one didn't also use banned substances.

Johnson believed his 1978 carding snub was not about his performances but had more to do with the CTFA's prickly relationship with his coach, Francis. Johnson would not be granted carding money for two more years, even though he was clearly one of the country's fastest men. This drawback did nothing to dampen Johnson's dedication to the sport. He'd anxiously await the end of the school day so he could rush to training.

"As soon as the bell rings, I'm gone, I take the bus [to the track]," Johnson said. "When there were [school] track meets, I'd have to skip school to go. I was so happy because I didn't want to go to school."

Education held no allure for Johnson. While most of his teammates went on to university after high school, he had no desire to become "book smart."

The Scarborough Optimists provided Ben Johnson with a second family. In the early days, the runners were united in fun by teasing Francis with their *patois*. "We'd always talk about what we did on the weekend while we were warming up and training, and Charlie couldn't understand what we were talking about," Johnson said. "He'd come over and say, 'What you guys said?' And we'd say, 'Don't worry, you wouldn't understand, we're speaking Jamaican.' When we are talking, Charlie is listening and listening, and after a while, we couldn't say anything else he picked it up. We'd say, 'Shhh, shhhh, Charlie's coming.'"

Francis would grow fond of and protective of his young group. When they traveled to meets, he'd discreetly slip money to athletes if they were short. On one trip to Montreal, Francis noticed the Johnson brothers were sharing a single plate of French fries as a meal. When he asked why they ordered that, the coach discovered they only had $6 between them for the two-day meet. As he often did with other runners whose families had little or no spare income, he bought the brothers proper meals until they returned to Toronto. It's likely that Francis's personal generosity kept many young athletes in the sport. Johnson said Francis never made anyone feel embarrassed about not having enough money and would deal with the matter quietly. "I never talked to Charlie about my personal stuff at home, but he knew I didn't have much money and that my mum was the only person taking care of us."

In 1980, the Johnsons officially joined another family. They became Canadian citizens. Gloria and her children dressed in their Sunday best on a summer day and traveled by bus, then subway, to a government office near St. Clair Avenue and Yonge Street in the heart of Toronto to be sworn in. "I believed it was the thing to do at the time," Johnson said of gaining Canadian citizenship, although he still holds a Jamaican passport. "It was just another step to living in Canada. My mother wanted to make it official, so we did."

The same year they became Canadian citizens, Gloria moved the family into a government-subsidized townhouse at 65 Varna Drive in northwest Toronto.

Her kids were getting bigger. They needed room to sprawl, and it was not too far from their first apartment, where they had friends. The larger home came with risk since Lawrence Heights was called "The Jungle" by those who lived there. Johnson recalled a neighborhood simmering with gun violence, drug gangs, and arson, especially in a parkette near him. Local families frequently complained to the city and police about the small green space rife with criminal activity or drinking parties at night. The city's answer was to plant thorny bushes in spots to deter loitering.

One evening in July 1984, Johnson heard a gunshot in the parkette. "I was in the house, playing music, and I heard something pop, like a car tailpipe blow," he said. "Everybody was running down the street, going to take a look, and my mum said, 'you're not going anywhere, you're staying in the house.'"

Johnson and his siblings remained inside, but word got out fast: Alex Morris, eighteen, had been killed. Johnson knew the dead teenager, a Yorkdale student. So did boxer Tony Morrison, whose family had moved into a townhouse almost directly across from the Johnsons. The fatal shooting was front-page news. But what appeared to be a cold-blooded murder by a third party was soon revealed to be a tragic accident involving best friends, Morris and Willard Haughton, then nineteen. Haughton was charged with manslaughter, but pleaded to lesser charges and was sentenced to one year in jail.

"It was the projects, man," said Johnson. "At sundown, people were in their houses."

His mother's guidance and his focus on running helped Johnson escape The Jungle's dangerous elements. His athletic reputation was growing. He was climbing the world rankings as a junior, then a senior sprinter. His achievements were announced over the school's public address system to the student body; his success was admired. Rather than lure him into trouble, Johnson's friends looked out for him. "They knew who I was, and it worked in my favor," he said. "I'd hang out with them for a bit. I just sit down with them while they smoke marijuana, drink their liquor, and chit-chat. I would always tell them I was leaving when it was getting late, and we'd always see the police cars cruising by."

He said kids from other neighborhoods would come around now and then, checking out the action. When any of them got up into Johnson's face, he'd mention it to one of his pals. "They'd go over and say, 'Are you bugging my friend Ben?' And when [the interlopers] realized where I live and where I hang out, they'd respect [that]," he said.

But there were other things going on in Johnson's inner world. Things that he didn't understand.

Although his athletic career was blossoming, other parts of Johnson's life were unsettled. He'd begun to feel increasingly anxious. Money was tight, his mother was now working two jobs, and even when he did qualify for low-level carding in 1980—about $250 a month, he recalls—it didn't make a big dent in the bills. He couldn't shake what he called "a funny feeling," swells of panic from knowing the family was floating just above the poverty line and that his track career was siphoning off precious household dollars.

"I don't know if it was anxiety or depression. I was just a young kid training, [but] seeing my mother paying the bills, putting food on the table, and making ends meet, I knew it was a struggle because the [carding] paycheck I got from the government wasn't enough and she was just making minimum wage," he said.

Johnson was never formally diagnosed with anxiety or depression, but, back then, he was hardly alone. Mental health issues weren't broached within families; they carried the severely shameful stigma of being weak or lazy. His remedy was to work diligently and tell no one. "I thought to myself, I just have to train harder, focus on doing all the right things, listen to what Charlie says, and believe in the training program. What he tells me to do, I do it. I never asked him why. I just do it. That's the reason I became successful, because I did as I was told, and I did it well."

The fact that Johnson was exceptionally coachable is not in doubt. But money was part of his motivation, since top-tier "A" carding pay was within his reach by 1980. He needed to race below 10.20 seconds at a reputable competition to register an eligible time. An "A" card was worth about $650 a month in the early- to mid-1980s. Not great wealth, but it would make a difference in the Johnson home.

There were the odd days when a fluttering of doubt ran through Johnson's mind, when he wondered if this challenging path in life was worth it. His days were full—bus to school, then bus from school to practice, train for hours, then bus home—leaving him exhausted. "[Charlie's] training was very hard and rugged, my God. Sometimes I'd ask in my mind: 'What the hell am I doing this for?'" Johnson said. "And then, I always think about my mother. 'This is for mum, this is for mum.'"

It would not be many more years before Johnson could proudly inform his mother that she no longer needed to work. He had enough money to take care of her.

CHAPTER SIX
OLYMPIANS WITH SECRETS

Angella Taylor Issajenko was Charlie Francis's first record-breaking international star, and the first to earn a top-five world ranking. It was a remarkable achievement for a rookie coach and a late-blooming nineteen-year-old athlete who, for a while, competed drug-free after joining the Optimists in 1978. She and Francis would blaze a trail into the covert world of steroids for others to follow, including Ben Johnson.

In 1979, Issajenko dominated the Canadian women's sprinting scene as its record-setting champ and burst to global prominence at the Pan American Games in San Juan, Puerto Rico, winning bronze in the 100 meters and silver in the 200 meters (American Evelyn Ashford won both). The 1980 Moscow Summer Games were on the horizon, and Issajenko's first Olympics looked promising.

Yet as she improved, she never seemed to gain a step on her foreign rivals, especially the noticeably muscular East Germans. Francis believed he knew the reason: some of her top opponents were juiced.

"Numbers define one's place in the track world. Now our place was receding, and I felt sure I knew why. Angella wasn't losing ground because of a talent gap. She was losing because of a drug gap, and it was widening by the day," Francis wrote in his memoir.

He broached using anabolic steroids in the fall of 1979 with Issajenko. The gist of his counsel is that a sprinter could not expect to win international competitions without them.

He knew the drugs wouldn't make "a plodder into a champion," but for an elite runner, they'd function as a tool to amass muscle strength, enable heavier workloads in training sessions, and increase power and speed for race days. Francis assured Issajenko that this steroid-fueled ability would close the gap on rivals who he was certain were doing the same thing.

She agreed. It was a risky venture by amateurs with no formal education in pharmacy, chemistry, or toxicology. They sought medical help, consulting Issajenko's personal physician, who agreed to prescribe Dianabol, a popular anabolic steroid used for decades by competitive bodybuilders, including actor/politician Arnold Schwarzenegger during his Mr. Universe days.

Issajenko took one five-milligram Dianabol pill daily for three weeks, then cycled off the drug for three weeks. Francis later testified at a public inquiry that he, Issajenko, and her physician didn't believe the intermittent dosing would compromise the sprinter's health. She had her blood tested regularly to monitor her body's chemistry. Francis claimed to know two British female sprinters who were taking 35 milligrams a day, seven times Issajenko's dose. Based on his own research, Francis thought smaller steroid doses were just as effective for Issajenko while avoiding potential masculine side effects like hair growth and voice deepening.

Her doctor also gave her a gift, a book called *Compendium of Pharmaceuticals and Specialities*, a source of drug information in Canada. Francis already had a copy. Issajenko, like her coach, consulted the book religiously, trying to understand how substances like steroids, human growth hormone, and anti-inflammatory drugs would affect her. The *Compendium* provided her comfort in navigating her steroid cycles, which she would track daily in her diary along with personal thoughts about training, teammates, finances, and romances.

Issajenko's results improved steadily while on the drug regime. She set the 200-meter indoor world record in 23.15 seconds in a semifinal heat at the 1980 national championships in Toronto. As indoor performances are indicative of outdoor readiness, Issajenko was viewed as a credible contender at the Moscow games. The Optimist men were also rounding into shape to qualify for the Canadian Olympic team—Ben Johnson, Desai Williams, Tony Sharpe, and Mark McKoy, a 110-meter hurdler—although they were not considered medal threats.

In January 1980, US President Jimmy Carter announced the US Olympic team would boycott the Moscow Games to protest the Soviet Union's invasion of Afghanistan. Canadian Prime Minister Joe Clark followed Carter's lead in a bewildering political move that gutted a generation of exceptional athletes across every sport. Not surprisingly, the lightly challenged Soviet athletes dominated their own games.

Moscow would have been a strong Olympic entry point for Issajenko. The four-year wait until the next games is a lifetime for an athlete. Still, she ended 1980 as the fifth-ranked 100-meter sprinter in the world, a spectacular accomplishment after two years of training.

For the Optimist men, the Moscow blow landed differently since they were not yet podium material. The remainder of 1980 was a period of progress. Williams, Sharpe, and Johnson, who was named to the Olympic relay pool of runners, were notching better placings in star-studded fields, gaining strategic experience in running heats and finals. Some of those fields included an American junior phenomenon named Carl Lewis, who also excelled in long jump.

At the 1980 Canadian outdoor championships, Optimists finished first and second in the senior men's 100 meters. Williams was first, and Johnson, only eighteen, was second in a personal best of 10.36 seconds. He would lower that to 10.25 the next summer, a performance that hinted at greater potential.

Francis decided it was time to have his anabolic steroid chat with the skinny kid who, three years earlier, couldn't run a whole lap of the track.

* * *

Doping was a perilous practice. When athletes were caught breaking anti-doping rules, they faced sanctions ranging from temporary to lifetime competition bans; the forfeiture of achievements such as records, medals, and berths on national teams; and, in Canada, the suspension of government funding.

Charlie Francis knew the risks and accepted them. He'd competed at the 1972 Munich games and seen open use of performance enhancers, including steroids. He'd experimented with them himself as a runner and saw no effective doping clampdown, even after steroids made the banned lists.

As odd as it may seem, Canada's Richard Pound, the IOC vice president who in 1999 directed the launch of the World Anti-Doping Agency, an independent global body whose primary role is to coordinate anti-doping rules across all sports and countries, understood how Francis concluded that competing steroid-free was a detriment to clean athletes.

"Canada tried to get serious testing done at track-and-field events and foundered," Pound said of the pre-Seoul years. "Then [Francis] said, 'All right, if the rules are not the rules that are written, then it's a very different paradigm and I won't be part of that.'"

The Hon. Hugh Fraser is a retired Ontario provincial court judge, a former Canadian Olympic sprinter, and a recognized international expert on sports law. He followed Francis as Canada's sprint champion, then pursued a career in law around the time Ben Johnson picked up the sprinting torch. Like Pound, Fraser didn't condone cheating but described Francis and Johnson as a product of their time—a time during which many athletes doped but few were captured in lab dragnets.

The inaugural world track-and-field championships, held in Helsinki in 1983, produced zero positive doping results. This was the same year scientists announced they'd made breakthroughs in steroid detection, yet somehow, they didn't catch a soul in Helsinki. "It was the Wild West," said Fraser of the era. "I can easily understand how someone could look at that and say, 'This is the environment I'm in, these are the rules I have to play by, and to get to the top, I need to do what everyone else is doing.'"

Fraser knew Francis and had numerous trackside conversations with him. The Optimist coach believed "everybody" was doping and stubbornly stood his ground when the young law student pushed back, saying that wasn't true.

"Charlie was very big on this 'everybody is doing it' type of thing," said Fraser, who in 1996 began presiding over doping appeals as a frequent arbitrator for the Lausanne-based Court of Arbitration for Sport. "We had many of those discussions, and I'd say, 'No, Charlie, I don't think everybody is doing it.' And he'd say, 'No, no, no, Ben doesn't have a realistic chance at the top if he doesn't follow the same regimen.' He didn't make that too much of a secret."

Ben Johnson was nineteen when Francis raised the subject with him one-on-one.

The sports community is better informed these days about what constitutes a healthy relationship between a coach and athlete. Broadly, it's one where an athlete can improve physically and mentally in a safe manner under the guidance of a skilled coach without fear of exploitation or harm.

Then there is Charlie Francis. Brilliant, driven, unselfish, and devoted to his athletes. And the architect of the most explosive drug scandal in Olympic Games' history. What to make of him?

The fact that Francis truly cared for his sprinters is not in dispute.

He began as an unpaid coach who famously quit his insurance job, moved into his parents' Toronto home, and sold his prized Aston Martin sports car to fund his coaching passion. He would fight for his runners to get Sport Canada carding, modest sponsorship deals, and decent appearance fees at meets. Francis made all his sprinters better; his technical skills were superb, and his dry sense of humor was a bonus. He arranged training camps, travel, athletic therapy, and competition schedules with the care and precision he didn't receive when he competed for Canada. It mattered to him that his athletes were treated with dignity and respect.

Francis was also contemptuous of stodgy CTFA rules and risk-averse administrators. His embrace of steroid culture flowed from that contempt.

Ben Johnson, shy and naïve, had come to regard Francis as a father figure. Did Francis abuse his influence by suggesting that a teenaged Johnson break drug rules that would destroy his career if found out?

Johnson was young but not blind. By the time Francis approached him, he'd trained six days a week for nearly five years and competed frequently across North America and Europe. He absorbed the international scene in a quiet way. He saw changes in the bodies of his older rivals, their muscles sculpted, their times dropping. He listened to track gossip. Closer to home, he noted Issajenko's racing successes and suspected the chemical reason behind them.

"I had an idea that Angie was using some stuff because she was setting world records indoors and her muscles were bulging," said Johnson. "She was the best [in the Toronto group], she was making money, and she was a star."

Johnson also noted that Francis paid Issajenko the most attention, as befitting her world-ranked status. So, when the coach invited Johnson for a serious talk about steroids, he listened.

In September 1981, the pair met to recap the past year's efforts and discuss competition goals for 1982, which included a trip to the

Commonwealth Games in Brisbane, Australia. The Commonwealth Games are a major quadrennial event for "colonies" of the former British Empire and an important gauge of progress toward Olympic preparation. Francis felt Johnson could do well in Brisbane and opened the chat by suggesting they tailor training sessions accordingly. Francis knew Johnson disliked the club's 300-meter "special" endurance runs and wanted his longest drills capped at 200 meters. They agreed to this. Then, Francis dived into the topic of steroids.

In Francis's opinion, the steroid advantage at the elite level represented about one meter, or a full stride, in the 100 meters. In running clean, Johnson was always going to be a meter behind his doping rivals. Years later, the coach would famously describe the steroid effect like this: Johnson could either put his starting blocks on the same line as his international competition or set them up a meter behind.

Johnson said he wanted in. Like his coach, he didn't consider it cheating if his rivals were doping.

"I didn't see it as a problem for me to say yes or no to Charlie," he said, denying Francis pushed him into the steroid pool against his will. "He believed that people were already breaking the rules and were not getting caught. We were trying to do it clean, and we were going to be in last place, so to speak. So I said, 'Hey, if these guys are breaking the rules and I'm trying to do it clean, it doesn't make sense.' Might as well join the club."

Pat Reid, the former high-jump coach who was on the same flights as Johnson out of Seoul, knew the sprinter and his coach well. He liked them. He also understood their dynamic—that Johnson was highly coachable and would unconditionally accept Francis's advice. "Ben was an easy mark for Charlie to influence," Reid said.

Others feel Johnson didn't need much of a shove. Tony Sharpe, a former Optimist teammate and Olympic bronze medalist, who is now an award-winning certified sprint coach, said Francis didn't need to browbeat his runners about steroid enhancement. Like Johnson, Issajenko, Desai Williams, and others, Sharpe agreed to use steroids because they were so commonly taken across the elite competition landscape. "There was this theory that you have to decide if you want to watch the finals or be in the finals," said Sharpe, who founded The Speed Academy, an athletics club near Toronto, after a successful commercial sales career at blue-chip companies that included Xerox and Bell Canada. "It was a culture influence more than a Charlie influence, though obviously he played a major role."

The culture of the times, as Sharpe points out, is important to what was happening in the Canadian sporting context, especially after the no-gold embarrassment at the Montreal games. Canada wanted Olympic medals. The government, through sports federations, was starting to throw money and support at sports and athletes who showed promise as world beaters. Track was one of the prized sports, with Francis's elite sprint group at the top of the heap.

Francis became a paid coach in 1981. He was named coach of the national sprint center at York University and earned a $25,000 salary (paid equally by Sport Canada and Sport Ontario). He would hold that top job through 1988. He remained convinced that to meet Sport Canada's goals of winning medals at major events, writing in his memoir, "steroids were an essential part of a world-class program."

"We were prepared to fulfill Sport Canada's mandate: to develop sprinters who could compete at the highest level. No one familiar with international track and field could have imagined we would get there drug-free."

Optimist team doctor Jamie Astaphan would later echo that sentiment. He was frank about steroids' place in the sport and how athletes perceived their benefits: "The axiom among track-and-field athletes was if you don't take it, you won't make it."

It must be noted that several of Francis's other top Optimist athletes did not take steroids and always competed drug-free. But for some young Optimist athletes constantly reassured by their coach and physician that using steroids wasn't a big deal, acceptance was easier. There was also little fear of being outed during the off-season since random dope testing at home and abroad was rare to nonexistent. Johnson was never tested out of competition prior to the Seoul Olympics.

After their private steroid chat, Francis and Johnson met with a Toronto physician to discuss potential side effects. He was told bad health outcomes were not a concern on a low-dose, intermittent program. Johnson thought about his decision for a week, then told Francis he'd like to start.

Johnson began his first Dianabol cycle in late 1981. While he maintains he didn't know the pills Francis initially gave him were steroids, a full understanding emerged during competition and training in 1982.

His initial steroid round was five milligrams of Dianabol pills taken daily for three weeks, then off for three weeks. Francis soon fiddled with Johnson's dosage, using five milligrams and then ten milligrams on alternate days. Francis bought hundred-pill bottles of Dianabol from his friend, Canadian shot put champion Bishop Dolegiewicz. He instructed his runners not to take any pills twenty-eight days before a competition and to visit their personal physicians for regular blood tests.

Johnson said it was easy to manage his doses and avoid race-day detection. In the early years, Francis would give him the exact amount of pills to take and no more. The sprinter said he never free-lanced doses, as others sometimes did, and stuck rigidly to clearance times.

Ten of the twenty-four carded elite athletes Francis coached eventually used drugs under his direction. It was unlikely that Johnson or any of the other nine were ever worried about being caught in a massive drug scandal. The Optimist group would avoid detection for nearly a decade, thanks in part to the all-but-useless process of testing athletes only on competition days. Athletes would joke that only the stupid or rookies ever got caught on race day.

Tight lips also helped. Rule-abiding athletes and coaches could report the Francis group to authorities, so dosing and steroid possession had to remain clandestine. Even Johnson, who told his mother Gloria everything, would not divulge this to her until long after he'd handed back his Olympic gold.

Keeping the secret brought the small group closer, sometimes out of necessity. If they weren't taking pills on a particular cycle, they needed injections into their glutes. Francis would give injections in his apartment near the York track center to those who couldn't bear needles, which included Johnson. Sometimes athletes injected each other. Issajenko and discus thrower Rob Gray both gave Johnson shots into his backside.

There were also supply chain issues: how to surreptitiously acquire thousands of dollars worth of drugs meant for the ailing, not for Olympic athletes. If physicians could not, or would not, provide prescriptions, shopping on the black market or buying from other athletes were the dicey alternatives. Vials weren't always labeled. Additionally, in Canada, steroids fell under the federal-controlled drugs and substances act, making trafficking a crime.

The group caught a break in 1983. Issajenko's medical contacts in a west-end clinic led her and Francis to a Toronto physician who, after hearing about her needs, agreed to act as team doctor for the elite Optimist sprinters. His name was George Mario "Jamie" Astaphan, a native of St. Kitts, licensed to practice medicine in the province of Ontario, where he lived with his family. Francis approved of the affable Astaphan, and the Optimist athletes came to like him. Not only was this doctor skilled at understanding and treating sports injuries, he quickly learned how to secure supplies of anabolic steroids and seemed trustworthy in protecting their consumption.

Under Astaphan's care, the athletes used both pill and injectable forms of anabolic steroids, including Dianabol, Winstrol (the brand name for stanozolol), and straight testosterone. They also used the banned human growth hormone (HGH), which is an anabolic hormone often prescribed to regulate growth and development in children. From his cramped office, Astaphan doled out anti-inflammatory medications and vitamins by the bushel, too. A mixture of inosine and vitamin B-12, both legal supplements, was given as a regular shot in the buttocks, sometimes in combination with steroids, HGH, and whatever else the doctor would tailor for certain athletes.

Athletes from other sports visited Astaphan, too, according to Johnson, Sharpe, and other Optimists. The sprinters have never outed them.

The runners' results progressed steadily on their way to becoming stellar. They won Olympic medals in Los Angeles, Commonwealth Games medals, and Pan Am Games medals. All kinds of records were set along the way. The Toronto sprinters were suddenly in demand to fill lanes in European and Japanese stadiums, earning thousands of US dollars in appearance fees.

By 1985, Johnson was a star. He began closing the gap on Carl Lewis after the LA Olympics and, now, was beating him. Johnson also managed to remain largely injury free, enabling his steady ascent, while rivals dealt with nagging soft tissue damage. He kept winning and getting faster.

"Ben really rocketed to the top. He was like a machine," recalled Sharpe, whose own career was curtailed by injury. "We called him Robocop for a while; remember those movies? The Americans would call him Robocop when he broke the world record in Rome. It was insane."

Through it all, the Optimist runners did not fail doping tests. Johnson said their clearance times were perfect.

With so much success, the athletes asked Astaphan few questions when he distributed the potpourri of steroids, vitamins, and anti-inflammatories to be consumed. They did what he said.

Johnson never dreamed the doctor who took such good care of him would one day betray him and his teammates in a most intimate way.

* * *

In late 1985, Jamie Astaphan introduced a new injectable steroid to the Optimist group. He called it Estragol, a wonder drug favored by the East Germans.

Astaphan told Francis and his runners that Estragol was an anabolic steroid generically known as furazabol. The beauty of this Estragol steroid was that it was undetectable in anti-doping labs, and therefore, a safer alternative to the popular steroid Winstrol, or stanozolol. A test to identify stanozolol metabolites in urine was being developed by German chemist Manfred Donike, so it would soon be riskier to take. In addition, Johnson and the others complained of muscle stiffness when they took stanozolol for too many days. The doctor assured Johnson that furazabol would be gentler on his muscles, leaving them looser and less prone to injury.

Astaphan told a fabulous backstory about how he stumbled onto Estragol.

The doctor claimed a Montreal man called him out of the blue, saying an East German athlete he knew wanted some of Astaphan's inosine and vitamin B-12 mixture. In return, the East German would provide a cache of an injectable steroid used by elite East German athletes. The two unnamed men traveled to Toronto to make the exchange. Astaphan received forty-eight steroid vials and gave the men 144 bottles of his inosine/B-12 mix.

Issajenko was wary. She wrote in her memoir that she couldn't find Estragol in her drug bible, *Compendium of Pharmaceuticals and*

Specialities. She mentioned her doubts to Francis. When confronted, the doctor said Estragol was a phony brand name for furazabol and claimed his Montreal contacts instructed him to use the fake name just in case any nosy American athletes overheard careless drug conversations.

Johnson knew Issajenko was suspicious of Astaphan's Estragol story but kept his thoughts to himself, as he often did. "I used to hear Angie and Charlie talk about those things at the track, but I never really got into it," he said. He figured if this Estragol steroid was good enough for the East Germans, he'd give it a shot, too.

The Toronto sprinters referred to Estragol as "the white stuff" because the solution turned milky-white when shaken. It came in 30-milliliter vials. The paranoid East German had removed all labels, apparently for additional security.

Astaphan sold Estragol to Johnson and the others for $50 (CAD) a bottle. Like most steroids, it worked its muscle magic, and "the white stuff" became part of the chemical jet fuel that propelled Johnson to a world championship, a world record, and, briefly, a record-smashing Olympic gold medal.

But the Estragol story was a web of lies. There was no East German pipeline. There was no Mr. Big in Montreal. There was no Estragol or furazabol in those vials.

Astaphan never told his patient-athletes what he was really injecting into them or what they were injecting into each other. It was a masterclass in deception by a physician who'd sworn an oath to do no harm. It would take a federal subpoena to learn the disturbing truth.

CHAPTER SEVEN

BEN AND CARL

Carl Lewis failed a doping test just weeks before Ben Johnson failed his in Seoul. In fact, Lewis failed three at the 1988 US Olympic trials after competing in the 100 meters, the 200 meters, and the long jump. The alleged violation: traces of different stimulants in amounts that, according to anti-doping rules in 1988, should have removed him from the Seoul-bound American team.

US Olympic Committee officials initially disqualified their star before quickly and quietly reversing that decision on appeal. They agreed his trouble stemmed from inadvertent use—Lewis claimed he used a herbal supplement that, unbeknownst to him, contained the contamination—and absolved him. This information was not disclosed to the public for fifteen years, which protected Lewis's reputation as a drug-free exemplar of Olympism. That American silence also served to intensify the post-Seoul villainization of Johnson as the "dirty" half of the rivalry and the lone doped-up wolf in all of men's sprinting.

Lewis had a chance to address the matter in his 1990 memoir, *Inside Track: My Professional Life in Amateur Track and Field*, but there's no mention. He does, however, mock and berate Johnson for doping and spray a fire hose of grievances at others. Had the public known prior to Seoul that Lewis had narrowly escaped his own doping disgrace, perhaps the frenzy around Johnson's drug failure would have been different.

Anabolic steroids aren't the only banned performance-enhancing drugs on the IOC's long list of forbidden substances. Stimulants, which can goose the central nervous system, are on it. There is a key difference between the two items. The mere presence of a steroid, in any amount, is an automatic positive. Stimulants are measured against a scale with a predetermined threshold to trigger a fail, meaning an athlete can have a little in their system and not register a violation. On occasion, crossing that stimulant threshold can be successfully explained away as accidental ingestion, as Lewis managed with an audience of sympathetic ears. In Seoul, Britain's Linford Christie wriggled out of a stimulant infraction in the 200 meters with a similar "oops" defense.

Lewis's brush with disqualification surfaced in 2003 only because former USOC director of drug control, Dr. Wade Exum, leaked thousands of confidential doping documents, including those of Lewis, to the media. It made for scandalous news coverage, fanned further when Lewis crashed his new Maserati in Los Angeles and was charged with drunk driving. (He later pleaded no contest to a misdemeanor and was sentenced to community service hours and attendance at alcohol management meetings.) But by then, the running rivals were no longer in the game. Lewis had retired and brushed off his doping matter as irrelevant.

After all these decades, Lewis's testing disclosures still raise a few "what ifs?" about the Seoul Olympics. If Johnson had won the 100 meters with Lewis kicked off the US team for a stimulant infraction, what type of doping discussions would have developed once Johnson tested positive for stanozolol? How would Johnson have been defined if Lewis was sitting at home, a disgraced cheat, with a trio of failed drug tests in his pocket? These are questions worth asking since, over the passage of time, information surrounding that Seoul race continues to surface, its historical framing shifting with each reveal. Lewis's testing record is just one part of it.

The American's free pass to the 1988 Summer Games sticks in Johnson's craw. He believes US Olympic officials improperly protected Lewis's chance at gold in Seoul. "[American] officials said, 'We will let him run in the Olympic Games because he's the only one who can beat Ben Johnson,' so they let him run," said Johnson, calling Lewis a hypocrite for attacking him but not confessing his own red-flagged history. "He'd been bragging to the whole world he'd been clean all along. Anyone who's bragging that they're clean, they're the ones who are guilty, they're the ones who are taking drugs."

Johnson was not alone in his view that American Olympic officials let Lewis off easy. In 2003, Richard Pound was head of the World Anti-Doping Agency. He said "the USOC was not prepared to enforce rules on its stars" and that he didn't buy accidental ingestion excuses from the experienced Olympic and world champion. "[The] USOC has some explaining to do for calling it inadvertent for a guy who had four gold medals [from Los Angeles in 1984]," Pound told the *Globe and Mail*, explaining, as he did to Johnson in 1988, that athletes are responsible for what they put into their bodies.

Pound also suggested that "at the very least, the results of the [US] trials should have been nullified and Lewis should not have been allowed to represent the United States in Seoul." The oft-repeated Lewis defense is that compared to modern doping rules, his 1988 stimulant readings would not be considered positive.

The 2003 whistleblowing revisited the Johnson-Lewis enmity. What is interesting, as sporting rivalries go, is that the rivalry was not a rivalry in the beginning, far from it. The two competed for years as junior sprinters, and Lewis was without question the superior talent. Johnson was just another sprinter, a Canadian guy trying to keep up with the flashy American.

* * *

Ben Johnson was in a group of younger Optimist runners told to grab a set of blocks to practice their starts. No one had shown him how to configure them, and at fifteen years old, he wasn't about to ask for help. Surely, he could do it himself.

He placed the blocks in a lane and spaced out the foot pads, with the left foot slightly in front of the right. It felt weird, though, when he pushed off for his first practice start. Something seemed wrong, even though he was the fastest out of the blocks. Charlie Francis, running the drills with a small starter's pistol, didn't notice anything amiss. Johnson's brother, Eddie, did.

Eddie had been sitting on a patch of grass, taking a break from practice with friends. He stared in disbelief at his brother, who was again about to crouch into the blocks with his spikes scraping on bare steel instead of rubber footpads. He stood up and wandered over.

"You know your blocks are in backwards, right?" Eddie said. Ben had no idea.

The early track careers of Johnson and Carl Lewis, who is six months older, had little in common. As a fifteen-year-old high schooler, Lewis was winning age-group sprints and long jump titles in and around his Willingboro, New Jersey, home. NCAA university recruiters would soon line up to woo him. The son of two high-school teachers, he was well-spoken and a strong student. He knew how starting blocks worked.

Francis looked on, bemused, as the Johnson brothers turned the blocks around so Ben could do the next drill. Other runners snickered, but the snickering didn't last. Johnson was faster each time out, gaining a better grip from the rubber matting beneath his spikes. It felt good and right.

"From that day on, they all knew I could start," he said.

Johnson developed an unshakeable confidence in the blocks from those days, although there was still some trial and error before he settled on his technique. "When I was trying to start back in the early days, I tried the way everybody normally comes out of the blocks.

When the starter says, 'On your mark,' most people put their heads down," he said, demonstrating the move by lowering his head with his eyes looking directly at the lane. "I tried that and nearly fell on my face coming out of the blocks. I thought, wow, I don't like that. It felt very unnatural, very different."

His head had to be up more. He raised it slightly so his eyes could see ten, maybe fifteen, meters ahead. His arm position also defied textbook norms in the set position. "My arms were a little bit bent while everybody [else] had their arms straight. I have mine bent and wide, so I can react faster and drive out with my hands faster."

A bullet start means nothing without smooth speed endurance over the full 100 meters. At first, Johnson's start was neutralized by stronger competitors who could outlast him over the last third of the race. Teammate Desai Williams was one of them.

Williams showed up for the first time at an Optimist practice in 1977 as an eighteen-year-old with an extensive soccer background. He had immigrated to Canada from St. Kitts, and for the next decade, his running career would be twinned with Johnson's. Williams logged impressive early results; his soccer training had developed his speed and stamina. That first year, he won the Canadian junior national 100-meter and 200-meter events and nudged his times down to 10.52 seconds for the shorter race. Johnson plodded along at 11.5 seconds.

More new faces joined the club, including the gregarious Tony Sharpe and the reserved Mark McKoy, two key figures as training partners and Olympic teammates in Johnson's future. Sharpe and McKoy were also best friends who grew up together in Scarborough after immigrating to Canada from Jamaica and Guyana, respectively. Johnson recalls looking at the 15-year-old Sharpe for the first time and being stunned to learn the tall, muscular kid was his age.

"I thought, 'This guy doesn't look like a junior, he looks like a senior guy. He was big,'" Johnson said. "He was a lot more developed than me, a lot stronger."

Sharpe was also faster than Johnson initially. Until he could start beating Sharpe or Williams regularly, taking on Lewis wasn't a consideration.

Ben Johnson's first major road trip was to a ten-day camp at East Tennessee State in March 1978. It opened his imagination to new possibilities for a sprinting career. He also witnessed the terrifying reality of racism at the end of an American gun.

The trip came between seasons for the Optimists. The club's winter indoor permit at the Swine Pavilion had ended. Francis refused to make the team slog across outdoor tracks slick with icy puddles from receding snowbanks. With the help of Ross Earl's bingo revenues, he planned a professional-quality training camp in the United States for his most promising and hard-working athletes. The Johnson brothers were part of it. They would travel to the Tennessee school where Francis had contacts, stay in motels, and train outdoors in warm, dry weather. It would lay a strong foundation for the runners' upcoming season.

Johnson was excited about the excursion. He was crammed into the back seat of an industrial-size van with Eddie and a few other runners, all wedged between equipment, luggage, and snacks. Francis was at the wheel, controlling the cassette tapes to the dismay of the athletes, who groaned at his selection of top-ten hits. The club's head coach, Peter Cross, was in the passenger seat, joking with the kids as Francis steered them through Ontario, Michigan, Ohio, Kentucky, and on to Johnson City, nestled in Tennessee's Great Smoky Mountains.

Once in the city's core, Francis's light mood abruptly changed. He turned to the runners and sternly told them to lie flat on the van seats. Bewildered, they did. "We all ducked down so no one could see us through the windows," said Johnson. Francis quickly explained that "it's not safe going through downtown with a bunch of Black guys in the back of the van."

The runners didn't understand why the move was necessary and stifled giggles until they were closer to campus and could again sit up. At their motel, they unpacked. A few athletes decided to go for a late-night stroll to stretch their legs. "It was around midnight, and we were walking behind a strip plaza, talking and laughing. I saw some of the unit doors propped open, you know, so you could throw out the garbage," said Johnson, recalling large dumpster bins behind the businesses. "Then, this one guy sees a bunch of Black guys walking by, and he comes out and shouts, 'Where you n------s come from? I'm going to get my gun.'"

The scared group ran, except for Eddie. When Johnson looked back to check on his brother, he saw Eddie strolling along. "I yelled, 'What are you doing? Run!'" said Ben, horrified when he saw the angry man return to the open unit door with a shotgun. "I just ran like hell."

The man brandished the weapon but didn't fire. Eddie kept walking until he joined the shaken group. Johnson exploded at his brother, furious that he'd taken such a chance by not running. They returned to their rooms and now understood why Francis ordered them to hide. The threat of racist violence was real. "In the van, we were all laughing and cracking up at the time, but it was serious; that's how bad it was," Johnson said. "Not a pleasant day."

Fortunately, the rest of the training camp was smooth. Francis and Cross ran two sessions daily, plus weight training. It was an exhausting routine, but Johnson was invigorated. His start, speed, and strength began to improve under intense instruction. The camp also coincided with his substantial growth spurt, which left him inhaling food like any growing teenage boy. Francis filled his motel room fridge with groceries for his athletes. By the second day, supplies were substantially depleted. Ben was identified as the food bandit. "In those days, I could eat. Charlie would buy these big packs of cheese, ham, eggs, bread, and butter, and every time I go (into his room), I just keep eating. Charlie would kill us at practice, and I was always so hungry."

Francis wasn't angry with Johnson for cleaning out the team's food. In fact, the coach rarely got angry, at least not in a loud, threatening manner. All he asked was that athletes give their best effort every time out, and those who didn't paid the price, Johnson said. "If Charlie got pissed off at you, he never shouted. Never. He held back." If someone was struggling, "he'd keep calm, he'd talk to you and ask if you had any soreness, cramps, aching pain, that kind of thing. But if you were doing something out of the ordinary that he didn't like, he will quietly punish you on the track, and you better well do what he says, because if you don't do it right, you're going to be there all day until he's satisfied."

Johnson embraced the training camp routine in Tennessee: stretching, tempo running, speed work, weight training, and massage. He accepted the requirements that an athlete be rested, fueled, and unconditionally invested in the coach's playbook. He was also patient, understanding that if he did exactly what Francis asked, he would improve in small and large increments. Details mattered to him as an athlete, and that made him a coach's dream, open to instruction and able to execute instructions with precision.

His obsessive attention to detail was a trait Johnson showed as a child and one that undoubtedly assisted his rise through the sprinting ranks, said sister Jean Hanlan. She recalled that her younger brother could focus for extended periods working with toys or crafts that required nitpicky assembly. "He was very focused as a child." Hanlan said her brother also had the ability to shut out extraneous noise while performing tasks he enjoyed because he "wanted to make sure it was done properly and that he understood everything about what the message was."

A year after that trip to Tennessee, Johnson began to blossom. He won the 1979 Canadian junior 100-meter championship, not in a knock-your-socks-off time (10.66 seconds), but it was a remarkable achievement, considering he was only in his third year of serious training and had packed on forty lean pounds and grown several inches in the interim. His improvement was steady. He was perfecting that explosive start.

Johnson hoped to be named to a European tour with the senior national team that same summer, a trip led by Canadian sprint coach Gerard Mach, but he didn't make the cut. Mach, however, liked the young runner with the unusual start. He told Francis he'd keep Johnson in mind as an alternate if anyone got injured. A few days later, a senior runner pulled up lame.

"Charlie comes up to me at practice and says, 'Guess what, Ben? You've been selected and you're going to Europe.' I was so happy," he said. "I'd never been to Europe, and at that point, I believed this [sport] was my destiny." His mother, Gloria, was thrilled. She discreetly gave Francis $100 to hold for her son as spending money. It touched the coach, who understood what a sacrifice it was to part with that much cash. So did her son.

"It was a lot of money for her," Johnson said. "She believed in me, and I was determined to get the job done, no matter what."

It was a big step up for Johnson, but nothing like what Carl Lewis was experiencing at the time. Lewis committed to the University of Houston in the fall to train under legendary coach Tom Tellez. Though it was against NCAA rules to pay athletes then, Adidas sponsored him for $5,000 (US) during his freshman year plus bonus money for major victories, enabling him to buy, among other things, a burgundy Trans Am. Johnson was not yet approved for a modest monthly athlete's assistance sum from the government. He took the bus to practice if he couldn't bum a ride.

On that summer tour under Mach, Johnson did well at a dual meet in Italy, running a strong first relay leg against veteran Italian Olympic star Pietro Mennea. The teenager had been too nervous to look at, never mind recognize, the older man in the next lane. "Charlie came up to me after and said that it was a good race. You really held your ground—and you know the guy beside you was Mennea, right?" recalled Johnson.

"I said, 'Holy fuck, really?' That was the same year Mennea set the [200-meter] world record in Mexico City. Then I started shaking, because I didn't know it was him."

Sometimes, the best athletic learning experiences don't come in the form of a medal. Sticking close to a sprinting icon was foundational to his confidence.

When the 1979 Canadian tour swung into the northern English city of Gateshead a few days before a meet, Johnson killed time in the hotel watching his sprint teammates playing cards, betting a few dollars a hand. He soon became bored. He wandered off and heard what seemed like a party going on in another room: uproarious laughter, shouting, music, and clinking bottles. Johnson peeked in the door and saw the big men of Canadian track and field: the throwers. Discus thrower Rob Gray, a burly fellow Torontonian with a beer in one massive hand, looked up.

"What do you want?" asked Gray, eyeing the slender teen.

"I just want to hang around with you guys," said Johnson.

"Okay," Gray said, waving him in. "Get yourself a beer."

Johnson took a bottle from the cooler, sipped from it, and watched the men carry on. They chatted with the sprinter, pleased to have a new person to entertain with their oft-told war stories. They delighted in making him laugh.

"Rob would tease me, he'd always say, 'you little fart,' and the way he talked sometimes was so funny, like, 'If you mess with me, I'll squeeze you like a grape,'" he recalled. "Back then, I was probably only 160 pounds, a scrawny kid hanging out with these guys who are 280, 300 pounds. But I wasn't intimidated by them, even though they were all so much bigger than me."

Gray, the group's *bon vivant*, said the throwers liked Johnson because he was not a "diva" sprinter. He would drink a beer, maybe two, and could shoot back funny lines. He also endured jokes about his stutter without complaint. In retrospect, Gray, a former Canadian champion and Commonwealth Games record holder, who has remained friends with Johnson, said he deeply regrets teasing him about his speech impediment during their competition years. "Ben, to me, was a very shy guy when he was younger, and part of that was probably due to his stutter. We were cruel to him in many ways. We'd say, 'Hey B-b-ben, how ya doing, man?' He would kind of laugh, but, clearly, it would bother him. Today, you'd get in trouble for making fun of someone's stutter, but in those days, we were all jocks, athletes. You know what it's like, you treat [athlete friends] the same way you'd treat your family, like, shut up and get used to it."

Years later, Gray and Johnson would end up having more in common than just good times on the road. In 1986, Gray and two shot-putters were banned from competition for life after testing positive for steroids at the Canadian national championships. The throwers' experience predates Johnson's doping failure, but similarities between the cases exist.

Gray, a rookie lawyer in 1986 while still competing at the national level, represented the throwers at a formal hearing. He requested copies of the three urine tests analyzed by the IOC's Montreal lab. The hearing's independent arbitrator supported Gray's request and ordered the production of the tests, but the doping documents, inexplicably, were not delivered by the lab, said Gray. The throwers never saw the scientific evidence against them, and yet the bans were upheld by the arbitrator, according to documents outlining the arbitrator's 1987 decision.

* * *

Ben Johnson had a healthy respect and appreciation for Carl Lewis as the best junior sprinter in the world in 1980, not to mention his dominance as a long jumper. One of the early head-to-head meetings between Johnson and Lewis was at the 1980 Pan Am Junior track-and-field championships in Sudbury, a northern Ontario city about a four-hour drive from Toronto.

Lewis had shown up in great shape, and Tony Sharpe, too. Johnson, for his part, was struggling. He'd badly sprained an ankle in a pickup soccer game two months earlier.

Lewis won the Pan Am title handily in 10.43 seconds. Sharpe was third in 10.56. Johnson showed up in 10.88, a disastrous result since he expected to be on the podium.

"I was strong, but I had no speed," he said, noting the ankle injury prevented him from training. "I made it to the final; I came out of the blocks okay, but I finished second last. I was so mad at myself."

That year, 1980, provided another fascinating snapshot of the not-quite-yet rivals as they began transitioning out of the junior ranks. Lewis was still on his superstar trajectory. He'd been named to the boycotted Moscow Olympic team, was dominating NCAA meets, and was pulling in rich sponsorships, including a $200,000 (US) Nike deal with $40,000 bonus pay for each gold medal at the LA Games. He'd also met Joe Douglas, head coach of the famous Santa Monica Track Club in California and later Lewis's manager. The two would form a bond through the 1988 games in Seoul.

Johnson followed a less gilded path. He started receiving appearance fees at European races, about $300 (US) a meet in cash, most of which went to Gloria Johnson. And he was provisionally named to Canada's 1980 Olympic team for the relay. As for postsecondary education, there were no big-time NCAA offers. He'd taken one brief run at community college, attending a "small motors" course and learning how to assemble, repair, and rebuild machinery like lawn mower engines. After a week or two, he decided his future was not in a classroom. He got up from his desk, gave his textbooks to needy students he'd befriended, and shook the shocked instructor's hand while explaining that life as a mechanic was not for him. "I said to myself, 'Ok Ben, this is it.'" He decided to become an Olympic champion one day. "I'm going to put all my eggs in one basket, and I'm going to make sure no eggs get broken."

If ever there was a perfect showcase for one athlete, the 1984 Los Angeles Games was it for Carl Lewis. He was the reigning world champion in the 100 meters, a title earned a year earlier with a 10.07 victory in Helsinki. He also won long jump and relay golds in Finland. In the summer of 1984, Lewis swept his three individual events at the US Olympic trials: the 100 and 200-meter sprints and the long jump. The sprint relay would be his fourth race as part of Team USA.

Lewis was receiving comparisons to another American track-and-field hero, Jesse Owens, who earned Olympic gold in the same individual events, plus a fourth in the relay, at the 1936 games in Berlin under the nose of Adolf Hitler. The expectations of a nation were that Lewis would win four, too, but it was a historic mantle Lewis found uncomfortable. "I could no longer be Carl Lewis. I had to be Carl Lewis, the next Jesse Owens," he wrote in his memoir. He devotes an entire chapter in the memoir to a "new event" on the international circuit called "Carl-Bashing." He wrote there were "basically three bashing categories: Carl thinks he's better than everyone else and he loves to show it. Carl does drugs; Carl is gay." Lewis said those denigrations were unfair, inaccurate, and due to jealousies.

Lewis was also smarting from a massive pre-Olympic feature written by Gary Smith, a reporter he described as "the all-time champion of Carl Lewis-bashing." Smith wrote an article for an Olympic edition of *Sports Illustrated* that, among other themes, explored Lewis's sexuality, his singing career, and his ample ego. It upset the sprinter, especially when other reporters picked up on the Smith piece and amplified parts Lewis said were false.

Anything Lewis said or did grabbed headlines leading up to the LA Olympics. Inadvertently, he was helping to deflect the political theater creeping into the games. This time, the Soviets were leading a boycott, mounted as payback for the Moscow Games snub. It hurt fields in many sports, including track, although it meant little when it came to the men's 100 meters. Americans owned the event. They swept the medals at the 1983 world championships in Helsinki: Lewis first, followed by Calvin Smith and Emmit King. The only Canadian in the Helsinki final was Desai Williams, who was eighth. Ben Johnson, suffering tendinitis in his knee, didn't get out of his semi.

It was understandable, then, that with all Lewis was handling on and off the track, Ben Johnson was not on his radar. The American had beaten him the first six times they'd met prior to the 1984 games.

"[At] the Olympics in Los Angeles, I didn't know much about Ben, and I didn't really care about him. He was just another sprinter, a Canadian who claimed he could beat me, but nobody paid much attention to him back then," Lewis wrote.

What Lewis likely didn't know was that Johnson's poor performance in Helsinki was an aberration. Until then, he'd been making gains under Francis's tutelage, covertly supported by the ever-evolving steroid program. At the 1982 Commonwealth Games in Brisbane, Australia, Johnson narrowly lost to defending Olympic champion Allan Wells, settling for silver in a wind-aided 10.05 seconds. Johnson was also part of Canada's sprint relay with Sharpe, Desai Williams, and Mark McKoy, which took silver in Brisbane.

Though Johnson did poorly in Helsinki, a few weeks earlier he'd nailed a career breakthrough, winning his first European Grand Prix meet in Munich in a personal best of 10.19 seconds. He was gaining attention on the international circuit for his unmatched reaction time to the starter's pistol and his quirky leaping start. Lewis would soon take notice.

* * *

Johnson's financial health was improving along with his times. Francis negotiated modest but welcome endorsement contracts with the sportswear company Adidas. Angella Issajenko was still the club's marquee athlete and received $500 a month, while Johnson collected

$250. It was not a princely sum, but it helped. Johnson gave most to his mother Gloria, and she, in turn, returned some to him to save or spend. He did both and was able to pursue another passion: car ownership.

He fell for a used 1976 Trans Am he'd spotted in a small dealership on Queen Street East in Toronto two years before the LA Games. It was his ticket to liberation. No more bumming lifts, no more public transit. And a bit of private time with girls he liked. He just needed some help to finance his first ride.

Again, Francis came through. He cosigned a $3,500 loan for the white muscle car, since most banks don't consider an amateur athlete's income to be reliable. In a serious moment as they were signing the papers, Francis reminded the sprinter what the Trans Am purchase was for: "He said, 'This is not a car to drive around, this is a car to get you to practice,' and I said, 'Yes, don't worry, I'll be at practice.'"

Francis paused, then discreetly asked: "Do you need any money?"

"Well, maybe just a little bit," Johnson said, nervously thinking of his first auto insurance bill.

Francis reached into a pocket and pulled out $300 in cash. He handed it over and asked if Johnson needed any more. The sprinter thanked him and said that gift was enough.

"When I got the car, I didn't miss a practice. I came to practice every day, I was never late," he said. Soon, the sleek car with the Firebird emblazoned across the hood was a familiar sight at the track center.

* * *

Media flooded sunny Los Angeles for the first Olympic Games that featured Hollywood razzle-dazzle in its opening ceremonies—remember the guy in the jetpack?—and delivered a two-week party atmosphere. They were also the first games to make a profit, thanks to the guiding hand of Peter Ueberroth, chairman of the Los Angeles

Olympic Organizing Committee. I was there, at my first Olympics, as a rookie reporter for the *Toronto Sun* newspaper. *Sun* sports editor George Gross was part of our team and parked himself at high-profile venues, like swimming and track, to write his columns. My assignments included taking a bus to Chino, California, to cover Olympic shooting of some sort, and stumbling into a gold medal moment for Canadian springboard diver Sylvie Bernier. Four years later, Gross would become a key figure in publishing Johnson's highly orchestrated "not knowingly" defense of his steroid use after Seoul, which ultimately did Johnson more harm than good.

While Canada's medal hopes in LA were pinned on the swimmers, the track contingent also provided thrills, especially in the men's 100 meters. A pair of Optimists, Johnson and Sharpe, were among the eight finalists, the first time two Canadian men had advanced to an Olympic 100-meter medal race.

Johnson lost his biggest advantage almost immediately when he was charged with a false start; he heard a nearby camera click and jumped out before the pistol shot. Runners were allowed one violation. The second was disqualification. He'd have to hold back when they lined up again.

The second start was clean. Lewis tore down his lane, hitting the tape first in 9.99 seconds. Compatriot Sam Graddy was second in 10.19 with Johnson ruining an American sweep by clinching bronze in 10.22 seconds. Sharpe was eighth.

Johnson claims the false start cost him silver, but not gold. He described himself as having to play catch-up from the blocks, surging around the 50-meter mark, and then running out of gas in the final strides. Lewis was simply too fast, and Graddy outlasted him at the tape. "I could have beaten Sam Graddy. I wouldn't have beaten Carl Lewis, but I would have run much better than 10.22."

Lewis was in a class by himself in Los Angeles, looking so relaxed, even at top speed. Francis and Johnson decided he was worth studying.

When the games ended and the athletes returned home for a short break, Francis obtained a VHS tape of the 100-meter final for Johnson. Like the little boy in Falmouth who loved watching movies over and over, he absorbed every detail of the race, especially the efforts of the top three finishers.

"I went home and studied the tape for almost an entire week," he said.

"Replays, from different angles, in my basement. After hours of doing that, I got the message of what I needed to work on, and that was the last forty meters of my race. I had to work on my finish."

Johnson believed Lewis was the only runner in the world substantially better than himself. He also felt Lewis had maxed out his top speed, whereas Johnson knew he had more capacity to develop.

"I said to Charlie that Carl Lewis was not going to improve that much. He's reached his peak, so to speak, and he's not going to get much faster," said Johnson. "But I can improve a lot more because I have more room to improve to get from 10.22 to 9.99 or 9.98—that was the key for me to get there."

Two of Johnson's first decisions were to take less time off from training after the summer season and to spend more time in the gym lifting weights to bulk up his upper body and core strength. He wanted to be "ahead of the game" while his chief opponent was resting.

History's greatest sprint rivalry was officially underway, even though Lewis had no idea Johnson was gunning for him.

CHAPTER EIGHT
THE PLAYBOY

It was two days before the 100-meter heats for the 1987 world championships in Rome. Ben Johnson was stark naked in a hotel hallway, banging on the locked door of the room where he'd just had sex with a woman he'd just met. The woman had already departed, blowing him a kiss before returning to the lobby, where she worked at an information kiosk. The hotel room was not Johnson's. A friend on the Jamaican national team reluctantly loaned it to him for the romp on one condition: don't use the bed.

Johnson had needed an unoccupied room for the quickie because his girlfriend was staying with him in a different Roman hotel. The pair weren't getting along. As he tells it, he wanted to have middle-of-the-day sex but his girlfriend did not. She suggested he save his energy for the 100 meters. "She said, 'This is the biggest race of your life,' and I said, 'Don't you worry about that, let me worry about that,'" he said. "I said, 'I'm going to sleep with someone else if you don't want to sleep with me.'" His girlfriend was unmoved. He paced the room, then left to find a willing partner.

The search didn't take long. Johnson's athletic cachet and good looks—photographers often snapped him bare-chested, wearing only shorts and spikes, his heavily muscled torso and legs on display—were catnip to a wide range of women. He was mobbed at track events and in public. That he was as understated as rival Carl Lewis was brash added to his mystique for his growing legion of groupies.

Johnson had hurried over to the Jamaican team hotel to locate an attractive Italian woman at the lobby kiosk. He'd been eyeing her for a few days. He flirted with her and made his pitch for a hookup. In the process, he'd tracked down his Jamaican friend, who handed over his room key.

The woman agreed to the tryst. She accompanied the sprinter to the borrowed room. When he unlocked the door, he saw a problem: some European hotel rooms are not as spacious as North American accommodations, which often contain extra furniture like big, comfy chairs. This one in Rome was on the small side. The bed beckoned. "There was nowhere else to do it," said Johnson, sheepishly. "I wasn't going to do it on the floor."

When the sex session ended, the woman dressed and strolled out. Johnson remained sprawled across the mattress for a few happy minutes too long. His Jamaican friend came snooping, pushed open the unlocked door, saw the sated Canadian in the rumpled sheets and yelled, "I told you to stay off my fucking bed!"

"He shoved me out of the door, butt naked, into the hallway. I said, 'Come on, man, open the door, I'm naked out here' . . . I had nowhere to do it, I'm sorry, it had to be on the bed." Johnson covered his eyes, laughing and shaking his head at the memory of it. "He refused to open the door for, maybe, two minutes."

When he finally relented, Johnson grabbed his clothes, dressed, apologized again, and jogged back to his own hotel in a giddy mood. If there are believers in the adage that sex weakens the legs before a competition, Johnson is not among them. He was a man who liked the company of beautiful women, and romancing them close to race days did not drain an iota of his energy. Just the opposite, he said.

"I feel so good now, nice and relaxed," said Johnson, describing the memory as if he were floating down the hotel hallway. "I thought, 'Holy shit, I hope this feeling doesn't leave me before the race.'"

In that moment, now spent of tension, he said he was able to turn his full attention to the 100 meters. In the final, he would go on to obliterate the world record with authority in a country that adores track champions.

Rome was one of Ben Johnson's favorite destinations, and it remains so. Not only had he raced well in the Eternal City over the years, but he also enjoyed shopping there: he bought tailored Italian suits and fine jewelry when he started making good money. And he was extremely popular with local women.

He recalled a 1986 experience in a restaurant. A "good-looking woman threw down a napkin with her number on it" in front of him and walked away.

Johnson later called her. She spoke English and invited him to her home, where she asked him to wait in her bedroom while she put the finishing touches to her make-up and dabbed on perfume. Johnson sat primly on the edge of her bed. He glanced around and recognized photographs of several men placed throughout her bedroom. Some were athletes.

"I looked around at all these famous people on the wall, and I thought, 'I guess I'm the next guy,'" he said. "I asked her, 'Who are all these people? Do you know them all?' and she said, 'Yes, of course.'"

It wasn't to be the evening Johnson expected. The woman, a professional model, simply wanted to stroll through the ancient streets, showing off her twenty-four-year-old Canadian eye candy.

"She's beautiful, she has her arms around me, everybody was just looking at us walking around downtown Rome. She had this dress on that was slit up high, not too high, and the dress was flip-flopping around her legs."

To this day, Johnson vividly recalls the pleasant evening and how he was charmed by a stranger. He didn't end up in her bed. His framed photo was not going up on her wall. And they never saw each other again. "I don't remember her name, but I remember her."

* * *

Coach Charlie Francis described Ben Johnson's appetite for women as prodigious. The stuttering kid who was bullied in grade school had, by the mid-1980s, stormed the world stage as a hot, eligible, nightclubbing bachelor who favored Italian silk shirts, magnums of Dom Perignon, and dance floors lined with stunning women, even though he didn't dance.

His amorous adventures were occasionally a source of amusement to Francis and his Optimist teammates. They'd see women wander into the training center looking for him, unaware he was sometimes with another date. Johnson was not always successful in scrambling fast enough to keep them from seeing each other, resulting in awkward confrontations.

Once, he had to take evasive action when he invited a new date to watch him train. The young woman sat under a shady tree on a small hill inside the fenced-off facility while groups of athletes worked out in the heat. Johnson planned to spend a nice day with her when he was finished. Then he spotted trouble.

"I forgot I'd invited someone else to come to the track that day, and suddenly, she showed up," said Johnson. She wandered into the outdoor complex. "She didn't see me and was asking everyone, 'Where is Ben?' I panicked, so I had to scale the fence to get away."

Once over the chain-link fence, Johnson darted behind thick shrubs to hide. He was safe: the women didn't know each other, nor had they noticed him fleeing. He bolted to his car and sat inside until he saw a couple of athletes he knew walk by. Johnson asked them to go back to the track to tell his newest date, the one under the tree, to meet him at the car. She did as requested, and unpleasant drama was avoided.

This scene was not an everyday occurrence. Johnson had several long-term relationships in his running days. Among them were a former beauty pageant winner, models, and a woman from Germany with whom he keeps in touch via social media three decades after they dated. He's also had some complicated romances.

About a decade after the Seoul Olympics, a relationship with a Canadian woman cost him his treasured gold Cartier necklace.

"I fell in love with this girl, and she stole it from me," he said, grimacing.

He'd given her the gold-link chain to wear as a token of his affection, but she later told him she'd lost it. Johnson said he suspects she sold it, although he has no proof. He broke up with her. Losing it wasn't about the $9,000 price tag. The necklace held deep sentimental value for Johnson; he'd worn it during his race in Seoul, and to him, it symbolized success, not disgrace. He vows to replace the original chain one day with a duplicate to fasten around his own neck.

Though some love affairs broke his heart, Johnson's zeal for pursuing gorgeous women never dimmed. His appreciation for longer-term girlfriends was shown in the form of gifts, jewelry, long-distance phone calls that cost thousands of dollars each month (in the pre-cell phone age, such calls were punishingly expensive to make on landlines), and first-class vacations to sunny places.

"My mum always said that was my one weakness—women," he said.

In the late 1980s, as today, Toronto nightclubs attracted crowds of single twenty- and thirty-somethings who liked to drink and dance. When Johnson squealed into a club parking lot behind the wheel of his $275,000 (CAN) Ferrari Testarossa, women would start lining up to get his attention, said Tony Morrison, who acted as Johnson's first line of defense.

"I'd play his bodyguard, and I'd say, 'No you can't talk to him,' and all the girls would hate me, but I was trying to keep the gold diggers away from him," Morrison said.

Even with Morrison's protective interventions, Johnson was not lonely for long. And girlfriends, whether they knew it or not, had to earn Gloria Johnson's approval for her son to maintain the relationship. Few cleared this hurdle, especially if a companion seemed more interested in the VIP trappings of her son's celebrity status and his growing wealth than in him. Gloria Johnson had the ability "to size them up right away," her son said. "My mother's standard was about honesty, loyalty, understanding who Ben is, and what Ben is about."

He respected his mother's opinions. He vowed he would not threaten the bond they shared by marrying while Gloria was alive. "My mum thought if I got married, she might end up alone." Johnson would remind her that his love for her was paramount, and no girlfriend would remove him from her side. "I would go up to my mum, look her in the eyes, and hug her and say, 'Mum, I would never leave you, so you never have to worry about me getting married. I'm going to stay with you.' And she'd say, 'I know son, I know.'"

Gloria often traveled with her son after he convinced her to retire from the workforce in 1985. At that point, he could take care of her financially. She attended the 1987 world championships in Rome and spent time with his girlfriend, who was not interested in daylight sex. Johnson described that girlfriend as beautiful, intelligent, and career focused, but he was also aware of Gloria's disapproving glances toward his companion. "She was not the one for me," said Johnson of his mother's assessment.

He would come to the same conclusion. By the end of the summer, Johnson was a world champion and, once again, an eligible bachelor.

He has never married.

* * *

Ben Johnson did not attend the birth of his only child, a daughter named Jeneil. It was in April 1988, five months before the Olympics in Seoul.

Johnson and the child's mother had been in an off-and-on relationship, and he was not seeking a long-term commitment. He was also, effectively, an absent father in Jeneil's earliest days, a function due in part to heavy travel and competition schedules.

Johnson's baby news was kept private, not just from the public but also from some in his social circle. At least one long-time teammate had no idea he was a dad.

"I didn't even know the guy had a daughter until she was about twenty," said Tony Sharpe, who raised a son and twin daughters with his wife Colene over their thirty-plus-year marriage. "That freaked me out."

Even now, Johnson is reluctant to discuss much about his daughter, saying he wants to protect their collective private lives.

This is an extremely sensitive area for Johnson. He wasn't prepared to be a father and didn't understand the extent of his parental obligations, but he provided child support for a period.

By spring 1988, the world-champion sprinter was firmly established as the Johnson family breadwinner. He bought his first house, "for my mother," in Scarborough in 1985. Optimist club founder Ross Earl and his wife, Sylvia, helped him shop for it, checking windows for drafts and the basement for leaks. He shared it with his mother, family members, and a pet parrot. He also purchased a second house nearby for his sister, Jean.

To protect his status as an amateur athlete earning money from his sport, Johnson, like other Canadian amateurs across all sports, was required to deposit sport earnings in a trust account. In Canada, it was called an Athletes Reserve Fund, or ARF, account, which was administered by CTFA officials for its members. In 1983, amateurs were permitted by their sports' ruling bodies to use trust funds, meaning they no longer had to hide under-the-table earnings. They could withdraw money from those accounts for reasonable expenses, the "reasonable" part sometimes a judgment call by federation officials. Withdrawals were subject to tax.

The riches in Johnson's ARF account and what constituted reasonable withdrawals—his Testarossa was deemed a reasonable training expense to get him to practice—would later become areas of scrutiny at a public inquiry, while child support went unmentioned.

Johnson said he provided money for Jeneil's care and assisted with baby items, dropping off clothing, diapers, boxes of infant formula, blankets, and more, but the new father was shaken financially after the Seoul disqualification. No new revenue was coming in, and he now had legal fees on top of his usual expenses. He'd return to the sport in 1991, but Johnson's earning power never came close to its 1988 zenith.

Johnson began to play a more active role in Jeneil's life when she began school. Today, he is a grandfather of three.

* * *

Di-anne Hudson has known Ben Johnson since 2001 and remains his most trusted confidante. She also acts as his business manager, an unpaid, protective role she serves after seeing predatory friends and strangers trying to take financial advantage of him. They met at a social event and became friends during a period when Hudson was working at the *Toronto Star* as an executive assistant to the corner-office suits, including the late publisher John Honderich. When Johnson was out of the country on business, Hudson stepped up to help drive his mother, Gloria, to medical appointments and Sunday church services right up until her death. Johnson said he is grateful for this platonic friendship.

"She took care of my mother when I was away for months at a time, and I didn't have to worry about my mum," he said. "That's why I am so loyal to Di-anne."

Johnson, who has had a steady girlfriend for years, also relies on Hudson's judgment. "She's the only person who understands me. She's the only person that I can't lie to. She's the only person who loves me, no matter what, regardless of what I do. She just loves me."

Like all good friends, they've had fights, sometimes about dumb things. Hudson tells a story of Johnson running out of gas on Toronto's busy Don Valley Parkway in the wee hours of a weeknight. He calls her, wakes her up, and asks for help. She is annoyed that he can't summon roadside assistance for himself. Enterprising, she finds a service to bring him gas on the side of the freeway, but he's not there when the service arrives. She becomes frantic because he doesn't phone her, doesn't answer her calls, and she fears he's been murdered by some maniac in the dark.

Hours later, after sunrise, she gets him on the phone. Johnson explains that a good Samaritan came by and got him back on the road. He didn't bother to tell her. He just drove home to get some sleep.

* * *

Of all the date nights Ben Johnson experienced during his competition years, one in Zurich held a significance unlike any other.

This is how he first met his "mystery man." On the morning of August 13, 1986, Johnson climbed into a courtesy car waiting to take him from his hotel to the stadium track. He was running in the famous Weltklasse meet and would line up against Carl Lewis in the 100 meters that evening.

He placed the bag carrying his spikes on the seat beside him and then noticed a tall man hovering close by. The Canadian asked if he was going to the track and whether he wanted a ride. The tall man with an American accent said yes to both.

En route to the stadium, the American introduced himself as Andre Jackson. He was laid-back, making small talk, then asked Johnson if he was interested in going out for a night in the town.

"I'd seen him around at different meets before. I didn't know who he was, but I knew he was American," said Johnson. "He asked if I wanted to hang out later because he knew two girls in Zurich."

Johnson said Jackson didn't volunteer that he was a close friend of Carl Lewis, nor did Johnson know that was the case. Regardless, Johnson was interested in a fun night, and they made plans to meet. But first, he had a race to run.

Johnson had recorded a series of important victories that summer going into Zurich. He'd beaten Lewis soundly in San Jose, California, hitting the tape first in 10.01 seconds and Lewis second in 10.18. Johnson's finest achievement was his 9.95-second triumph at the Goodwill Games in Moscow. It was the first time he had broken the 10-second mark. Nigeria's Chidi Imoh was second, with Lewis well back in third in 10.06.

Thirty-four years later, the 1986 Goodwill Games win again made headlines when former Russian anti-doping chief Grigory Rodchenkov claimed Johnson tested positive for stanozolol but the result was not reported. It was one of fourteen suppressed positives in Moscow, according to Rodchenkov, who in 2014 "masterminded" the sample-swapping scheme at the Sochi Winter Games to protect doped-up Russian athletes.

Johnson dismisses Rodchenkov's claim as false. He said if that were true, he'd have been reported immediately, disqualified, and suspended by the IAAF to the benefit of Lewis's career because Canadian officials would not have challenged the findings.

After the Goodwill Games, Johnson won three medals at the 1986 Commonwealth Games in Edinburgh: golds in 100 meters and sprint relay, and bronze in the 200 meters. Queen Elizabeth II draped the 100-meter gold around his neck and shook his hand.

There were lower caliber meets interspersed through the competition schedule that year, and Johnson recalled being worn out with the heavy demands of racing, travel, and increased media attention. Now his dominance over Lewis was about to be tested at Zurich's Weltklasse meet. It was not an option to run poorly because he was fatigued, especially not at the Weltklasse, an exclusive stop on the European Grand Prix circuit. Paying fans wanted a show. So did Johnson's sponsors and the meet director who paid him.

They were not disappointed. Johnson leapt from the blocks, arms slicing high over the first few steps, to win the 100 meters in 10.03 seconds, a decent time for a tired guy. Lewis was third in 10.18 seconds. The outcome cemented Johnson's unofficial ranking as the world's No. 1 sprinter, which became official at year's end when he usurped Lewis in the top spot.

After this drubbing of Lewis, Johnson took a taxi to join Jackson and the two women at an exclusive club. Champagne was uncorked, the dance floor was full, and the night ended with a woman on his arm. Johnson said he saw Jackson again the next day at the track, and they chatted briefly. Johnson didn't remember crossing paths again and soon forgot his clubbing buddy's name. When Jackson appeared in Seoul, Johnson said he didn't recognize him because he had gained weight and had less hair, looking different from what he had in Zurich.

The two would meet again years after the Seoul Games to discuss the sprinter's positive test, according to Johnson. He was so desperate for answers to restore his reputation, he would leave his mother's deathbed to seek them.

CHAPTER NINE
I DON'T TALK BULLSHIT

The proving ground was the eight-lane track at Rome's Olympic stadium on August 30, 1987, the day of the 100-meter world championship final. Two of the fastest men alive had a score to settle.

The Carl Lewis-Ben Johnson showdown had been brewing for three years. Their public sniping was escalating, and as a by-product of the animosity, there was global interest in the race. The appeal of the two athletes as hero and antihero, depending on one's allegiance, was massive.

Johnson held the upper hand going into Rome, having beaten the American each time they'd met since August 1985. Lewis became resentful and aggrieved during this streak, while Johnson grew confident and vocal.

A late-May race in Seville had ratcheted the hostility to an extreme, in a very public manner. Going into the outdoor season of 1987, Johnson felt ready for a world-record attempt. He and coach Charlie Francis knew he was strong enough to break American Calvin Smith's 1983 mark of 9.93 seconds, but a nagging calf cramp, akin to a muscle strain, surfaced during a ten-day spring training camp in Provo, Utah. A record attempt would have to be delayed by a few weeks. By the Seville meet, Johnson felt close to full strength. Maybe the timing would work since Lewis was also scheduled to be in the race. His rival's presence would push him.

Johnson recalls warming up nearly two hours before the Seville sprint when he saw Lewis in the stands, chatting with friends. Why was he not on the field? Johnson wondered if his rival was going to skip the 100 meters and dodge him. The two had been accusing each other of ducking races in recent months. Maybe Lewis was only going to long jump or run the 200 meters. He discussed that possibility with an impatient Francis, who blurted: "Who cares? Just do your thing."

Johnson had moved on to speed drills when Lewis walked to field level and commenced what Johnson considered an unusually short race prep. "Man, I'm out here busting my ass for two hours warming up, and this guy comes in with less than forty minutes to go," he mused.

The spectators didn't mind Lewis's late arrival and cheered him wildly. With head-to-head contests between the rivals infrequent, the crowd was excited for the Canadian too. He had his own fans clapping, calling out his name, and asking for photographs and autographs whenever he moved close to the grandstand. Johnson pledged to sign programs and pictures after the race.

When the runners were called to their mark and the starter's pistol fired, the sprint began as it always did. Johnson was out of the blocks first, moving well and accelerating smoothly. Lewis's long strides began eating up ground. Then Johnson sensed his left calf tightening. He decelerated slightly. He didn't want to aggravate the muscle before Rome, even though he sensed Lewis at his shoulder.

"I barely slowed down at the finish line, maybe about two meters out, and he leaned into the tape, trying to beat me," said Johnson.

Then things devolved. "After he crossed the finish line, he put his hands up in the air like this," said Johnson, waving his own arms in the air as Lewis did. "He was clapping like this, like, 'I won the race.'"

Johnson was annoyed at the playground move but stayed silent. He jogged in his lane to cool down, certain he'd beaten Lewis again, while race officials studied the photo finish to sort it out. He may have remained silent, except he heard Lewis boasting about his performance to trackside reporters.

"All the media was around him talking about the race, saying, 'I think I beat him,'" he said.

Johnson lost his temper. He strode angrily toward the gathering and elbowed his way in.

"I was so upset, I pushed the [media] crowd open, and I said to him, 'In Rome, it won't be this close,'" he said, pointing his right index finger at Lewis.

Lewis was shocked and said nothing. It was widely reported that Johnson also called him a "clown." Johnson doesn't remember saying that but concedes it was possible.

In the end, Johnson's win streak remained intact. He was first in 10.06 in Seville, with Lewis right behind at 10.07. He had not lost to the defending Olympic and world champion in three years.

After the Seville episode, the press was all over the sprinters' rivalry. Stories on the flow of bad blood and the personality differences of the men were all part of the hype leading to Rome.

The personality gulf was on full display in the pre-race press conferences in Italy before the start of the 1987 world championships.

Lewis's was staged in the palatial Villa Miani, an eighteenth-century marbled wonder overlooking Rome from one of its famous seven hills. There, amid ancient tapestries, and ornate columns, and breathtaking views, *Globe and Mail* journalist and author James Christie captured the "perfectly orchestrated" scene:

> For the hundred or so press scribes on hand to record Carl's every word, bottomless bowls of pasta were paraded out by uniformed waiters. When the beer taps inexplicably ran dry after only a dozen or so glasses had been drawn, champagne flowed freely . . .
>
> The Villa Miani also just happened to be where the press photographers could get their film processed and lounge about.

King Carl appeared, looking typically cool in a shirt with the slogan "California Beach Patrol." He wore a heavy gold watch on each wrist. His entrance was accompanied by the eruptions of flashes and the tempers of competitive, noisy lensmen who elbowed one another to get a better angle of the track celebrity.

Lewis had his English remarks translated into Japanese and Italian, gracious nods to his sponsor, Mizuno, and his Roman hosts. Lewis avoided saying anything controversial about Johnson or anyone else. He chatted about his singing career, confessed the long jump was his favorite event, and in the 100, he would "run the way I can run in my lane and let everything else take care of itself."

Johnson's press conference was comical in contrast. It was held the same day, but in a small hotel conference room, without translators or a microphone. Reporters peppered Johnson and coach Charlie Francis with questions about the rivalry, with Francis intercepting most of them. The coach was "running interference all the time for Ben, you couldn't get to Ben, you had to go through Charlie," said Steve Simmons, covering Johnson for the *Toronto Sun*.

Simmons recalled how Francis simultaneously shielded Johnson and played favorites with the media. The coach adored the European press for their track knowledge and treated the ice hockey-loving Canadian reporters with open disdain. Getting a coveted one-on-one interview with Johnson was out of the question for most Canadian media.

"With Charlie, boy, was he easy to dislike in those days," said Simmons, who later became friends with Francis. "He was a bit of a bully, a bit of a control freak, and the smartest man in the room. He kind of looked at you like, 'I know that you know nothing, so therefore, I'm not going to tell you anything, *but* I might tell *him* something because *he* knows something.'"

During the Rome press conference, Francis repeatedly insisted there was no animosity between Lewis and Johnson. He deftly deflected the rivalry talk until the presser was about to wrap up, and one last question about Lewis was shouted at the sprinter. Johnson, who'd remained relatively silent for most of the event, spat out this gem: "I just want to kick his ass."

That remark made headlines, as did Johnson's prediction of a record-breaking performance under perfect race conditions.

He said on a hot, dry day, with a stacked international field and a fast surface like the one in Rome—a performance-boosting Mondo track—he would hit a world record time of 9.85 seconds. Few took this as anything but fantasy.

Rome was the last chance to take a shot at the world record that season—all runners had peaked for this day—and Johnson didn't want to wait another year to topple it. More importantly, he wanted to break the record at sea level. He'd come close to Calvin Smith's mark in Cologne that summer, hitting the tape in 9.95 before tumbling over a photographer who'd stupidly crept into his lane. Francis got into a shoving match with another photographer, then Johnson, back on his feet, dragged that cameraman off his coach.

Smith's record set in Colorado Springs was legitimate and legal, but with most track-and-field records set at altitude, the thinner air is considered an advantage. It seems a strange point to seize on with so many athletes doping, but Johnson believed a record would be "much faster and much more impressive" if achieved at sea level.

The morning of August 30, 1987, dawned hot and still. The temperature would peak at 30°C. The Mondo surface ringing Rome's Olympic stadium infield was dry despite the humidity. The semifinals would be run in the early afternoon, followed by the final about two hours later.

Johnson's perfect conditions were set.

* * *

In his semifinal, Carl Lewis blazed through the finish line in 10.03 seconds while running into a gentle headwind. It was a meet record for the world championship, not to be confused with the world record, which can be set anywhere and at any time, and Lewis was pleased. His semifinal time was faster than his Helsinki world championship victory in 10.07 seconds four years earlier. It signaled he was ready to defend his title and take out Johnson.

Johnson breezed through the earlier semifinal in 10.15 seconds, also into a slight headwind. A run like that was typical of his style; when he knew who was in the field against him, he could predict with impressive accuracy the time he needed to run to advance to the next round and not a hundredth of a second more. He only emptied his tank in the final.

Charlie Francis said Johnson had "an almost mystical self-awareness" on the track. "More than any of my other sprinters, he could sense precisely how fast he was going and could alter his pace to order," said Francis in his memoir. "If I told him to run a 150-meter drill two-tenths of a second slower than his last one, an almost imperceptible difference, he modulated with ease."

He also owned an incredible competitive streak—a "will of iron," said Angella Issajenko in her 1990 biography, *Running Risks*. "Ben believed with every fiber of his being that he would win any race he entered. We had chided him, when he was still running in the 10.20 seconds, when he announced that he would beat Carl Lewis by the next year. Most athletes are pretty cocky, if only to keep themselves motivated, psyched up, but Ben *believed* it, and it happened."

The Rome final was shaping up to be an extraordinary contest. Johnson received a light massage on his legs from Waldemar Matuszewski, whom he called "the magician," then dozed on the treatment table.

Francis tried to rouse him about an hour before the race, but the runner wanted more sleep. With about thirty minutes to go, Francis returned for Johnson, who yawned and reassured his coach he was ready. His muscles were supple in the heat, and he hadn't overexerted himself in the semifinal. He didn't need much of a warm-up. Johnson told his coach that he felt great. Francis, running on Cokes and coffee and jangling coins in his pockets, paced nervously.

The eight runners lined up, with Viktor Bryzgin of the (now former) Soviet Union in lane one; Italian Pierfrancesco Pavoni, the local hero, in two; Jamaica's Raymond Stewart in three; and Hungarian Attila Kovacs in four. Johnson was in lane five, next to Lewis in lane six. American Lee McRae and Great Britain's Linford Christie were in lanes seven and eight, respectively.

Simmons said when the sprinters were paraded onto the track, the atmosphere in the stadium, including the press box, was taut with anticipation. He said it was the same tingling he'd feel when silk-robed prizefighters begin their walk to the ring. "As someone who's loved boxing his whole life, this was like the buildup to the big fight. It was Ali and Frazier going into the ring, except they're doing it over 100 meters. There's no feeling in sport that compares. You're shaking when it happens; it's that exciting."

When the stadium crowd was hushed, the starter's pistol discharged. Johnson bolted from the blocks with an unprecedented level of ferocity. No false start. He was flying.

His feet were photographed off the ground as he launched. His left push leg was fully extended behind; his right foot reached through the air to plant about a meter and a half ahead. Bulging arms were swinging high to propel his start speed.

His reaction time to the starter's pistol was 0.129 of a second, a reflex unmatched by his peers. Lewis, by comparison, was out at 0.196 seconds. The American lost the race in the first stride.

The seven trailing men watched the Canadian build his lead with every step. If anyone could close the gap, it would be the long-legged Lewis, whose remarkable acceleration and endurance were his weapons. On this day, they would not be enough.

Johnson's split at the 60-meter mark was 6.38 seconds, which, as a point of reference, was faster than the 60-meter indoor record of 6.41 he'd set in Indianapolis, Indiana, in the spring. He hit the tape and glanced at the stadium clock: 9.84 seconds. They'd need to rewrite the record book. He smiled.

At age twenty-five, Johnson was a world champion and world record holder. The little boy who raced friends across the hot, dusty streets of Falmouth was now, officially and irrefutably, the fastest man on earth.

The Olympic stadium's sixty-five thousand spectators erupted. They'd witnessed history. It was the greatest 100-meter sprint of all time, an astonishing human achievement akin to American Bob Beamon's (then untouchable) 1968 long jump mark.

Suddenly, the stadium clock went black, then flashed again with a different winning time. When that happened, the crowd's collective decibel level rocketed even higher. Johnson understood why when he saw the reposted result.

"The official clock said 9.84, and when it changed to 9.83, then the whole place went crazy," he said. "It was deafening."

He'd lopped a full tenth of a second off Calvin Smith's 9.93-second mark. It was a decimation of the world record accomplished at sea level, just as Johnson wanted. His margin of victory was so enormous that Lewis looked a distant second in matching the old record of 9.93.

"This is a landmark performance," Italian track-and-field expert Roberto Quercetani told the *Los Angeles Times:* "What is so incredible is that the man has broken the world records in the indoor and outdoor championships in the same year. . . . A man with a fast start may be able to win indoors at 60 meters, but he does not always maintain his speed over 100 meters. This man does."

On the track, Lewis chased Johnson down ostensibly to congratulate him, quickly shaking his hand, but also suggested to the Canadian that he'd false started and gotten away with it. Johnson brushed him off and continued jogging before the cheering crowd, waving.

He didn't seem exhilarated in the moment, which confused spectators. Johnson heard later that he was not "happy enough" and explained his on-track demeanor: "In practice, this is what I was doing all the time, breaking world records," he said. "So when it happened in Rome, it wasn't news to me. But for the world to see it, it was a shock to them."

Minutes after the race, Johnson was summoned to the broadcast pen near the finish line. More than half a billion people had watched the Sunday night race on television and were eager to hear from the Canadian, who'd definitively unseated Lewis as the world's best sprinter. Dwight Stones, the former American champion high jumper-turned-broadcaster, was the interviewer. He reminded Johnson, and in doing so, informed viewers as background, that the sprinter previously claimed he could lower the world record to 9.85 seconds. Stones had set up Johnson nicely to explain why he'd been even quicker by asking:

"Did you know you would run that fast?"

"I knew. I don't talk bullshit."

* * *

Canadian Paul Gains, then the meet director for the Hamilton, Ontario, indoor meet, visited a high-end men's shoe store on Rome's Via dei Condotti a day or two after Johnson's world-record romp. While browsing, Gains noticed an employee suddenly locking the door. People outside were pressing their faces against the store window. Gains walked into another section of the shoe shop and saw Johnson with security guards, checking out the pricey footwear. They knew each other, chatted, and when Gains made to leave, the door was unlocked, the crowd surged, "and everybody was reaching in with pieces of paper and pens for me to get them an autograph from Ben."

"Most of our sporting heroes could walk down the street and not be recognized, but everybody knew Ben," he said.

While still in Rome, Johnson was courted by new sponsors. He also elicited increased payouts from existing ones. Often billed as the Canadian "underdog," he'd knocked off his famous foe, and his popularity was off the scale. Security teams had to be hired to protect him from swarming fans.

The richest new deal came from the Italian shoe and sportswear company Diadora when he parted ways with Adidas. Diadora was to pay the sprinter $2.5 million (US) over four years, with provisions for royalties from the line of shoes and apparel bearing his name and bonuses for achievements such as winning gold in Seoul.

He attracted an impressive raft of Japanese endorsements, including the Kyodo oil company, Visa, a commercial real estate company, a car wax, and an encyclopedia line. Japanese auto giant Mazda signed Johnson and, in addition, financially supported Charlie Francis's elite sprint group, which was renamed the Mazda Optimist Track Club. About $200,000 (US) annually flowed into the club from Mazda.

In Canada, Johnson secured sponsorships from a national grocery store chain, Timex Canada, Purolator, and Toshiba. He had a second agent, Glen Calkins, just to handle his Canadian work.

The Canadian Track and Field Association got in on the act, too. It planned to sell 983 signed posters of Johnson and pay the sprinter for his participation in the moneymaker. This deal would later bring the CTFA unwanted scrutiny and accusations that it had been profiting from Johnson's success while ignoring information about his steroid use.

That Johnson was not a smooth-talking extrovert like some athletes plugging products in the 1980s was no hindrance to companies now throwing money at him. He was a fresh face, a brand, and a superstar athlete whose appeal was rooted in vulnerability. "It's strength, it's speed, it's being No. 1 in the world, but it's also being just Ben," explained his American agent at the time, Larry Heidebrecht to author Christie. "He has a slight speech impediment, but his level of acceptance is such that it doesn't seem like some big flaw. It just makes him more human. We can identify with him. He could be any one of us, trying to succeed through hard work."

Johnson's race day price rose dramatically. Once a $300 lane filler, he now commanded fees up to $40,000 (US) per meet. With rules in place that permitted amateurs to deposit earnings in trust funds, Johnson started amassing what promised to be generational wealth. His teammates and handlers got richer. Everyone close to Johnson earned more as part of the lucrative package deals Heidebrecht negotiated with meet directors and sponsors. The sprinter would also reward those important to him: Francis received $20,000 (US) as a year-end bonus.

Johnson still had a post-Rome set of European races to finish before the season ended. In a turn that illustrates the fickle nature of fame, the sport's brightest new star was booed off the track at one of those meets.

* * *

The *Toronto Star* had covered Johnson at the world championships, after which the reporter flew home. When it dawned on the paper's editors that Johnson was the biggest sports story on the planet, they decided to put someone else on him.

I had no idea this was in play. I remember going into the fifth-floor newsroom on a September morning and being asked by editor Gerry Hall if I had a valid passport (yes) and to spike my assignment that day (okay). Our editorial assistant in sports, Gay Leno, insisted I stay in the building. Something weird was going on. Hall and Leno slipped away, and an hour or so later they returned to the newsroom with envelopes in their hands. Leno was giggling.

"You doing anything tonight?" Hall asked.

"Uh, no."

"Good. You're going to Belgium."

He threw down plane tickets, a few hundred in US dollars, a packet of American Express travelers checks, and an itinerary. I was to be the "Ben Johnson" reporter. I'd be in Brussels, Lausanne, London, and Monte Carlo. Our travel agency had booked hotels in each city—a huge help. Finding Johnson and Charlie Francis in each city, however, would be my problem, and I would have to talk my way into press row at track meets.

I drove home, packed a small suitcase, carried my Tandy 200 laptop in a backpack, grabbed a few *Star* clippings as resource material, and cabbed to Pearson Airport to catch the evening flight. Landing in Brussels, I found the Optimists' hotel, connected with Johnson, and started writing about him every day, even when he wasn't competing.

Some of the highlights (and lowlights) over those days:

- In Brussels, Johnson said he could run even faster, closer to 9.75 seconds. Reporters, astonished at the prediction, dutifully wrote the stories, which were met with skepticism.
- In Lausanne, Carl Lewis was an unexpected late entry in the 100 meters, and Francis was furious with the meet director, arguing that a rematch so soon after Rome served no purpose and that good money could be made with a well-promoted head-to-head at some future date. The compromise was that Lewis would run the 100 meters and Johnson would attempt a world record in a separate 60-meter event. Fans cheered Lewis but showered Johnson with boos and whistles for apparently refusing to engage his rival.
- In Monaco, I asked Francis to write a column for the *Star*. Smart and opinionated, he came well prepared with notes, which made

it easy for me as his ghostwriter. It was an ode to Gerard Mach's skill as a technical coach, but there wasn't a word, of course, about Johnson's steroid program. I failed to ask about steroids, which spoke to my naiveté about the sport at the time.

- I saw how easily cash appeared for star athletes. A local Monaco TV crew asked to chat with Johnson while I was watching him practice. One man handed Francis a wad of US bills, which he put in his pocket for safekeeping. Johnson gave a brief interview.
- Still in Monaco, another car buff, Prince Albert, drove to Johnson's hotel and picked him up for a spin around the French Riviera. Johnson, Francis, and agent Larry Heidebrecht later went to a high-end car show, where the prince introduced the sprinter to the crowd. Johnson was peeved; no sponsorship or appearance fee was part of the auto show trip.
- After Rome, Japanese promoters coaxed one unplanned trip out of him. Johnson was paid about $35,000 (US) to jet to Tokyo, race, and head back to Toronto. His Japanese hosts rolled out the red carpet, even giving him front-row tickets to a Michael Jackson concert, but Johnson was so fatigued that he stayed in the hotel and slept through the performance.

When the 1987 track season ended, the sprinter collected a heap of awards, among them: performance of the year from *Track and Field News*; male athlete of the year from the news agencies TASS, Agence France Press, Associated Press, and Canadian Press; and the Lou Marsh Trophy as Canada's outstanding athlete of the year (a *Toronto Star* award that for decades was acknowledged as the country's top sports award and most often won by professional athletes).

Johnson was also invested that year as a member of the Order of Canada, an award established in 1967 by Queen Elizabeth II to recognize outstanding achievement, dedication to the community, and service to the nation. In bestowing this award, Canada enshrined Johnson as one of its most distinguished citizens.

Carl Lewis was not among those applauding Ben Johnson's record-breaking year. His camp had worked quietly in Rome to discredit Johnson's race, requesting an IAAF investigation into the validity of his blazing start. Officials had already confirmed Johnson's start as legal on race day, but a second investigation was launched, and it lasted nearly a year, ending shortly before the Seoul Games. The IAAF concluded, again, that Johnson's start in Rome was legal. Francis knew of the investigation but didn't tell Johnson, lest it distract him.

While still in Rome, Lewis took another approach to undermining Johnson's triumph. He hinted that Johnson was a cheater who was boosting his speed by doping. With the world championships still underway, he said to a British television reporter: "There's a strange air to this meet, too many runners coming out of nowhere, and I don't think they're doing it without drugs."

Johnson responded: "When Carl Lewis was winning everything, I never said a word against him. And when the next guy comes along and beats me, I won't complain about that either."

Whether Lewis or his entourage suspected Johnson was using steroids or had hard evidence is unknown. In the end, it didn't matter.

CHAPTER TEN
SEOUL DOUBTS

Ben Johnson almost didn't line up in the 100-meter race in Seoul. In mid-May 1988, he was at a personal and athletic crossroads. He was injured. He was exhausted. He was unhappy. In that moment, he was finished with track, with traveling, with Charlie Francis. He fled the sport and for six weeks buried himself in sand, surf, and long, lazy days on the Caribbean shores of St. Kitts, a dual island nation with Nevis and a sovereign state in the British Commonwealth.

Confounded teammate Desai Williams reminded Johnson that the Canadian Olympic trials, a mandatory event in advance of "the race of your life" in Seoul, were fast approaching: "Are you crazy?"

Johnson had already taken a short break with Williams in St. Kitts earlier in the year. Why did he need another at this crucial time?

Williams wasn't the only one questioning his friend's sanity. News of Johnson going AWOL made international headlines, framed as a bitter fallout with Francis during a critical period of pre-Olympic fine-tuning. It shocked Johnson's legion of fans, who were counting on him and Lewis to fight it out in the Olympics' most glamorous race.

Johnson's rivals meanwhile smelled chum in the competitive waters: the top-ranked sprinter in the world could hardly retain his title by lying on a beach, drinking beer, and cruising buffets while they were training and competing.

The rift between Johnson and Francis began innocently. Like many close relationships that break apart, it frayed over a series of misunderstandings and minor interactions, leaving hurt feelings. Unlike many relationships, theirs was under the new pressures that accompanied Johnson's status as a world record holder and world champion. There were increased contractual obligations from sponsors, more in-person appearances, extra travel for business opportunities, and round-the-clock interview requests from international media. All this was siphoning Johnson's patience and gobbling his free time. Fame was exacting its price.

None of these tensions were manifest on the track. The new year of 1988 had started off just fine. The runner enjoyed a successful winter season, which in track refers to indoor meets held during the colder months. Sprinters like Johnson and Carl Lewis usually ran 60 meters indoors, reflective of foundational speed prior to the outdoor season. Johnson won the short events in Canada, Spain, and Germany while also setting a world record in an unusual 50-yard dash. After Johnson strained his hamstring in Germany, Francis canceled the rest of his indoor season. It was nothing major. Johnson was not often sidelined with injuries. He simply needed rest and treatment.

"World-class sprinters are like exotic sports cars: superb in performance, but constantly in need of servicing and subject to breakdown," Francis wrote. "While coaches and physios do their best to prepare their athletes for the violent forces of sprinting, there are times when the strain is too much." He noted that the hamstring pull was Johnson's first serious injury since 1984.

While injured, Johnson stayed on the European tour with the rest of his Mazda Optimist teammates. Club massage therapist Waldemar Matuszewski worked on his hamstring. Even in street clothes, Johnson's star power remained intact. He was paid around $5,000 (US) by meet directors, usually in cash, just to show up at their events because he'd still draw crowds. Some fans were aggressive in their quest for autographs. At one point, he was swarmed and knocked over, with someone accidentally trampling his injured leg, necessitating more healing time.

When the winter tour ended around March, Johnson wanted a two-week hot-weather break in St. Kitts with Williams. He was not going to recharge in cold, slushy Toronto. Francis reluctantly agreed, although he knew Johnson would not get intensive hamstring treatment in the Caribbean since team doctor Jamie Astaphan was working with other athletes in Europe. Nor was Matuszewski available to travel to the island.

The trip to St. Kitts was uneventful, and Johnson returned to Toronto as promised, but his hamstring was not 100 percent. He couldn't train fully, and his physiotherapy sessions were interrupted three times for overseas business jaunts, two of them to Japan. Johnson also began a six-week anabolic steroid cycle, not his last before Seoul, as part of his outdoor season preparations.

Johnson slowly began regaining his old form and seemed ready to begin the outdoor season. Francis scheduled a May 13 race in Tokyo with a soft field that wouldn't unduly test Johnson's hamstring. The runner wasn't so sure.

"I couldn't say no to the organizers in Tokyo. I didn't want to disappoint them. Plus, I was the main attraction, so I said, 'I'm going,'" said Johnson, noting the Japanese were generous with appearance fees and always offered VIP treatment.

"I told Charlie, 'I can't open up too much or I'm going to pull my hamstring.' He said, 'Just get out of the blocks, nice and slow, and just maintain speed.'"

Johnson agreed to the plan but mentioned he'd be competing against a young Japanese runner who was starting to clock fast times.

Francis reassured him: "You know what to do."

When the gun went off in Tokyo, Johnson pushed out of the blocks just hard enough to stay ahead of the Japanese sprinter, a sticky opponent. "I was barely ahead of him. I just kept running, but I couldn't shake him off," Johnson recalled. "I changed gears around 60, 70 meters, and my hamstring went. I could feel it pull, and I walked off the track with my legs burning."

He didn't finish the race. He hobbled down the stadium stairs quickly, past a pale-faced Francis, and an aghast Matuszewski, past the cheering crowds pushing in to take photos and beg for autographs. "It was so painful; I didn't want anyone to know I was hurt so much," Johnson said.

He was whisked to a local doctor, who examined him with an ultrasound. A hamstring tear just below the original injury was detected. Johnson felt sick.

"When I heard that, I thought, 'Oh my god, my career is gone. It's over.'"

Coach and runner flew home. Francis suggested Johnson come on a European tour with his clubmates. He reasoned Johnson would get daily attention from Matuszewski to help with hamstring recovery. Johnson balked. Francis insisted. They argued.

"I told Charlie I didn't want to be traveling, dragging a suitcase and a bad hamstring all over Europe," he said. "I can't, I'm exhausted, I'm tired, I just want to go home to my mum."

A compromise was reached. Or so Francis thought. The plan was for Johnson to fly to the team's first stop in Malaga, Spain, to begin his personalized treatment. Matuszewski would meet Johnson at the Malaga airport and escort him to the team hotel. But the runner was a no-show. Johnson flew to another part of the globe instead. Four days later, he let Astaphan tell Francis he was back in St. Kitts.

Johnson was gone for more than a month. And on this trip, his spirit was most in need of repair. He didn't care what friends and foes were saying about him; bad hamstring or not, he was emotionally and physically spent.

Johnson moved into a resort hotel near the white sands of Frigate

Bay and spent hours each day at a beachfront pub called The Monkey Bar. He drank Carib beer, played dominoes, and chitchatted with whomever strolled in. He ate whatever he wanted, and when he needed refreshing, he slipped into the crystalline waters to swim. Snoozes under shady palms relaxed him, while the heat of each day deeply warmed his muscles. "I thought, 'Oh, this feels so good. I don't have to train anymore. This is a good life,'" he said. "I was having fun."

He also had time for self-reflection, some of it painful. He began to recognize the emotional toll immigrating to Canada had on him when, twelve years earlier, he left behind his father and the Caribbean island he loved and moved to a culture and a climate so removed from that of his birthplace. While trying to navigate a predominantly white, uptight city like Toronto in the 1970s as a young Black teen, Johnson also began the highly structured training, travel, and competition life of an athlete. That commitment meant sacrifice, which, for young people, can manifest in social isolation from friends when invitations to parties, movies, dates, and just hanging out dry up.

Already brooding over his spat with Francis, Johnson mulled over the value of his regimented career. He was successful, clearly. But was he happy? Did he always have to take orders from his coach with no room for negotiation? Johnson did as his coach wanted, always, but while alone with his thoughts in St. Kitts, regrets and grievances mounted.

"My childhood was taken away from me completely because I went from Jamaica to Canada and right into track and field. So I didn't have time to play with other kids or have fun. That was gone," said Johnson. Francis had forbidden him from even playing pickup soccer with neighborhood friends in case he got hurt.

Parenthood, too, was weighing on his mind. In April, he'd become the father of a baby girl. A new set of adult responsibilities dawned. Johnson needed to figure out how to balance the demands of fatherhood with his track career.

One determination from his time on the beach was that, as a 26-year-old man, he wanted more hands-on control of his life. He also knew he had more to give as an athlete, and yes, he desired Olympic gold. Johnson was unsure of the status of his relationship with Francis, but with a new perspective, the sprinter's first order of business was to heal his hamstring, on his own terms. Johnson didn't once speak directly to Francis while in St. Kitts, nor did the coach phone him. Astaphan, back living on the island, operated as the go-between with Francis, who was relieved that the doctor would be working daily on repairing the sprinter's leg. Part of that care was water-resistance exercise. Another part was a short cycle of steroids.

"I wasn't going there to take drugs," Johnson said of his initial decision to flee to St. Kitts. "I was going there for a break and to enjoy myself, but the world knew I was hurt. So I went to see Jamie."

The doctor prescribed pills. "I was taking all types of different pills: blue, yellow, white, red," Johnson said. Some were for circulation and inflammation issues. Some were vitamins. He knew steroids were again on the menu—round pink pills, the anabolic steroid Winstrol, generically known as stanozolol. "Whatever it takes," Johnson said of his mindset once he refocused on Olympic preparations.

Johnson and some of his teammates would occasionally take short doses of Winstrol/stanozolol from the doctor, even though three years earlier, when they tried long doses, it made their muscles stiff and sore. When supplies of their preferred steroids were low, they'd use the old drugs to bridge the gap. Johnson didn't ask for detailed explanations about what he was swallowing. He trusted Astaphan completely.

During that time, the doctor's mask as a genial host on his native island began to slip. He sought to become more indispensable to the sprinter than Francis. Johnson was paying him $10,000 (US) monthly to treat him, procure steroids, and keep his drug use secret. Astaphan wanted more: more credit from the sprinter and, eventually, much more money. He saw himself, not Francis, as the brains behind

Johnson's success. The proof was there in St. Kitts. Astaphan was attentive to Johnson's physical and psychological needs while Francis was off with his other athletes.

Johnson didn't push back on Astaphan's requests because his hamstring was healing. The water therapy was working. The hot weather helped, too, brightening his mood while loosening his muscles. His mind was back on Seoul and the race. "Every so often, I'd touch my leg, and the pain would get dimmer and dimmer and dimmer. I said, 'Jamie, I'm feeling much better,'" Johnson said. He was so pleased that he assured the physician that a fat payday would follow an Olympic gold.

Astaphan also tamed stubborn inflammation around Johnson's Achilles tendon by doing something highly unusual but effective: he invited an American athletic therapist named Jack Scott, who claimed to have worked with the Lewis camp, to St. Kitts to treat Johnson. Scott arrived with an electric muscle stimulator to use on the sprinter's tendon and hamstring. Johnson didn't mind the Lewis connection and asked Scott for a machine like the one he was using. Scott let him keep the model he'd brought.

What drug secrets Astaphan and Scott may have shared on the island are unknown. The men are dead. But one or both likely spilled a few beans at some point; the stunning *Sports Illustrated* article published days after Johnson's Seoul disqualification contained drug details from his St. Kitts stay.

Johnson left his island paradise, briefly, to make a mid-June appearance in Italy for his main sponsor, Diadora. There he ran into Francis, an unpleasant encounter that seemed to end their partnership for good. Francis recalled that he saw Johnson in Padua, but the two didn't speak until Francis spotted him in the team hotel. Francis was upset that Johnson had shown up for a Diadora event wearing street clothes, not a Diadora tracksuit as required by the $2.5 million endorsement contract.

It wasn't in his job description, but Francis monitored how his athletes honored their endorsement agreements. He chided Johnson about risking his Diadora deal by shirking something as simple as wearing the company's tracksuit. Johnson was in no mood to be lectured. He was angry and confronted his coach about not keeping in touch with him in St. Kitts and for pushing him to run in Tokyo when his hamstring wasn't fully healthy. Francis listened to the complaints, then suggested to his star sprinter that if he refused to heed his advice, maybe they couldn't work together anymore.

"Then I guess we can't," Johnson shot back.

The next day, the two split. Johnson returned to St. Kitts, and Francis headed off to Formia, Italy, with the rest of the Mazda Optimist runners. A partnership and friendship that had lasted more than a decade, culminating in Johnson becoming the No. 1 sprinter on the planet, had ended. Francis felt betrayed. Johnson felt free. He would coach himself, with Astaphan at his side.

He began gearing up to train on the island. He hadn't run at all for about a month, not watching his diet, and rarely hitting the gym. This enormous amount of time off was a dramatic departure from his habits under Francis, who allowed his athletes roughly a week off when the season ended. Francis's philosophy was to never let an athlete's peak drop too much; it was better to build upon existing levels of strength, power, and speed while opponents took longer rest periods.

Johnson was about to test Francis's theory. "When you're training for 12 years, you don't lose your muscle mass or strength that fast, you're still strong," he said of his downtime in St. Kitts.

Astaphan took him to a local grass field and suggested Johnson warm up, then "leg it out." The sprinter slipped on his spikes, ran a few 60-meter sprints. He felt good. He claimed he was running world-record times, even on the bumpy turf.

"I said to Jamie, 'Shit, I haven't been training for so long. Whatever you were giving me works very well.'"

* * *

The standoff between Francis and Johnson did not last. It would be resolved, indirectly, by their shared dislike for Lewis.

That summer, Lewis ran an impressive 9.9 seconds in a Paris meet. Francis dryly recalled the American's victory celebration as "a protracted show of mugging and bowing." More galling was what Lewis told the media: "All I know is I'm running better than ever, and [Johnson] isn't running at all."

Francis was furious. He wasn't going to let Lewis win an Olympic title in Seoul when Johnson was the faster man. Johnson, too, was incensed by Lewis's braying.

Their fury led to a detente, arranged and hosted by their mutual friend Ross Earl. Johnson flew back to Toronto to meet Francis at Buchanan Public School in Scarborough, where Earl taught. The pair discussed their lists of grievances, and with Earl's deft mediation, they reached an agreement. They'd make a fresh start and gun for gold in Seoul.

CHAPTER ELEVEN

UNKNOWINGLY

While Ben Johnson was jetting out of Seoul, after his disqualification two attempts to connect with him were underway. The motivations behind them were very different.

The first occurred the morning of Tuesday, September 27, 1988. Before catching his flight from Seoul to Vancouver, Charlie Francis made a phone call. It was to Toronto track coach Sue Snider, a certified doping control officer and someone he and Johnson trusted. Francis asked her to collect a fresh sample of his sprinter's urine for testing as soon as Johnson arrived home.

"Are you willing to do it?" Francis asked.

"Of course," she replied.

Still confounded by the Seoul findings, Francis hoped a clean screening by an independent lab would exonerate Johnson. It was a long shot.

The second attempt to get Johnson's attention began around the same time, half a world away. It was late afternoon on Monday, September 26 in Toronto. Paul Godfrey, then publisher of the *Toronto Sun*, took a call from an old political acquaintance, lawyer Ed Futerman. The two discussed ways to capitalize on Johnson's situation. These included organizing a $1 million match race between Johnson and Carl Lewis, which never materialized; getting Johnson's exclusive tell-all story for the *Sun*; and installing Futerman in a new Johnson management team.

Francis was successful. Johnson would provide another urine sample for Snider, which she then locked in a freezer in her condo until a credible testing lab could be found.

Before Godfrey and Futerman could be successful, they first had to contact Johnson, a stranger to them both. Futerman took aim at the sprinter's devastated mother, Gloria. Through contacts, he was able to reach Kay Baxter, then the Jamaican consul general in Toronto. Baxter had never met the Johnson family but had called Gloria Johnson directly.

Baxter told Gloria about a man named Kameel Azan who would like to visit the Johnson family and offer a solution to her son's problems. Close to Futerman, Azan was a popular Toronto hairdresser who owned a thriving salon in the city's fashionable Yorkville district. He had no sports management expertise. Gloria agreed to let Azan visit. They met three days after the disqualification.

"Let me tell you exactly what my mum saw. Kay said to my mother, 'I know this gentleman named Azan; he's very successful; he lives on a farm with acres of land with his family and horses, and he's very established.' And my mum sees that as a guy with a strong base, he knows how to make money, he knows how to do business right," he said.

But Johnson was unsettled by strangers rushing to his aid. "Just because these guys have big houses and big land doesn't mean that they're not crooks," he told his mother.

"No, son, you got it wrong. You don't know these people," she responded.

Meanwhile, Ben Sr. had frantically arranged a flight to Toronto from Jamaica, which had just been ravaged by deadly Hurricane Gilbert, to be at his son's side in the tense household. The media was camped out in front of the Scarborough house, making the Johnsons virtual prisoners. They were trapped indoors unless they wanted to run a gauntlet of reporters and photographers. They unplugged the home telephone for hours at a time to prevent its incessant ringing.

There was uncertainty in the house about what Johnson's next steps should be. His parents were divided on the issue, which added to the sprinter's anxiety. His mother wanted him to work with Azan and Futerman and had invited Azan to visit on Thursday, September 29. His father demanded that his son return to school to get a better education and eventually a better career—wasn't that the reason he was in Canada? Frustrated and angry, Ben Jr. shot back, saying that no one could make him quit track. "I said, 'Dad, this is what I do best. This is how I make my living. This is the only thing I know how to do; I don't know how to do anything else. I've spent my whole life running.'"

"Then I started crying."

Azan stepped in to smooth the raw moment. He reminded Ben Sr. that running was how his son supported the Johnson family.

Ben Sr. backed off, reluctantly, on one condition. His son was a Canadian citizen, and Canada should stand up for him. "I swear on the lives of my grandkids, this is what he said: 'The Canadian government must protect my son,'" recalled Ben Jr. of his father's request.

Azan assured Ben Sr. that he would do his best to enable that protection. That pledge made Gloria Johnson happy.

The same week, Johnson's agent, Larry Heidebrecht, came by, the only member of the sprinter's entourage to knock on his door. He relayed that the German magazine *Stern* would pay $500,000 (US) for Ben's exclusive story. Even this opportunity was divisive. Johnson was considering it. Azan scoffed at it, suggesting it would harm the sprinter's credibility with the Canadian public if he accepted the German deal before speaking to a Canadian newspaper or TV station.

Stern was throwing around money for Johnson material. Canadian photographer Claus Andersen, who was working in Seoul for the

Canadian Track and Field Association, said the magazine tracked him down when the disqualification news broke and offered him $50,000 for the immediate delivery of photos he'd taken of Johnson over the years. This was before the digital age, and Andersen, whose printed photographs and film negatives were in Canada, could not oblige.

Unsure what to do about *Stern*, Johnson called Francis.

"$500,000? Are you kidding me?" said Francis. "Do it. Take it. You're suspended anyway."

Gloria Johnson did not share that opinion. She agreed with Azan. She believed her son should speak directly to a Canadian media outlet first. She was swayed by Baxter's assurances that her son would be in good hands with this new group.

Amid all the back and forth, Johnson was an emotional wreck. He was exhausted. He couldn't sleep or eat. Deep down, he wanted someone else to fix his problem. As an elite athlete, that wasn't an unusual expectation. Much like pro athletes today, Johnson's job was to train and compete while his entourage handled outside details and deflected distractions. Even though he was nearly twenty-seven years old, his decision-making experience outside of the sports world was extremely limited. He was lost without his coach's in-person presence to calm and guide him.

Francis did not visit the Johnson house that week, but he hadn't abandoned his beleaguered athlete. He was scrambling to devise a face-saving solution for the main players in the Seoul scandal.

The coach had moved into a nondescript Toronto hotel with his fiancé, Canadian hurdler Angela Coon, to avoid the media. There he brainstormed with allies, including discus thrower-turned-lawyer Rob Gray, team physician Jamie Astaphan, and Optimist club founder Ross Earl. Their feeling was that with the games still going on in Seoul, a narrow window existed to make a statement while Johnson's electrifying run was still fresh in Canadian minds.

"We just couldn't get hold of Ben," said Gray, who favored an immediate public *mea culpa* from Johnson to explain he'd used steroids to repair a muscle injury and win gold for Canada. "His phone was unplugged all the time, or so it seemed."

Francis wanted to secure highly regarded Toronto trial attorney Robert "Bob" Armstrong for Johnson to safeguard the sprinter's interests. Rumors of a Canadian investigation into the disqualification were intensifying, and a battle-hardened legal warrior was required if the matter ended up in front of a judge.

Astaphan upended the group's cautious planning when he broke ranks to do a live, nationally broadcast one-on-one interview with veteran CBC journalist Barbara Frum on Wednesday, September 28. On camera, the doctor denied administering anabolic steroids to Johnson, but he came across as a sweaty, twitchy, and evasive man under Frum's relentless grilling. It was a public relations disaster.

Azan used the Astaphan interview as additional ammunition to persuade Johnson to leave the Mazda Optimist crew behind. Gloria Johnson agreed. Her despondent son surrendered. He picked up the plugged-in phone and reluctantly informed Francis he had "a new team now," leaving his coach to fend for himself.

The Johnsons would meet the Godfrey/Futerman group at Azan's farm on Friday, September 30, 1988, four days after the sprinter handed back his gold medal in Seoul.

* * *

Sue Snider knew she'd crossed a line with the Canadian amateur sport hierarchy when she agreed to help Ben Johnson. She suspected it would cost her. And it did.

Snider would never again be asked to act as a doping control officer by Sport Canada after she collected a urine sample from Johnson on Wednesday, September 28, the day after the sprinter landed in

Toronto. This specimen collection was for a private test, which Snider was certified to conduct, but word of it soon spread through the Canadian sports community.

"The minute they found out I'd [collected] the test, even though it wasn't sanctioned [by a Canadian sports body], I was a rogue," said Snider.

"They never said it out loud, but I never did another drug test [for amateur sports events in Canada]."

She has no regrets. Johnson was a friend, and she refused to turn her back on him. "I followed my heart," said Snider. "And it was B.J. . . . you're not supposed to take drugs, but I'm sorry, that doesn't change who he is as a person or who I am as a person."

Snider, known as Sue Heather in 1988, was a respected, award-winning track-and-field coach who trained national champions and Olympians. An anti-doping advocate, she became a certified doping control officer in the 1980s, volunteering her time to collect specimens at amateur events under the direction of Sport Canada, the branch of the Canadian government whose duties included overseeing national sport organizations and their anti-doping procedures.

Snider was popular with the athletes, including Johnson, for her coaching skills, exuberant personality, and interest in the lives of athletes she met. She was also a straight shooter. Raised in an extended family full of Toronto police officers, she made it clear where she stood on breaking rules. "Thou shalt not dope," was one of Snider's catchphrases, a no-nonsense summation of her personal fair-play values and the philosophy of the track club she founded, Top Form.

Snider was asked to appear on the evening broadcast of a Canadian news outlet on Tuesday, September 27, to explain how athletes' urine specimens were collected and prepared for testing. People at the time mistakenly thought Johnson had tested positive twice after giving two separate urine samples in Seoul. She described to CTV anchor Lloyd Robertson how a single urine specimen is split into two bottles, the

A and B samples, from one original specimen source. The public's anabolic steroid IQ would be ramped up considerably from that day on.

The next evening, which happened to be Snider's birthday, she arrived at the Johnson home around 7 p.m. with a male colleague who would witness the sample collection. She recalled pushing through a media crowd. "It was insane. There was every reporter from every news agency outside, and there were people from the neighborhood watching," said Snider.

When she and her colleague got to the front door, Gloria Johnson greeted them warmly and thanked them repeatedly. Johnson recalled giving his sample in a first-floor bathroom while the male colleague watched. Snider remained with Gloria, whom she described as "the epitome of a great mum, just protecting her boy."

Johnson, on the other hand, was emotionally stressed. Snider said it was difficult to see him this way, even though she'd suspected he was a steroid user. His deeply carved musculature was an obvious indication of artificial enhancement to her trained eyes. Still, Snider felt something was off about the testing in Seoul. "My mind wasn't, 'He didn't do it.' It was more like, 'Why the hell did this happen now? How did he get caught after all this time?' I truly believed something was wrong."

* * *

Ed Futerman had wanted to hold a press conference for Johnson to tell the international media he did not use banned drugs. Paul Godfrey had a better idea: give the exclusive to the *Sun* and let Johnson talk to the rest of the world later.

A former high-profile, media-savvy Toronto politician who wielded considerable backroom clout across the city, Godfrey was well connected at all levels of government and in the sports realm, too.

During his eleven-year reign as Toronto's Metro chairman, he led the charge to bring a Major League Baseball expansion franchise to Toronto. He later became the Blue Jays' club president. Godfrey thought an open press conference would be a mistake for Johnson. "I told [Futerman] I would get a sports guy who would appreciate the problems Ben had gone through. Whether he [used steroids] or not, at least it would be [an interview] with just one guy rather than a flock of curious reporters who would bombard him with questions."

The chosen "sports guy" was *Toronto Sun* sports editor George Gross, a popular columnist in the city. The skeptical Gross asked his boss if a Johnson exclusive was "a wild goose chase," but Godfrey was confident it would happen.

On the last morning of September, Godfrey's chauffeur-driven *Sun* car purred its way across the city's east end with the publisher and the sports editor in the back seat. Gross had a tape recorder, notebooks, and pens.

They were following Futerman's vehicle as he picked up Jamaican counsel general Kay Baxter. The cars then headed north of Toronto for about an hour or so to Kameel Azan's Newmarket farm, entering a long, sweeping driveway and passing horse paddocks, green fields, and loping dogs. Godfrey was struck by the beauty of the Azan estate as he and Gross followed Futerman and Baxter into the main house.

Earlier that morning, three limousines with tinted windows had pulled up to the Johnson home in Scarborough. Gloria, Ben, and his eldest sister, Dezrine, were spirited into two of the cars, which left one as a decoy. The passengers put their heads down, avoiding any chance of being seen through windows as the vehicles sped off toward Highway 401. The media followed, but few photographers made it to the Azan farm, and those that did were stuck at the gate of the long driveway, their zoom lenses unable to capture the action.

Gloria met Godfrey and Gross in a large room with a table holding coffee and snacks. Ben was not visible. "His mother was very cautious and said to us: 'He's been through a lot, please be easy on him because he's very sensitive. This whole taking away the medal did not sit well with him,'" said Godfrey.

Johnson emerged from another room. He was surprised to see Godfrey and Gross. He didn't realize the proposed *Sun* interview was to be that day while he was still an emotional mess.

Futerman introduced himself, described the services he could provide as Johnson's lawyer, and pushed a retainer agreement in front of him. The sprinter's internal radar sounded. Years later, he'd describe the scene as an ambush and file a $37 million legal claim alleging negligence against Futerman. Now he pulled his mother aside for a private conversation.

"I said to my mum, 'I don't like this guy. I just don't like the way he walks and moves, like he's too important [and] I don't feel comfortable,'" said Johnson. "But my mum said, 'Everything's going to be okay.' She just wanted proper legal advice, for me to be protected, so I said, 'Okay then, Mum.'"

Futerman's retainer was $40,000. Johnson scribbled his signature on the page. He now had legal representation, someone to protect and steer him.

Futerman's strategy as it evolved in Newmarket, based on the sprinter's claim he'd not used steroids during the Olympics, was to show that somehow, in some way, Johnson had been set up or possibly taken advantage of by powerful people in his orbit, namely, Francis and physician Jamie Astaphan.

Similar rumors swirled elsewhere. Richard Pound, the Montreal lawyer and IOC vice president, had publicly opined that Johnson's body may have been "guilty," but his mind is "innocent." Jean Charest, the federal cabinet minister who had banned him for life, suggested Johnson could not have acted alone.

Futerman wanted Ben to sit for a candid *Sun* interview in hopes of influencing public and political sentiment in support of his claim that he had done nothing wrong and that his medal was improperly seized.

Johnson grew uneasy listening to his new team plot his future and carve out their roles. Still staggered by his Olympic disqualification, he felt powerless to object, and he was still hearing Francis's frantic words from Seoul ringing in his ears: deny, deny, deny.

"We all sit down around the table, and now I look at all these guys, coming around like wolves, and in my mind I say, 'My heart was just ripped out in Seoul, and now I'm here with a bunch of people trying to get a piece of me,'" said Johnson. "They all talk about their strategies, what they're going to do, and that Ben should speak to George Gross [for] the first story, he's going to be the headline on the front cover, and Futerman will do all the legal work and Azan will take care of the financial part. Then they started to discuss that Ben's going to go outside with George, where he'll feel comfortable, relaxed, by the fence, and talk about the story, what really happened. . . . I saw my life going a different way from that moment. I was so hurt and so mad about how my mum saw this (plan) through and went along with it. It was a mistake."

Gross began making small talk at the table, trying to draw Johnson out a little before they headed outside, just the two of them, to conduct the interview. Gross asked Johnson in front of everyone if he was going to be truthful.

"I said, 'Yes, I'm going to tell you the truth.' [Then] I start to backtrack in my head; 'What does he mean about telling him the truth?' I mean now, I could get half a million dollars for my story, and now I'm getting nothing," he said of his sudden understanding that he was expected to give an exclusive interview to the *Sun*, on the spot, for free.

Godfrey had been listening intently to the exchange between sprinter and Gross. He said Johnson paused before telling Gross that he would be truthful. Godfrey didn't like that hesitation. He'd heard all the "hot rumors" about Johnson's steroid use and quickly interjected: "I said very politely, 'Ben, we all love you, but you know what? If you have to go on the stand and you tell a lie, you're in deep trouble,'" recalled Godfrey. He wanted to raise the prospect of penalties for perjury if a formal investigation went forward and the sprinter was untruthful.

The room fell still. Johnson, silent, bent his head. Tears rolled slowly down his cheeks.

Gloria Johnson scolded Godfrey. "I told you to be gentle with him."

"I basically shut up after that," Godfrey said, alarmed that he'd angered Johnson's mother and upset the sprinter. "If there was one emotional moment in this whole episode, I felt badly because he was crying. He's a big, tough guy, and I saw a soft spot."

Johnson composed himself. Yes, he repeated, he would be truthful.

And yet, when Gross led Johnson out to a spot by a paddock for the interview, he stuck to his story. He told Gross that he hadn't used steroids in Seoul, and if steroids entered his system, it had to be sabotage, or as Gross would write in a more sinister turn, he may have been administered the drugs without his consent.

Johnson insists he denied steroid use in that moment out of loyalty. "I wanted to protect Charlie."

Johnson was also seeking to project his own innocence. But in the post-Seoul frenzy of that week, there is a case to be made that a pilloried man under crushing pressure to explain himself might see denials as doing the least amount of damage. If Johnson confessed to his longtime steroid use, he knew he would instantly implicate his coach and taint others in the Mazda Optimist fold. He believed floating an "I didn't do it" scenario was harmless since he was already banned from the sport, no government investigation had been called, and it appeared, at that point, he was the only person to be punished.

Johnson had no inkling what his denials would unleash.

* * *

In Toronto, printing presses for the three major dailies—the *Toronto Star*, the *Globe and Mail*, and the *Toronto Sun*—were rumbling to life on Friday evening, September 30, 1988. There had been rumors all day that Ben Johnson had spoken to one of the papers, and newsrooms were on edge. Back then, being beaten on an enormous story was humiliating, and editors yelling at scooped reporters was an unhappy consequence.

Sports editor George Gross worked quickly that afternoon. His story was ready by deadline, and pictures of Ben Johnson shot by a *Sun* photographer at Kameel Azan's farm were in place. The pages were laid out with banner headlines and hyped by that delicious newspaper word, "Exclusive."

Few people at the *Sun* knew of the pending story. Godfrey kept it that way and even welched on an informal deal between the tabloid and the *Star* in order to maximize the *Sun*'s scoop. Prior to this night, the print rivals routinely swapped dozens of first-edition newspapers, hot off the presses. That way, if one newspaper had a scoop, the other would scramble to match it in subsequent editions.

"We thought this was a big blockbuster, and we decided that the first one hundred papers would not have the Johnson story in them," said Godfrey of the initial bundles sent to the *Star*'s One Yonge Street newsroom. "There was no reference to the story, so [the *Star* presumed] the *Sun* didn't have it."

The tabloid then replated its presses with the Gross article. The *Star* could not react in time to match it. Radio stations began blasting out the news of the *Sun*'s massive scoop in the early morning hours of Saturday, October 1.

When the *Star*'s publisher, the late John Honderich, learned of the trickery, he was "absolutely angry; he just went nuts," said Godfrey, but the only fallout was the *Star*'s refusal to send its first editions to the *Sun* for at least a year.

* * *

The crux of Johnson's interview with the *Sun* was his contention that he had not knowingly used steroids. The sprinter signed a statement acknowledging this under the approving eyes of his new lawyer, Ed Futerman. It ran as part of the *Sun* package:

> I want to state clearly now that I have never knowingly taken illegal drugs nor have had illegal drugs administered to me.
>
> I have always believed, and I certainly believe now, that illegal drugs have no place in our society.
>
> During the past two years, I have been tested about ten times. Every single one of my tests has been negative. My most recent test was on or around August 17. All of these tests, to my knowledge, were thorough and complete.
>
> I'm well aware that every Olympic medallist is tested and, as you all are aware, I wasn't going to Seoul to lose. I fully expected to win a gold medal and I fully expected to be tested.
>
> There can be no possible reason under those circumstances that I would have taken an illegal drug.
>
> If, indeed, it was my urine sample that was tested, then I invite a full investigation by the appropriate authorities to find out how all this happened.
>
> I'm innocent and I welcome the opportunity of proving it.
>
> I'm proud to be Canadian and I would never do anything to hurt the people who support me. The Canadian people should have the right to hear my story first.

Johnson was presenting himself as a malleable dupe. Public opinion split. Supporters were enthusiastic, eager to believe their hero would not cheat. Doubters wondered how an adult man would not notice striking changes to his body over time. The anti-doping circles kept mostly silent.

(Top) Sixteen-year-old
Ben prepares to get into
the starting blocks in
1978. (Bottom) Ben, far
right, and high school
track and field friends
after a meet.

(Courtesy of Claus Andersen)

Gloria Johnson (right) was her son's biggest fan and the centre of his universe. He told her "I would never leave you, so you never have to worry about me getting married." In 1977, Ben met coach Charlie Francis (below), who believed his sprinters needed to use banned anabolic steroids because many of their international rivals were doping.

(Courtesy of Claus Andersen)

Ben and Angella Issajenko were friends and Mazda Optimist teammates during their sprinting careers in Toronto. Issajenko was later a star witness at a public inquiry into athletic doping struck after his disqualification in Seoul.

Ben's greatest advantage as a sprinter was his flying start (top). "When the gun go off, the race be over," he liked to say. (Below) Warming up before racing at the Rome world championships. He said of American arch-rival Carl Lewis "I just want to beat his ass."

(Courtesy of Claus Andersen)

(Courtesy of Claus Andersen)

In the 100-metre world championship final in Rome, Ben set a world record and left arch-rival Carl Lewis and the rest of the field in his dust. His time of 9.83 seconds lopped a full tenth of a second off the old mark. Lewis later suggested Johnson was doping.

Italian automaker Enzo Ferrari told Ben that the world's fastest man should have the world's fastest car. Johnson agreed and paid $275,000 (CDN) for his Ferrari Testarossa.

Whether in a Canadian track uniform or a leopard-skin print under leather, he was catnip to female groupies. Ben enjoyed the attention, recalling his mother told him women were "my one weakness."

In 1987, Canada's Governor General Jeanne Sauvé (top) congratulates Ben on becoming a member of the Order of Canada. Ruth Owens presents him with the Jesse Owens International Trophy, named after her 1936 Olympic champion husband, as the world's top sprinter in 1987.

During a pre-Seoul split with coach Charlie Francis, Ben flew to St. Kitts for a rest and to have team doctor Jamie Astaphan (below, with Gloria) repair his hamstring injury. Astaphan also gave the sprinter a short course of steroids. Astaphan was later exposed for giving Johnson and other athletes veterinary steroids without their knowledge.

Ben led the 1988 Olympic men's 100-metre final from the instant he shot out of the blocks to the finish line, stunning American rival Carl Lewis with his world-record time of 9.79-seconds. Johnson dedicated the race to his mother Gloria.

(Courtesy of BBC)

After news of his disqualification leaked, Ben was crushed by media at Seoul's Kimpo Airport in the pre-dawn hours of September 27, 1988. Montreal's Richard Pound, a powerful IOC vice president, defended Ben before the IOC in Seoul, suggesting a "mystery man" in the doping control room slipped steroid pills into Johnson's beer.

(Courtesy of Ohio State University)

Ben needed police protection to enter his house after arriving in Toronto from Seoul. Reporters and camera operators camped outside the Johnson home, around-the-clock, for weeks. The Hon. Charles Dubin (bottom) was commissioner of the Canadian public inquiry struck shortly after Ben was disqualified in Seoul. Dubin would scold Johnson during his testimony for initially lying about his steroid use after failing his Olympic drug test.

(Courtesy of Digital Archive Ontario)

His first day of testimony over, Ben walks past a media crowd to an awaiting vehicle. He tearfully admitted on the witness stand that he had knowingly used anabolic steroids for years.

World Cup legend and Argentinian football star, Diego Maradona,
hired Ben as his personal trainer in the summer of 1997. The two
formed a friendship during conditioning sessions in Toronto and
Buenos Aires but in late August, Maradona failed a drug test in
Argentina.

(Courtesy of *International Business Times*)

Saadi Gaddafi, a son of former Libyan dictator Muammar Gaddafi, hired Ben as a conditioning coach in 1999 in hopes of establishing an elite football career in Italy. The two became friends, a relationship that years later brought the retired sprinter to the attention of the Royal Canadian Mounted Police.

Ben knew the word "Cheetah" was loaded but figured a $12,500 payday to film an energy drink commercial was worth it. His big line: "I Cheetah all the time." (Below) The so-called "mystery man," Andre Jackson (left), in Seoul's doping control centre with Ben, shortly after the 100-metre gold medal race, with cans of beer on the floor.

Ben was the featured sprinter in English filmmaker Daniel Gordon's documentary, 9.79*, about the infamous "dirtiest race in history." Canadian artist Bubby Kettlewell was commissioned to sculpt life-sized figures of Ben Johnson in four stages of his sprint, a project scuttled after his Olympic expulsion.

(Courtesy of Bubby Kettlewell)

Johnson's closest teammates were aghast, Angella Issajenko most of all. She knew Johnson was lying and, by doing so, had potentially set up Charlie Francis and Jamie Astaphan to take the fall.

Rob Gray, who was just beginning his career as a litigation lawyer with a Toronto law firm, was troubled by the plan to present his friend as a clueless dolt. "Ben was not a dummy," he said.

Francis, who had hired former Ontario attorney general Roy McMurtry as his lawyer, was panicked by Johnson's interview. The coach issued a carefully worded statement on October 3 that read in part: "Like all Canadians, I was shocked and dismayed to learn of Ben Johnson's disqualification at the Seoul Olympics, based upon a positive test for the drug stanozolol. Such a test result defies all logic and, in my opinion, can only be explained by a deliberate manipulation of the testing process."

Francis had raised the sabotage idea to the world, but it didn't register amid all the Johnson noise.

The day the *Sun* interview was published, Johnson appeared at the Canadian Black Achievement Awards, where he was honored for his contribution to sport and cheered by galagoers when he professed his innocence at the mic.

The media were gleefully cynical. Many didn't believe the sprinter and said so, especially after Futerman and Johnson doubled down on the "not knowingly" defense at a news conference at Toronto's Sutton Place Hotel on Tuesday, October 4. With his mother and father in attendance, Johnson stumbled reading the words "I didn't knowingly," while Futerman, who was not camera shy, handled most of the questions. "The Ed Futerman Show" is how the *Toronto Star* columnist John Robertson described the conference.

The next day, the federal government acted. Johnson's ordeal would be the subject of a royal commission.

CHAPTER TWELVE
UNDER OATH

Ben Johnson got what he requested.

On October 5, 1988, on recommendation of Canadian prime minister Brian Mulroney, who just two weeks earlier had called Johnson in Seoul to offer congratulations, the federal government established a royal commission of inquiry to investigate the sprinter's claims of innocence.

Johnson believed the probe would lead to his vindication and the return of his gold medal, and absolve key people like Charlie Francis of any transgressions. He could not have been more mistaken.

The commission was officially and awkwardly called the Commission of Inquiry into the Use of Drugs and Banned Practices Intended to Increase Athletic Performance. The Hon. Charles L. Dubin, an Ontario Court of Appeal judge with an affinity for sports, was appointed commissioner.

The Dubin Inquiry, as it would become known, would go beyond examining the specific circumstances surrounding Johnson's positive test in Seoul. It cast a wide net across the nation's amateur sports landscape and examined the roles of sports ruling bodies, including the IOC, regarding anti-doping testing, compliance, and enforcement policies. Dubin had the weapon of subpoena power at his disposal and the ability to recommend criminal charges should he see the need.

Dubin made the decision not to include active international athletes on the witness list. Carl Lewis and Linford Christie, for instance, would not be asked to testify. Only Canadian athletes were tapped, at a devastating cost for some.

Another of Dubin's early decisions was to hire Bob Armstrong, the skilled trial lawyer Francis had wished for Johnson, as the commission's lead counsel. Armstrong was an obvious choice: he'd articled under Dubin fresh out of law school in 1965, then worked with his friend and mentor until Dubin was appointed to the bench in 1972. Additionally, Armstrong had inquiry experience. He was a junior counsel at an infamous and contentious 1972 probe into claims of police brutality against the Toronto police force.

The affable, patient, and tenacious Armstrong was aware that Johnson had flatly denied that he was a willing and knowledgeable user of banned anabolic steroids. The obvious question was whether the sprinter was telling the truth. Was it possible he'd been tricked into cheating by his handlers? Was there another explanation?

Armstrong had just begun mulling these questions when Charlie Francis came forward through lawyer Roy McMurtry. Within days of the inquiry being struck, McMurtry had called Dubin. He wanted a private discussion on behalf of his client. McMurtry, Dubin, and Armstrong met at Osgoode Hall, a historic Toronto building that houses Ontario's Court of Appeal, where Dubin was a judge.

"Roy McMurtry told us the whole story," said Armstrong, who listened in amazement as Francis's detailed, years-long steroid protocols for a willing and comprehending Johnson were spelled out. "Obviously, it was extremely helpful."

Were Armstrong and Dubin shocked? "When Roy left our conference room, Charlie Dubin and I just looked at each other and said, 'holy smokes'—maybe something a little stronger than that," Armstrong chuckled.

Francis's willingness to cooperate left Armstrong with "a lot of work to do." If the coach's versions of events withstood scrutiny, the commission would be exposing Johnson as a liar. "Charlie's got one side of the story. Ben's going to have another side of the story, which is not all that novel if you've been involved in litigation, and I'd been a lawyer for a number of years," said Armstrong. "But the [witness] that really put it beyond question was Angella Issajenko."

Canada's premier female sprinter stepped up not long after Francis.

Angry at what she considered Johnson's attempt to shift blame toward Francis, Issajenko agreed to an initial interview with Armstrong, with her lawyer Dennis O'Connor present. "She was very open and frank, and she seemed to have this unbelievable memory about what she recalled of the steroid regimen she participated in," Armstrong said of the indoor world record holder.

Issajenko rattled off times, dates, places, types, and doses of anabolic steroids and other athletes involved, including the needle-averse Johnson, whom she'd injected periodically in the backside. Armstrong was fascinated by her narrative and eventually asked, "Do you have this written down somewhere?"

O'Connor reached into his briefcase. "Here it is," he said, holding up Issajenko's diary. Between handwritten pages capturing her personal life away from the track, Issajenko had scrupulously recorded details of her world-class sprinting career. That included descriptions of her training sessions, competitions, earnings, health, feelings, travel, and the particulars of the steroid routine she began under Francis and was later supervised by team doctor Jamie Astaphan.

"That was something else," Armstrong said of the moment O'Connor produced the diary. "That was probably *the* most important exhibit in the whole inquiry, her diary. And, of course, she was an amazing witness."

Issajenko would be one of the stars on a witness list that included a remarkable cast of characters, including the fallen Olympic hero, his beloved and now estranged coach, a compromised physician, a money-hungry entourage, oddball lawyers, sanctimonious sports officials, a parade of white athletes who would escape punishment for their steroid testimony while Black athletes did not, clean-cut RCMP detectives, and anonymous government pencil pushers.

Of course, every good story needs a villain. There was some serious competition for that role at the Dubin Inquiry, but one individual stood apart for his singular treachery.

* * *

Ed Futerman called Rob Gray "out of the blue" soon after the Dubin Inquiry was struck. Gray was familiar with Futerman's name. They worked in the same field of personal injury law, but he wondered why Futerman was calling.

The older lawyer confronted the rookie: "I've heard you directed Ben Johnson to take steroids, and you gave him injections."

Gray was astonished at the accusation. He told Futerman that any further conversation would have to be in person. "At that time, I really believed my phone was tapped," said Gray.

"It might have been paranoia and imagination on my part, but when you are talking to people [on the phone] and you are hearing clicking noises and things like that . . ."

It was no surprise that the inquiry would knock on Gray's door. His name had come up in post-Seoul gossip as one of three national team throwers banned from competition after positive doping tests in 1986. He met Futerman at his downtown Toronto law firm, with Gray's boss sitting in to listen. Gray told Futerman that Johnson's steroid denials "were going to be a real problem" if he clung to that defense. Gray told Futerman that while he'd never directed Johnson to take steroids, he'd injected the banned drug into his backside once when Charlie Francis wasn't around to do it. "I specifically told [Futerman] that you're going to be faced with a bunch of credible people, including myself, who will say Ben knew exactly what he was doing."

Gray gave Futerman valuable information that day. Witnesses from the sport would testify that his client was lying, and Johnson was doomed to be outed if his inquiry preparation was not handled carefully. Gray's urgent message was that Johnson needed to be truthful now, not later.

He suggested a solution: Futerman take Gray on as a temporary associate during the inquiry to help him understand dope-testing procedures, the sport's ins and outs, and how the IOC operates. In that legal role, Gray could influence the early strategy to best position Johnson before the inevitable facts rolled out. The discus thrower-turned-lawyer also wanted to keep his steroid history off the witness stand. Working with Futerman would prevent a subpoena from coming his way. "I was hoping he would agree with that kind of approach, but I never heard back from him."

To Gray's dismay, the Johnson camp would not budge from steadfast denials for months. "To try to present Ben as a dolt, as a guy who didn't know what was going on, was totally the wrong strategy. Look, lawyers fight about strategy all the time. I've been a litigator for thirty-six years, and my strategy may be different from that of the guy next door to me in my office or a lawyer in another firm. To me, if you know there are people out there who are going to discredit the approach you're going to take, why take it?"

* * *

As the old saying goes, the Mounties always get their man. A crew of top-notch investigators from the RCMP and Toronto police was seconded to the Dubin Inquiry. Most of their duties took the form of old-school detective work—tracking down witnesses, interviewing people, and searching for documents. Just weeks into their sleuthing, officers, with a little help from Angella Issajenko, made a bombshell discovery that would turn the inquiry on its head.

It involved the anabolic steroid that Jamie Astaphan introduced to the Optimist sprinters in late 1985. It was the milky white injectable solution Astaphan claimed came from a mysterious East German. He'd been calling it Estragol, claiming it was a code name for the undetectable steroid furazabol. The Optimists, including Johnson, believed they'd been taking furazabol.

On the advice of her lawyer, Issajenko turned over a dozen unused, unlabeled vials of Estragol to investigators in November 1988. Francis had asked her in January 1988 to store this extra Estragol, given to him by Astaphan, at her home, which she did. The vials were sent to different labs for analysis, including the health protection branch of Health and Welfare Canada. The certified findings were jaw-dropping.

Testing revealed the milky white substance in the unlabeled vials was the steroid stanozolol, not Astaphan's so-called wonder drug, Estragol. The Optimist sprinters had, in fact, been using the very detectable drug that tripped up Johnson in Seoul. It was stanozolol, marketed under the brand name Winstrol.

Investigators next began tracking the source of the fake Estragol to discover where these stanozolol vials were purchased from. Was it on the black market or from a legitimate pharmaceutical company in Canada, the United States, Mexico, or elsewhere? Astaphan would not be of much help. He'd returned to St. Kitts after his disastrous national television interview with Barbara Frum, and he was making noises about not returning to Canada.

The investigators discovered furazabol was only produced in Japan, under the brand name Miotolan. They obtained a batch. Next, they turned to respected American forensic toxicologist Dr. David Black, head of the Vanderbilt laboratory in Nashville, Tennessee. They asked Black to conduct a series of studies to compare furazabol and stanozolol. Was it possible to have mixed up the two steroids during the anti-doping testing in Seoul? Black agreed to the request, and the answer was no; the two compounds could not be mistaken for one another.

Back in Toronto, police investigators were on the stanozolol trail. They hit the jackpot at Sterling Drug Ltd., north of the city in the suburb of Aurora. The company confirmed to police detectives that Astaphan had purchased stanozolol in injectable and tablet forms, under the brand name Winstrol V. According to Sterling Drug records, the doctor bought a total of six thousand and five hundred pills and sixty-eight bottles (30 milliliters each) of the Winstrol V products. Astaphan purchased so much Winstrol V that a company sales manager would later tell Dubin, "I was under the assumption he was a veterinarian."

Veterinarian? There are two Winstrol brand name versions of stanozolol: one is manufactured for humans, and the other is made for animals. Winstrol for human consumption comes in pill form only. Winstrol V is a veterinary product. It, too, comes in pill form and is identical in composition to the tablets made for people. Winstrol V also has an injectable steroid solution that has a slightly different makeup and is manufactured for veterinary use only.

The bottom line: Astaphan was feeding Johnson and his teammates an anabolic steroid intended for animals and lying to them about the drug's true purpose.

* * *

Charlie Francis decided to cooperate with inquiry chief counsel Bob Armstrong shortly after reading Ben Johnson's interview in the *Toronto Sun*. Francis was sharp enough to see his potential criminal exposure if his star sprinter's denials were believed. Above all, he later wrote that he was deeply wounded by Johnson's public stand. "While I empathized with Ben and the impossible situation he'd been placed in, I was shaken and hurt by the falsehood," said Francis, then forty years old.

"If Ben stuck to these statements, they would support the theory that I had deceived him by giving him steroids without his knowledge or assent, a scenario that would lead to criminal charges against me," he said.

The phone calls between the coach and athlete stopped.

Armstrong had several in-person interviews with Francis and his lawyer, Roy McMurtry, prior to his testimony. He was impressed by Francis's candor, intelligence, and mettle. On the stand, the coach would have to reveal steroid users, including Johnson. "Our conversation with Charlie Francis was entirely focused on him and his fundamental philosophy that 'to compete successfully at the international level, we had no choice but to do what others are doing,'" said Armstrong.

The inquiry had a short opening phase in Montreal in January 1989. The purpose was to examine the sport of weightlifting, since many of the witnesses performed in that arena. The beefy men called to testify provided endless tales of steroid stupidity, from being busted at customs with bags of pills to failed doping tests, to cringey stories of catheters used to "transplant" clean urine to beat doping tests.

"Seven men were selected to represent Canada at the 1988 Olympic Games in Seoul as members of the weight-lifting team," Dubin would say. "Before the competition even began, four had been disqualified for cheating, and the three who did compete previously cheated or helped others to cheat. How was this disgrace allowed to happen?"

How indeed? The public would soon learn that weightlifting wasn't the only sports federation, domestic or international, not aggressively searching out drug cheats.

* * *

In February 1989, the Dubin Inquiry returned to Toronto for its main phase, focusing on track and field. I covered the hearings daily, along with my *Star* colleague Joe Hall. I represented the sports department, Hall the city desk. It was a massive story and a two-person job.

In 1989, the *Star* still had an evening edition for the city's core. That meant we had to dictate our copy to a rewrite desk over the telephone, sharing the receiver to read from our notes in advance of the noon deadline. When the afternoon session concluded, we cabbed back to the newsroom to write a second, more complete story for the next day's morning edition. After filing, we'd often hit the now-defunct Print Room bar on the ground floor of the newspaper's One Yonge Street headquarters, living up (or down) to the reporter stereotype.

Riveting testimony emerged from the Dubin Inquiry. It opened the inner sanctum of elite athletics to the general public. Many of the revelations weren't about doping. We heard a lot about the dedication, discipline, sacrifice, and fortitude of amateur Canadian athletes competing at the highest levels. It astonished me that so many were managing it with so little support. They were carrying a share of the training, financial, travel, and therapeutic burdens themselves. That deep commitment to excellence was evident in athletes who doped as well as those who didn't.

Nevertheless, the juiciest news of the day was always who was juicing. And the big questions on the public's mind were when will Ben Johnson take the stand and what will he say? That day did not come for nearly five months. Johnson, as requested by Futerman, would be the last Optimist sprinter to testify.

The inquiry heard from Sport Canada and CTFA officials, as well as athletes and coaches. In the strategic rollout of the witness list, Francis would be the first of the Optimist group to testify in early March.

Francis spent eight days on the stand in a hearing room packed with Canadian and international media and members of the public. Some days, there were upward of two hundred media covering the inquiry, far more than the room could hold. Squeezed-out reporters were crammed into a small overflow area in which the proceedings were broadcast.

In his early testimony, Francis spoke of how he learned about rampant doping when he was competing for Canada and attending Stanford University on a track scholarship in the United States. He asserted the sport's ruling bodies—the domestic and international federations—were lax or uninterested in ferreting out cheaters, especially if they were from powerful nations like the United States, Great Britain, or countries behind the Iron Curtain or were individual superstars who drove ticket sales and TV ratings.

Francis's revelatory account of the how, when, why, where, and who of steroid use was captured on television cameras daily. While many people would have heard of anabolic steroids in 1989, few understood much about how they worked and how widespread was their use. Francis mesmerized audiences with his admissions, explanations, and encyclopedic knowledge of banned substances and how they were obtained.

One of the coach's blockbuster claims was that top CTFA officials conspired to help athletes cheat drug detection in Canada and other countries. In one instance, Francis alleged that then-CTFA chairman Jean-Guy Ouellette promised to warn Canadian athletes of upcoming unannounced drug tests and that he'd try to delay launching random testing in Canada until after the Seoul Olympics. Ouellette would vehemently deny the allegations under oath, and Dubin, finding him credible, would write that Francis misunderstood their drug-testing conversations.

The coach recalled the details of Johnson's final doping cycle that commenced nearly a month before the race in Seoul, his disbelief upon learning Johnson's A sample was positive, and his ensuing despair at the Olympic disqualification. Francis also raised the possibility that Johnson's drug test in Seoul was sabotaged by the American mystery man, whom he claimed breached doping control security. No one linked to the inquiry yet knew the mystery man was Carl Lewis's friend, Andre Jackson.

Francis's theory about a US-linked sabotage plot was roundly rejected by inquiry witnesses as bunk. The allegation of lax security in doping control was shot down by IOC medical commission member Arne Ljungqvist, who said no unauthorized person had gained access that day. Neither was Dubin moved by Francis's finger-pointing. He would dismiss saboteur schemes and conspiratorial gripes about the IOC's handling of Johnson's case in just three paragraphs in his final report.

In contrast, the commissioner accepted most evidence from IOC medical commission members regarding the Seoul testing as sound, including that of Manfred Donike, who developed and introduced at Seoul the endocrine profile test that suggested Johnson was a longtime doper.

Francis hotly disputed the singling out of Johnson for the endocrine profile and never backed down from his position that his athlete was targeted to fail his drug test. "Until the day he died, Charlie believed Ben had been set up in Seoul," said Rob Gray, who remained close to Francis until his passing in 2010.

Francis's motivation to cooperate with the inquiry wasn't entirely about coming clean. He wanted to get as close as he could to outing other international dopers and their handlers without naming them. He was going down swinging. On the stand, Francis was adamant that other athletes were artificially boosting their speed. He made it clear in his memoir that he believed that Johnson "had won on a level playing field in Seoul and that his spectacular accomplishment should be returned to the record book."

The inquiry would be told repeatedly that Johnson only doped because he and his coach believed much of their competition was doing the same thing.

* * *

Charlie Francis's testimony under Bob Armstrong's meticulous questioning was spellbinding. During cross-examination, Ed Futerman would do his best to break the spell. He swung hard at the coach, accusing him of playing Russian roulette with the career and health of an athlete incapable of understanding the consequences of using the drugs Francis pushed on him.

Futerman suggested Francis, as the most influential person in Johnson's life after his mother Gloria, used that influence to further his own ego and ambition as the architect of Johnson's success.

Francis insisted that Johnson was an adult capable of making his own decisions in all aspects of life and was aware of every risk tied to taking the banned drugs. Plus, said Francis, he'd never jeopardize his own coaching career by introducing a steroid program to an athlete who might fail a drug test because they didn't understand how clearance times worked.

Futerman alleged that Francis misled his athletes on the subject of steroids: "You were able to persuade your athletes of two important facts: number one, everyone in world-class prominence in track and field was doing it, and therefore, there was nothing morally wrong, and number two, there were no known side effects in small doses."

Futerman asked about Johnson's intellectual capacity. Francis responded that he had staked his career on Johnson knowing what steroid use meant. "I was fully in the belief that he understood what he was doing, that he was capable of listening to the instructions, understanding the clearance times involved with the drugs, so that he could then be able to pass the [doping control] tests."

When Futerman described Johnson as a struggling high school student with limited scholastic ability, the coach countered that Johnson was bright, capable of doing better in school if he wanted, and smart enough to pursue a career after his track days ended.

"At that time, I felt, on the basis of my discussions with him, the considerable hours I spent with him every day, his sense of humor, and other indications to me, that in fact he was someone who could advance himself, who could have a career in the future."

Francis gave examples to illustrate Johnson's steroid acumen. For instance, on January 15, 1987, Johnson set a world indoor 60-meter record in Osaka, Japan. The panicked sprinter called the coach in Toronto because meet organizers were demanding a urine sample. Johnson hadn't expected he'd have to provide one and was worried he might fail the test. Francis reassured him that the intensive off-season steroid cycle he'd been on ended early enough that he was clear. Johnson passed that test. Futerman's takeaway from Johnson's worried call to his coach was that it showed he was so naïve about steroid use, he didn't understand he could not refuse to give a urine sample after a race.

Futerman got Francis to admit that he did not order comprehensive liver tests for his athletes before they embarked on steroid programs and did not have extensive discussions with medical experts about possible side effects, particularly on the liver, which the inquiry was told was the organ most vulnerable to steroids. Johnson's medical records showed that tests two months before Seoul found his liver function to be abnormal, but not seriously so.

When Futerman asked Francis to show the commission his rear end and point to the exact place where a steroid injection would be made, Dubin shot him down, saying such a display would only embarrass the witness, who had described the injection process at length during his time on the stand.

* * *

Angella Issajenko was fiercely loyal to Charlie Francis. Besides being her coach, he was also a friend. So when Ben Johnson stated he had not knowingly used steroids, Issajenko was enraged. She knew better. In the Optimist sprint group, athletes were frequently discussing their steroid use, what drugs they liked and disliked, and which made their muscles tight or increased libido. Johnson was part of those chats, and Issajenko was adamant that he'd been aware of what she was plunging into his glutes.

Frustrated, she gave an explosive interview to the *Toronto Star* four days after the Dubin Inquiry was struck. "Ben takes steroids," she said. "I take steroids . . . Jamie gives them to us, and Charlie isn't a scientist, but he knows what's happening."

She took the stand immediately after Francis, the first Mazda Optimist athlete to do so. It was obviously a difficult moment for her since she was implicating, directly or indirectly, teammates as doping brethren in the course of detailing her own steroid journey. She wept as she told the hearing who would be most hurt by Johnson's public denials: "I came to the conclusion that B.J. was going to lay the blame on Charlie and Jamie. And this could not be because I felt at that time that when someone has been very good to you, someone who has done you a good turn, that has been responsible for making you great, then you shouldn't turn against people like that."

Over three gripping days, Issajenko stated that maintaining the conspiracy of silence among steroid users was a serious matter, and "but for the inquiry, the truth would never have been discovered and the athletes would have gone to their graves with their secret."

She told the inquiry that Charlie Francis directed her and other Optimist athletes to strike out the portion of their 1987 CTFA contracts that dealt with random drug testing. That signaled their refusal to be drug tested at any time, with little or no notice outside of competition days, even though it was a mandatory requirement for receiving financial support from the Canadian government.

Issajenko also said that Astaphan sold her $1,200 worth of human growth hormone prior to a training camp in Guadeloupe and that

Johnson and fellow sprinter Tony Sharpe snuck it through customs in a cooler bag. She told how she had begun to suspect that the Estragol that Astaphan provided was stanozolol in 1987 because it made her muscles stiff.

Her diary, of course, was an important part of her testimony, detailing her cycles of vitamins, human growth hormone, and anabolic steroids. Johnson's steroid cycles could be traced through her writings. He remains angry at Issajenko for volunteering her testimony, saying, "She threw me under the bus at the Dubin Inquiry" with her record-keeping.

* * *

If Issajenko's testimony was a betrayal, it was nothing like the one involving fellow sprinter Desai Williams, who the inquiry heard had ratted out Ben Johnson to a CTFA official.

Williams and hurdler Mark McKoy split with Charlie Francis and the Optimists after the 1983 world championships in Helsinki. They rejoined the Francis group four years later. Glen Bogue, then the CTFA's manager of athlete services, testified that Williams called him in either 1985 or 1986 to alert him to the doping practices of some athletes coached by Francis at the York University training center, including Johnson. Bogue already suspected the group was doping; he was ready to listen.

Bogue said Williams was concerned about Johnson's health due to the quantity of steroids he was taking. During that phone call, the two devised a sting operation to entrap his former teammate. Williams would alert Bogue when a steroid shipment arrived for the group, and Bogue would arrange an unannounced random test for Johnson. Bogue would keep Williams' name out of it.

Before proceeding, Bogue reported the tip and the planned sting operation to Wilf Wedmann, the CTFA president. Wedmann stopped the scheme in its tracks. Incredibly, the top man in Canadian track and field wanted nothing to do with investigating an alleged doping ring involving a star athlete and a national team coach operating out of the CTFA's high-performance center at York University.

Wedmann testified that he did not consider Bogue's information from an anonymous source as "very substantial." He also rejected any surprise drug testing at the York training center, claiming the CTFA "did not have sufficient authority to conduct such tests since there was no agreement by the athletes in their contracts with the CTFA to permit out-of-competition testing."

The CTFA, in fact, did have that authority. By 1986, carded Canadian athletes were required to agree to drug testing during competitions and on random days. As a condition of receiving funding from the government and their respective national sports federations, they were not to possess or use anabolic steroids. As Dubin concluded, the CTFA had contracts with its athletes but "did not enforce this requirement."

Athletes such as Johnson and Issajenko were never challenged when they simply crossed out the random testing clause in their CTFA agreements.

Bogue told the hearing he also spoke to Gerard Mach, the national sprint coach and Francis's mentor. Mach dismissed the idea that steroids were a problem in the sport. Bogue then stopped pursuing Williams' tip.

As a witness, Williams refuted parts of Bogue's testimony. He agreed he'd called the CTFA official to discuss Johnson's steroid use but denied he wanted to set him up. Dubin didn't find Williams's explanation convincing and suggested that Williams's true motivation behind the call to Bogue was to get rid of his younger, faster rival. "I do not think it was Mr. Johnson's health that Mr. Williams was concerned about since, if it were, a private chat with Mr. Johnson would have been the appropriate means of dealing with it," he wrote.

Johnson had no clue that Williams was trying to turn him in.

* * *

For months after the Seoul Games, Jamie Astaphan bunkered down in St. Kitts. Through his lawyer, David Sookram, he said he wouldn't return to Toronto unless he was paid $100,000 to cover his legal costs. He would eventually have a change of heart. His role in the scandal was leaking out. Charlie Francis laid out everything during his testimony, which was backed up by Angella Issajenko and others.

Astaphan's license to practice medicine was under review by the province's medical licensing body, the College of Physicians and Surgeons of Ontario. Not only was his steroid involvement problematic, but he was also accused by the college of falsely billing the province's health-care system for treatments for at least one athlete that the doctor didn't perform.

Inquiry lead Bob Armstrong and associate counsel Kirby Chown flew to St. Kitts to interview the mercurial doctor. Over the course of three days with the Canadian lawyers, Astaphan agreed to appear as a witness. He would support previous witness testimony stating that he'd given Ben Johnson anabolic steroids and that the sprinter understood exactly what the banned drugs were for. "The visit went well in the sense that he was frank about everything," Armstrong recalled.

Astaphan, then forty-three years old, seemed to enjoy being the center of attention when he took the stand in May 1989. His arrival after months of "will he or won't he?" was front-page news. He was by now being referred to as the "personal physician" of Ben Johnson, who'd paid him $10,000 (US) a month for his services.

The doctor used his inquiry time to minimize his culpability, laud his steroid expertise, and implicate Johnson as a pampered mama's boy who was lying about being tricked into doping. Astaphan also told Commissioner Charles Dubin that it was his duty as a physician to supervise and regulate the steroid intake of the Optimist athletes who, when he met them, were taking an assortment of performance-enhancing drugs. "If I didn't monitor them and if I didn't give it to them, they were going to get it elsewhere, and most of them had gotten it from elsewhere," Astaphan testified. "They came to me for advice and for supervision, and I thought it was my responsibility to do this."

Astaphan said he injected Johnson with steroids fifty or sixty times between 1984 and 1988, and the sprinter was "very inquisitive" and "knowledgeable" when the pair discussed the banned drugs. It came out at the inquiry that Astaphan had taped telephone conversations about steroids with Johnson, Francis, and Issajenko without their knowledge in January 1988. The poor-quality recordings were played during the inquiry. Astaphan said he did this for protection after Johnson allegedly told him that he or Francis would "take the rap" if the sprinter's steroid secret was discovered. He secured the tapes in bank vaults in Toronto and St. Kitts with written instructions for an ally to use them if the doctor became a fall guy. He'd also taped Italian sprinter star Pierfrancesco Pavoni, who periodically trained with the Optimist group and who later denied he'd ever used steroids.

Dubin learned that Astaphan's medical records of Optimist group sprinters, including Johnson's, disappeared in 1986. Armstrong reminded the doctor that a 1986 break-in at his Toronto medical office, where the records may have been lost, occurred a day before a scheduled probe of his practice by the College of Physicians and Surgeons of Ontario. Astaphan moved back to St. Kitts around this time.

While Astaphan claimed he could beat any doping test with his clever use of masking agents, he took no responsibility for the Seoul positive. He blamed Johnson, suggesting the sprinter took stanozolol near race day, an allegation that seems unlikely given Johnson's 8 years of perfecting clearance timing.

The doctor clung to his story that he'd been given injectable furazabol, not stanozolol, from an East German athlete he refused to name before the inquiry. When Armstrong told him the Japanese drug manufacturers of furazabol did not produce an injectable form of that steroid during the period, Astaphan continued to reject the assertion that he'd given stanozolol to athletes. He claimed his Winstrol purchases over two years were for a St. Kitts farmer friend, who bought the drugs to fatten his scrawny goats, sheep, and cattle. The friend, who was an inquiry witness, said he would then sell the animals to an island veterinary college for dissection and experimentation. No transaction records were produced.

David Sookram, Astaphan's lawyer, asked sprinter Tim Bethune if he felt the urge "to get down on all fours" like an animal to graze on grass after taking the veterinary steroid, Winstrol V, raising gasps of disbelief in the hearing room and enraging Dubin. In his report, the commissioner would veer from his usual neutral observer demeanor to scold the doctor for betraying his Hippocratic Oath to do no harm and for engaging in schemes to make money off his patients.

CHAPTER THIRTEEN
THE TRUTH

Canadian Track and Field Association officials had a tricky issue to address long before Ben Johnson took the stand at the Dubin Inquiry: how to explain to a judge why they turned aside multiple opportunities to investigate claims of a doping ring involving Charlie Francis, a national sprint coach, and Johnson. That the CTFA was one of Canada's federally funded national sports organizations made things more uncomfortable for officials: they were accountable to the public.

The inquiry heard of other coaches and athletes, some from the University of Toronto's track club, who had offered the CTFA credible information prior to Seoul about the Optimists' steroid use. These tips were shelved, often by the man at the top, President Wilf Wedmann, to the astonishment of Commissioner Charles Dubin.

One of the crazier examples involved Toronto shot-putter Peter Dajia a few months before the Seoul Games. He wasn't offering a tip. Dajia threatened to expose Johnson's steroid use to the media if the thrower's own doping suspension wasn't quickly commuted.

Dajia had tested positive for a steroid in 1986 and was suspended for life, although athletes could and often did successfully apply for reinstatement after about eighteen months. Dajia believed his appeal was being slow-walked. He confronted a CTFA staffer about it. The shot-putter testified he didn't utter the word "steroid," but threatened to "turn in the world's fastest man" to reporters if his case didn't speed up.

Dajia was soon reinstated, although the federation maintained that his threats did not cause a speedier resolution. No one had acted on the shot-putter's cheating allegations.

In another instance, Jean-Guy Ouellette, the CTFA's board chair, testified that he feared lawsuits from Optimist members if doping rumors about them were investigated. Ouellette claimed he had a kind of honor system with Francis. He'd informally asked Francis if his athletes were doping, and the coach always answered no. Case closed.

Yet another official said he was afraid Francis would beat him up if he asked about steroids, so he didn't.

As previously noted, Johnson wasn't drug tested at the 1988 Canadian Olympic trials in August in Ottawa. The random selection process had two of the top three finishers provide urine samples, and Johnson's position, as the winner of the event, was not one of them. This, apparently by sheer luck of the draw, ensured Johnson wouldn't be outed before Seoul if his clearance timing was off.

Given how often red flags were overlooked or dismissed by the CTFA, it wasn't a stretch for Johnson, Francis, and others to interpret their federation's inaction as tacit approval to keep winning and keep beating the Americans—just don't get caught. It also emerged that the CTFA had foot-dragged the launch of its long-planned random drug-testing program until *after* the Seoul Olympics.

Pat Reid, the former director of the Ottawa indoor meet, said in retrospect that it's understandable why Johnson believed he was untouchable in any doping room: "You can see how Ben thought he was safe . . . he was getting help from his own federation. The context [of 1988] is, 'You're not doing anything wrong, we'll protect you, we'll tell you where the red-light cameras are.' Then they all denied it, but Ben was left hanging. I can see why Ben says, 'Why did this happen to me?'"

Dubin was clearly disturbed by what he was learning about the governing body's reluctance to police doping allegations. His written conclusions regarding CTFA inaction read in part:

> The information was of such a serious nature that inquiries should have been commenced. No such inquiries were ever made. The information was consistently discarded as rumor and of no weight and was often attributed to mere expressions of jealously. It is true that in some cases the information could have been described as rumors, but over the years these stories became increasingly prevalent and worthy of some inquiry into their basis.

How did sports officials in Canada, including the CTFA, allow it to happen? Hugh Fraser, the retired judge and now Court of Arbitration for Sport adjudicator, suggested the hands-off approach officials took with Johnson involved "some willful blindness and the hope it was all going to work out."

"When little old Canada is getting these kinds of results from one of the glamor events in athletics, I think a lot of people just said, 'Pray to god nothing happens to blow this up, but we're not going to be the ones to go after it in a really proactive way,'" said Fraser, who was part of a sports advisory panel to Dubin. "It [was] at the point where he's getting those great results. Who's going to try to upset the apple cart?"

Money also played a part. Johnson was a cash cow. His handlers, the CTFA, meet directors, sponsors, teammates, family, agents, doctor, and more, made money off him when he ran. He cast a wide, lucrative spell few wanted to break.

The CTFA budget jumped by about $1 million over the fiscal year 1988–1989, due largely to Johnson's star power. Then-CTFA president Paul Dupre told the hearing that the extra cash, pushing the budget to $4.2 million from the previous year's $3 million, was due to increased marketing, sponsorships, special promotions, and track meet attendance featuring Johnson.

The CTFA created an exclusive poster to celebrate Johnson's 1987 world championship in Rome, one he would sign for buyers as a fundraiser for the federation. Johnson recalled being at a three-hour signing session in early 1988 at a Vancouver mall. The CTFA was to pay him $30,000. The sides settled on a lesser sum post-Seoul.

Between 1985 and 1988, the money coming Johnson's way was often cash. When he received cash appearance fees, he wouldn't always deposit the full amount into his trust fund as required, sometimes storing it in a safe in Ross Earl's home. (This practice partly caused the sprinter's later tax troubles.) Johnson recalled that it wasn't unusual for him to have up to $50,000 (US) tucked into a satchel he carried as he competed on the European circuit. Other sprinters noticed his earnings. Angella Issajenko claimed Johnson was notoriously cheap and that he once refused to share $300 from an appearance fee with younger club sprinters. Johnson rejects greedy depictions of himself as untrue. "All anybody had to do was ask me for money if they needed money. I would have given it."

There were instances when the sprinter wasn't aware he was being used as a moneymaker for others. Polish-born massage therapist Waldemar Matuszewski testified that Astaphan plotted to take over as Johnson's coach after the sprinter and Francis split in the early summer of 1988. Matuszewski said the doctor promised to pay him $250,000 (US) if he'd treat Johnson exclusively through Seoul and if the sprinter won Olympic gold. That, of course, didn't materialize as Johnson and Francis reconciled.

However, in August 1988, while sitting in the stands at the Canadian Olympic trials in Ottawa, Matuszewski testified that he was offered $25,000 (US) to sign an agreement not to discuss matters relating to the Optimists. This money didn't come from Johnson. It was provided from Mazda club funds through arrangements made by Johnson's agent, Larry Heidebrecht, and Ross Earl, Dubin was told. Matuszewski received $18,750 (US) in cash when he signed the handwritten deal drawn up by Earl; the remaining $6,250 was to come after the Olympics. Matuszewski said he understood the contract meant he was not to discuss steroid use by club members, but Earl denied this interpretation. Under cross-examination, Earl told Bob Armstrong that the agreement was meant to plug leaks to the media, like the ones that exacerbated the summertime rift between Johnson and Francis.

In May 1988, Astaphan had received $25,000 (US) as a bonus, again from funds obtained from Mazda "for its sponsorship of the Francis sprinters."

* * *

One of Bob Armstrong's more brilliant inquiry accomplishments was to demonstrate that the anti-doping programs carried out by Canadian and international officials for more than a decade before Seoul were virtually useless.

CTFA and IOC medical commission witnesses reluctantly admitted under Armstrong's questioning that competition-day drug testing, the method that caught Ben Johnson, was largely ineffective because most doping athletes were adept at calculating clearance times to provide clean urine samples. Armstrong also extracted admissions that anti-doping experts had known since the 1970s that the best way to battle steroid use was through short-notice, out-of-competition testing conducted randomly during training periods when athletes were using the drugs, not on competition day.

Armstrong asserted that sports bodies continually pushed upon the public the fallacy that competition-day testing was the gold standard for steroid detection when they knew that was not true. The fallacy left the impression that the few who failed competition-day tests, like Johnson, were using steroids but that others in the same sport were not, Armstrong said.

While questioning Robert Dugal, head of the IOC-accredited Montreal lab, Armstrong said it took the "fluke" detection of Johnson's steroid use in Seoul and not the actions of the IOC brain trust to finally initiate effective out-of-competition testing programs. Dubin also scolded Dugal for "claiming great kudos" after Johnson's disqualification by giving the impression to the public that competition-day testing "was effective."

The commissioner doubled down on this theme in his final report: "Evidence from this inquiry proves that the athletes caught at Seoul were not the only drug users. They were the only detected ones."

More alarming doping news dropped during the inquiry regarding protections given to doping American athletes by US Olympic officials leading up to the 1984 Los Angeles Summer Games. The United States Olympic Committee announced that seventy-five American athletes tested positive for banned drugs in the months prior to the 1984 Olympics but faced no sanctions because the USOC had a nonpunitive testing program in place from November 1983 to March 1984. The USOC statement came shortly after Francis testified in 1989 about the existence of the program.

The USOC explained that the penalty-free testing period was not to help their athletes cheat, even though all or most of the seventy-five doping Americans were likely competing internationally during this phase, but to familiarize themselves with doping control processes. A USOC spokesperson called the testing "educational and informal" and said that athletes failing tests were not punished because "the possibility of error existed."

* * *

By the time he was to appear at the Dubin Inquiry, there was no way that Ben Johnson could keep up his charade. There had been too many witnesses. There was too much evidence that he'd knowingly taken anabolic steroids for years and reaped the benefits that the drugs enabled: faster times, world titles, wealth, and fame.

He'd watched the televised testimony at his home. He'd heard Charlie Francis tell all, followed by a string of teammates who did the same. Johnson was cornered, and the whole world knew it. As the former discus thrower Rob Gray had warned Futerman would happen, all of the Optimists' secrets were spilled.

The months preceding Johnson's appearance had been difficult. The predictable and lucrative life he'd built had blown up. He was an anxious wreck. He couldn't sleep. He had savings but no money coming in. He was suspended from competition for life while guarding a doping lie. How could he be anything but stressed (at best) or traumatized (at worst)? Even those highly unsympathetic to Johnson's predicament, and there were many, including angry teammates subpoenaed to testify, could probably today appreciate how global shaming could cause debilitating suffering.

Johnson was twenty-six when nabbed in Seoul, old enough to quit doping if he'd wanted to. He was responsible for breaking his sport's rules. But when it all came crashing down, the sports system that quite literally had cashed in on his success and winked at rumors of doping swiftly abandoned him, as did the government that embraced him on the world stage. He'd become an embarrassment and a political liability. Johnson said no one from any Canadian sports body offered him professional counseling or mental health support.

Throughout the ordeal, Johnson remained under a steady media watch, with cars and cameras chasing him whenever he left his house. There were strange scenes in which Johnson would hand-wash his $108,000 Porsche in his driveway, ignoring the assembled reporters asking about inquiry witnesses who had confirmed his steroid involvement or international doping experts who had laughed at his sabotage theories.

He did manage to enjoy himself from time to time. He'd hit nightclubs with the help of his sister, Clare, and a friendly neighbor. After dinner, Clare would drive Ben's third car, a champagne-colored Corvette, from the family home. The media wouldn't bother following her. She would park the car unnoticed around the block. Her brother would then lope across his backyard, hop the fence into his neighbor's yard, and continue through the property to the Corvette waiting at the curb. He would drive to his favorite midtown hot spot, coming home after last call when most of the media encampment had packed up for the night. "I wasn't going to stay inside for the rest of my life," he said.

This fun was undermined by two unfortunate incidents that landed Johnson on the front page and in court.

A motorist reported that Johnson had waved a gun at him while driving his black Porsche along Highway 401 in Toronto. Police later seized a starter's pistol at the sprinter's home, and on October 11, 1988, he was charged with assault and possession of a dangerous weapon. Johnson entered a not-guilty plea. The following summer, he would be given a conditional discharge and twelve months' probation when he pleaded guilty to common assault and the crown dropped the weapons charge. The presiding judge had been told that the day before the incident, Johnson received a speeding ticket on the same highway while trying to escape journalists chasing him. He admitted to a "certain degree of compassion" for the sprinter in light of the fishbowl life Johnson had led since his Olympic disqualification.

The second incident occurred in May 1989. The world's fastest man had just dropped off his friends and fellow Olympians, Desai Williams and Mark McKoy, and was driving his mother's Nissan along the trendy Yorkville Avenue. He attempted to steer around a stopped car blocking the narrow road, a move that led to a confrontation with a group of men who recognized him. He got out of the car, was sucker punched, broke a tooth, and split his lip. At least one man jumped on the hood, kicking in the windshield as Johnson tried to drive away. Johnson chased the offender, catching him a block away. Williams and McKoy helped hold the suspect until police arrived. One man was charged with two counts of mischief in connection with $700 in damage done to the Nissan.

These were upsetting events for Johnson. Apart from piles of speeding tickets, he'd avoided situations that involved the police, and now, he couldn't even turn to Francis for moral support. On Futerman's instructions, Johnson was increasingly isolated.

Ross Earl, the Optimist track club founder, recalled that he and Charlie Francis were summoned by Futerman to his law office just after the inquiry was called. They went to the office together, but only Francis was waved in by Futerman for a closed-door discussion. After a few minutes, said Earl, Francis emerged, pale and upset, saying they must leave immediately. The coach said Futerman threatened to sue each of them if they contacted Johnson during the inquiry.

Jamie Astaphan had a similar experience. It arose during the inquiry when Futerman badgered the doctor about not conducting follow-up liver tests on Johnson after Seoul. Astaphan shot back that he'd been prevented from doing the tests by Futerman, who'd told him not to contact the sprinter.

In addition to watching the Dubin testimony at home "to see who were my friends and who was saying what," Johnson drove to Ed Futerman's law office daily to be briefed on developments. He remembers this routine mostly as an additional expense, not a productive endeavor. "I was going to Futerman's office almost every day for six months," he said. "I paid for my own parking, $20 a day, $100 a week, and I didn't even write it off because my mind wasn't in the right place. I wasn't thinking."

* * *

Lead counsel Bob Armstrong had given the Johnson camp latitude to reconsider the sprinter's position after Charlie Francis and Angella Issajenko began cooperating. He had courteously granted Futerman's request that Johnson testify last in the track-and-field portion of the inquiry. Counsel for witnesses received full disclosure about the results of inquiry investigations and the evidence expected to arise from those findings, so they were "armed in advance with what might be said about their clients by witnesses who preceded them," Dubin would later write. Nothing had been withheld from Futerman and Johnson.

At Futerman's request, months before Johnson testified, a young associate at his firm, Lorne Lipkus, privately grilled the sprinter in a mock two-hour cross-examination to test the credibility of his denials. Futerman then had Johnson submit to a lie detector test in the United States, which he passed, although some areas of the test suggested deception. The lawyer also arranged to have the runner clinically assessed by a psychiatrist, who concluded Johnson had the intellectual capacity of a child around seven years old.

Johnson's first day on the stand was Monday, June 12, 1989. Canadians were riveted to their television sets just as they had been for his gold medal race a year earlier in Seoul. The behind-the-scenes understanding among all parties in the days leading up to his testimony was that despite his denials, Johnson would admit he had knowingly and willingly used anabolic steroids.

He arrived at 1235 Bay Street the morning of his appearance dressed in a suit, tie, crisp shirt, and polished shoes. After getting out of his vehicle, he was surrounded by his four sisters; mother, Gloria; and a security team. They made their way through the throngs of media and curious onlookers into the building and up to the second-floor hearing room.

Under Armstrong's steady guidance, Johnson began answering routine questions about his background, his immigration to Canada, and his early days in track and field with brother Eddie under the coaching of Charlie Francis.

When Armstrong veered into how Francis had introduced him to steroids, Johnson began to equivocate. Everyone in the hearing room was wondering the same thing: was he going to stick to the story that he'd been fooled?

Johnson told the hearing that he didn't fully understand the purpose of his blue (Dianabol) and pink (Winstrol) pills during the first two years he was given them by Francis. The commissioner didn't believe him.

"Dubin stepped in and said, 'You're telling me you don't know what you were taking?' And I said, 'No, I didn't know what I was taking,'" Johnson recalled. He still insists he was not entirely sure initially what the pills were for, although Optimist members scoff at that notion.

Dubin confronted Johnson. He said the sprinter's answers didn't ring true—a string of witnesses had given convincing testimony to the contrary. Johnson became emotional, his eyes welling. His "not knowingly" defense was being undone on national television. He asked for a short break to collect himself.

In a private backroom, Johnson sat with Gloria, holding both her hands in his. He turned to her, knowing she loved him unconditionally. He asked a question to which he already knew the answer: What should I do?

"I start crying. My mum hugged me and said: 'Don't worry son, just tell them the truth,'" Johnson recalled. "I didn't want to tell them the truth. Even with all the testimony that was in front of me, I didn't want to tell the truth. I wanted to protect Charlie as much as I could because Charlie did nothing wrong, considering what other people were doing." Francis, of course, had already testified to what everyone, including Johnson, was doing.

The brief recess ended. Ben Johnson was back on the stand,

braced for impact. Bob Armstrong calmly guided Johnson through his admission.

"Did you become . . . aware . . . that some of these drugs that you had been taking were in fact something called steroids?" asked Armstrong.

"Yes."

"And you became aware at that time that Dianabol, the blue pills, were steroids?"

"Yes."

"And you, of course, became aware that steroids were drugs that were banned and that if you took a test and it was found that you had them in your system, you'd be disqualified?"

"Yes."

In the heartbeat of silence after that last answer, a short, muffled cheer from the overflow media room was heard by some in the main hearing gallery. Not a proud moment for the profession, but that reaction reflected the country's intense need to hear the Olympian speak the truth under oath.

Johnson's staggering about-face was international news. He also said he wouldn't have taken steroids if he'd known about their potential side effects. He'd had a mild, temporary one, called gynecomastia (swelling of breast tissue in males due to hormone imbalance). Health risks were a main theme during the inquiry because athletes were using drugs for which they had no medical need and were guessing at the "safe" dosage. Johnson asserted neither Jamie Astaphan nor Charlie Francis had properly explained steroids' health implications to him as the pair had previously testified, a claim both refuted on the stand.

Under the skeptical eyes of Dubin and Armstrong, Johnson stuck to his contention that he wasn't aware until 1983 that the "blue and pink" pills he began taking in 1981 were steroids, although he conceded he understood they were likely banned substances because Francis warned him not to let anyone see him taking them.

What changed in 1983? That was the year of the steroid scandal that engulfed the Pan American Games in Caracas, Venezuela. More than a few athletes fled Caracas before the games began when word leaked out that anti-doping scientists had improved steroid detection. Others failed drug tests, including two Canadian weight-lifters.

While on the stand, Johnson was asked about the still-unnamed mystery man in doping control, but the sabotage theory and the spiked beer story gained no traction in this setting.

* * *

Charles Dubin and Bob Armstrong had made periodic statements informing the public that the inquiry would probe the larger story behind banned substances and practices in sport and that it was not a Ben Johnson inquiry. But for most people, it was always and only about the sprinter.

Johnson's confession did not satisfy Dubin, a keen observer who missed nothing in his hearing room. He had previously challenged witnesses about testimony, and Johnson would not avoid accountability. The commissioner chided him for lying about doping after his Olympic expulsion and, by doing so, triggering a $4 million inquiry that required a legion of staff, investigators, witnesses, and their counsel.

Dubin: On Sept. 30, a rather carefully orchestrated interview was arranged with Mr. [George] Gross of the *Toronto Sun* at your friend's farm?

Johnson: Yes

Dubin: And you knew, by this time, that stories had been spread about sabotage, even someone rubbing stanozolol (in cream form) into your leg?

Johnson: Yes

Dubin: You knew that what was being published in the paper

would be published to all of Canada. You know how important that was.

Johnson: I was wrong to say that, yes.

Dubin: And in that statement, you denied ever having taken any banned substances, and you said you didn't knowingly take any illegal substances and wanted a full independent inquiry into how all this happened.

Johnson: Yes.

Dubin: But didn't you realize that by making that public statement, you . . . were concealing the fact there had been steroid use? Did you not realize how important that was? What a disservice it was to sign a statement like that and make the interview with Mr. Gross?

Johnson: I did it wrong. But, like I said, I was confused at the time.

Dubin: But you didn't consider what an impact it would have to ask for a full investigation . . . knowing all along you had been on the steroid program for some years?

Johnson: Yes

Dubin: Mr. (Ed) Futerman has said you got a lot of letters of support from young people.

Johnson: Thousands of letters, yes.

Dubin: Who all believed you were innocent, right?

Johnson: Yes.

Dubin: Now you'll be trying to give a message—and an example of how to be on your own—without cheating.

Johnson: Yes.

Dubin: All right. Thank you very much for your evidence, Mr. Johnson.

With his head hanging and tears brimming, the man who reigned as an Olympic sprint champion for less than three full days apologized for cheating and lying, with special reference to children who'd supported him. "I was ashamed for my family, friends, and the kids who looked up to me [and] the Canadian athletes who want to be in my position. I know I did it wrong. I was confused at the time," he said.

Johnson also pleaded for the chance to compete again "for my country, for Canada." He predicted he could run drug-free and beat anybody in the world and that he'd help to rid track and field of drugs, especially among youth.

There was a degree of public sympathy for Johnson. It was difficult to watch him admit a humiliating truth, especially after learning how pervasive steroid use was in Canada and other nations. But Optimist clubmates were more aligned with Dubin's view that his doping denials were costly and damaging. "It could have all been avoided if he had told the truth from the beginning, that's the sad part," Angella Issajenko told *Star's* Gail Swainson after his admissions. "The question is, why was the charade carried on for so many months? If the guy had admitted it from the beginning, we could have avoided all the staging and the dramatics."

Former teammate Tony Sharpe agreed. Blaming Francis instead of immediately taking personal responsibility showed Johnson's lack of "integrity" in the matter. "I still can't get over the fact that Ben wouldn't take ownership of his positive drug test and [instead] took it to a level where you absolutely cripple all of your teammates, your coach, and everybody else, and it's not your fault," said Sharpe, twice named Athletics Canada's Development Coach of the Year for his work at The Speed Academy. "That, to me, is what I remember of Ben, not owning up and doing the right thing. And it's not even doing the right thing; it's integrity. It's hard for me to understand that as a twenty-six-year-old man, you're going to tell the world that you're such a dumb ass, you're taking needles and paying $10 grand a month, and you had no frigging idea it was steroids—and that it was Charlie's fault? Come on, man."

Francis wrote in his memoir that he was disappointed that Johnson apologized for doping. At the same time, he recognized the no-win situation his Optimist athletes faced on the witness stand, Johnson most of all. "[T]he sport's pervasive hypocrisy put them between a rock and the hardest of places. The worst dilemma belonged to Ben. He had two choices, neither of them palatable. He could deny his drug use and attempt to limit the sanctions against him, a tactic that would alienate the Canadian public. Or he could admit to using steroids at the cost of severe penalties from the IAAF."

Johnson's belated admission also drew praise, including some from Carl Lewis, "I really admire the fact that he finally came out and told the truth," Lewis told *Toronto Star* reporter Randy Starkman. "There are a lot of people who wouldn't have done that."

Decades later, Johnson regrets how the inquiry unfolded. If he had a do-over, he would not have given the *Toronto Sun* interview. He said the "not knowingly" excuse was pushed on him by Futerman and former manager Kameel Azan—"I don't talk like that," he said of the infamous wording—as was the call for an inquiry. Once the commission was formed, he felt he couldn't back out because his mother believed it would prove his innocence. "My mother was very trusting, very loving, and they took advantage of her kindness," he said, referring to Azan and Jamaican consul Kay Baxter wooing Johnson through her. "She was a Christian woman who believed what goes around, comes around, perhaps not in this lifetime, but in the next life. She always believed that."

Does he also regret that so many others were involved in the inquiry that he requested and that many were punished for telling the truth?

He thinks about that for a while. Johnson does have blind spots about the Seoul fallout, including the Dubin Inquiry. He understands friends were hurt in the process—they faced public scorn, their careers were derailed, and their government funding was pulled—but his remorse is muted. Or perhaps, with so much emotional scar tissue built up over time, he can't fully express that specific regret.

Johnson's answer, in the end, is that the witness list should have been only him, Francis, Issajenko, and Jamie Astaphan. No other Optimist should have been subpoenaed.

Armstrong disagrees. He doesn't believe the story could be fully told by only a few players. "My approach, not only to the Dubin Inquiry but to other things I've done as a lawyer, was to leave no stone unturned," Armstrong said.

"I mean, jeez, if we just called Charlie Francis and Angella Issajenko and just left it at that, then all these other athletes would have been saying, 'Well, Charlie and his two or three or four select group of athletes all cheated, but that's not the rest of us.'"

* * *

While the Dubin Inquiry was ongoing, International Amateur Athletic Federation boss Primo Nebiolo took troubling action. He rammed through a new retroactive doping rule that affected only two athletes on the planet: Ben Johnson and Angella Issajenko. Nebiolo ignored Mr. Justice Charles Dubin's general entreaties to respect athlete evidence given under oath, meaning, do not punish them for telling the truth. He did it anyway.

The pompous Italian, once so enamored of Johnson that he'd spirited him from Rome's doping control room to parade before his rich horsey friends, weaponized Dubin Inquiry testimony during the IAAF's general meeting in Barcelona in September of 1989. The new rule would strip from athletes who admitted to doping under oath both world titles and world records, going back six years. There was a weak pushback from federation delegates at the meeting.

Perhaps Nebiolo had heard enough truth out of Toronto. Maybe he was nervous about his doping control chicanery in Rome. Or he obliged outside influences by scrubbing Johnson's victories from history. We'll never know. Nebiolo died of a heart attack in 1999.

Regardless, the IAAF expunged Johnson's 1987 world title and world-record 9.83 run. Carl Lewis assumed the 100-meter crown, with the rest of the field moving up accordingly, just as happened in Seoul. Johnson also lost his indoor world titles and world records. (He kept his two Olympic bronze medals from the 1984 games in LA, governed by the IOC, not the IAAF.)

Issajenko was stripped of her 50-meter indoor world record set in 1987.

The chilling effect of retroactively rewriting the books was unmistakable. It insured doping silence from other athletes and coaches and became the first clue that Canadians would be waging the anti-doping fight alone for some time.

Charles Dubin released his 637-page report in June 1990. It's a fascinating exploration of a complex subject, not least for the interpretations and context he provides from hundreds of hours of testimony. It contains a long list of recommendations for the Canadian government, most of them housekeeping matters about anti-doping improvements. When it came to sports executives and administrators, particularly those linked to the CTFA, Dubin refrained from recommending firings, demotions, or sanctions, despite his opinion that there was shared blame between athletes and their federations.

Dubin recommended that Johnson's suspension from federal funding be maintained but that he had a right to appeal to an independent arbitrator after serving his two-year IAAF competition ban, which expired in September 1990.

The judge followed Sport Canada policy in recommending that a group of track-and-field witnesses, who had testified to past steroid use, lose their federal funding for being in breach of doping rules. These athletes, said Dubin, should be allowed to appeal the loss of funding.

Angella Issajenko had retired. Dubin praised her inquiry cooperation and recommended she be given consideration to return to the sport should she want to coach.

Francis received the same loss-of-funding recommendation, again with the right to appeal "at the end of any suspension period imposed by the sports federations."

Two of the main inquiry characters held separate press conferences in Toronto after the report's release. Charlie Francis called it quits. He said Canadian athletes working with him would be poisoned by the association. Later on the same day, Johnson asked for a chance to compete for Canada again and apologized to the nation for doping. He briefly lost his cool when reporters pestered him about *why* he should be forgiven. "What do you want me to say? Bow down and kiss their feet, and say, 'Yes, I'm sorry?'"

In January 1991, eight months after Charles Dubin released his report, Canadian sports minister Marcel Danis delivered a list of fourteen names to Athletics Canada (renamed from the old CTFA) for punishment. Charlie Francis took the biggest hit. Athletics Canada banned him from coaching for life but suggested he could apply for reinstatement after seven years.

Athletes on the minister's list had their monthly "carding" stipends suspended for one to two years before they could apply for reinstatement. The sanctioned included Desai Williams, Tony Sharpe, Molly Killingbeck, Mark McKoy, Rob Gray, and Peter Dajia. Many would retire from competition shortly after.

Dubin's chief counsel was enraged at Francis's lifetime coaching ban. Bob Armstrong called it "a professional death penalty" and took a shot at Athletics Canada officials who'd been exposed during the inquiry for ineffectively handling an array of doping matters. "Charlie Francis is being dealt with very harshly by an organization that doesn't have a particularly admirable record in the field of anti-doping," Armstrong said.

It should also be noted that while athletes from other sports, including bobsled, football, and weightlifting, testified before Dubin about their own doping or failed drug tests, none were sanctioned by their respective bodies. That may have been because those witnesses had retired or hadn't violated their specific governing body rules regarding doping. But alert observers raised another possible reason; the majority of punished sprinters were Black and the others were white.

"There are a lot of people I saw at Astaphan's office who went on living life as though they'd never visited his office. We saw some of them at the Dubin Inquiry," Sharpe recalled. "Nothing became of it, and that's where I think the racist element came into play. We got buried with it. All the young Black kids got buried, and all the white kids I saw in Astaphan's office [walked away]. It was like: you're banned, you can't coach, you can't do this. Most of us were young Black kids from the Scarborough Optimists with no real legal representation. We were just doing as we were told with our little subpoenas."

Jean Augustine, the former Member of Parliament, said she can understand why Johnson balked at coming clean in a hearing room with a clear racial divide: white judge, white lawyers, and white media versus a small group of young, scared Black athletes under subpoena. She said the situation was compounded by Johnson's inability to advocate for himself immediately after Seoul and on the witness stand. "This happens to so many of us: Black people in a room where we are powerless, surrounded by the powerful white world. One has to be really affirmed . . . to get that confidence to say you are an equal, you are not less than. So, when you are in the courtroom and you look at all these powerful people, you are traumatized when you don't have the ability to explain yourself."

Johnson, decades after inviting the inquiry to exonerate him, now regards it as a deliberate bulldozing of his career to score international brownie points for Canada as doping's white knight. The whole point of the inquiry, he laments, "was to clear Canada's name and to punish me."

* * *

The fate of the urine sample that Ben Johnson provided to Sue Snider at Charlie Francis's request after his return from Seoul is a strange footnote to the Dubin Inquiry.

In early 1989, Snider alerted inquiry investigators to the existence of the Toronto specimen, which she kept in a locked upright freezer in her condo. They arranged to have it analyzed at the IOC-accredited lab in Calgary, the site of the 1988 Winter Games. Yet when Snider and an RCMP officer arrived with the specimen—labeled with a code number, not Johnson's name, as per standard procedure—a lab official refused to accept it. Snider said it was obvious to her that the official suspected it was Johnson's. The Mountie argued, but to no avail. They returned home, and Snider placed Johnson's sample back in her condo freezer.

Soon after, a thief broke into Snider's home, pried the lock off the freezer, and grabbed some test kits lying on top. It's a reasonable assumption that the goal was to obtain Johnson's sample: none of the others were of particular interest. Nothing else in the condo was taken, not jewelry, not electronics, and no drawers had been rifled.

Fortunately, Snider had tucked Johnson's test specimen under several layers of frozen packaged goods. Pulling everything out of the freezer, she found that his urine sample was still there. The thief had grabbed the wrong kits.

Snider contacted Toronto police and the RCMP to report the break-in. Officers, including RCMP detective Ken St. Germain, then working as a Dubin Inquiry investigator, arrived at her home to take a report. The break-in was never solved.

Later, St. Germain took Johnson's A sample from the specimen to American forensic toxicologist Dr. David Black for analysis in

Nashville. Johnson remembers that the test was negative. Black could not recall the result nor had access to the long-ago file. Regardless, Dubin Inquiry staff didn't use the information. The results were likely deemed irrelevant as this urine sample was provided five days after the medal final and would have little to no bearing on Johnson's post-race results from Seoul. Yet someone thought the vial was important enough to steal.

Francis's hope to clear his sprinter ended when Snider invited Johnson to her condo, with St. Germain there as a witness, to pour his B sample down a sink drain. Johnson then placed the vial on the floor and crushed it with his foot.

CHAPTER FOURTEEN
SECOND CHANCE, SECOND FAIL

If he had the chance to do it over again, Ben Johnson would never have returned to the track in 1991. He would have retired from sprinting and likely become a coach or personal trainer in any sport other than his because the happy ending he envisioned eluded him.

At first, however, Johnson was delighted at his reprieve. A new federal sports minister, Marcel Danis, cleared the way for his return in August 1990 by overturning the lifetime Canadian competition ban his predecessor, Jean Charest, had imposed.

Athletics Canada (formerly the CTFA) next stated the federation would welcome Johnson back after he'd served the short balance of the IAAF's two-year suspension. Canadian Olympic Association president Carol Anne Letheren announced on September 27, 1990, two years to the day, that she retrieved Johnson's gold medal from him in Seoul, that the COA executive had reinstated his eligibility to represent Canada at the Olympic Games should he make the national team again. "We believe he's suffered enough," Letheren said.

Johnson was twenty-eight years old, turning twenty-nine in that December. That's getting on in age for a sprinter, but it was possible to believe he'd again be competitive, at least in Canada. "I'm just happy the government gave me the okay to run for this country again," Johnson told reporters crowding his Scarborough driveway. "I want to thank the Canadian public who supported me. This is one of the happiest days of my life, so far."

He also addressed his prospects at the 1992 Barcelona Summer Games with typical bravado: he'd win gold in Spain, of course. And what about doping? Could he run world-class times unaided? "I have to prove to myself all over again that I can do it without drugs," he said.

He had no choice. Johnson knew he would be subjected to frequent drug testing, and now, with random out-of-competition testing finally in place in Canada, doping control officers had the right to demand a sample from Canadian athletes with no notice.

Johnson had kept in shape. He'd returned to the national training center in 1989 to hit the weight room and the track. He ramped up the pace in 1990. He'd see familiar faces there, including former coach Charlie Francis, Desai Williams, and Mark McKoy, but his old, comfortable pre-Seoul existence was gone.

His father, Ben Sr., died unexpectedly of a stroke in 1990, leaving a deep emotional wound. And for the first time in his sprinting career, Johnson would compete as a one-man club, handled by outsiders.

The new Ben Johnson team was anchored by lawyer Ed Futerman and Kameel Azan, the sprinter's manager. Largely because Azan had no connections, agent Larry Heidebrecht was in the mix for a while to set up a series of rich events to ease Johnson's reentry to the circuit.

As for the key element, the coach, it was no longer Francis, juggling a Coke in one hand and a stopwatch in the other. Francis was eligible to return to the Canadian fold after serving seven years of his lifetime ban, but as Johnson describes it, "Charlie told them to go fuck themselves. He wouldn't do it."

Instead, Johnson hired American university coach Loren Seagrave. It was a relatively short partnership, but one that got Johnson back to racing for the 1991 indoor season. And instead of making a splashy

Rocky-like comeback at a venue like New York's Madison Square Garden, Johnson chose Hamilton, a solid, blue-collar steel town about an hour's drive west of Toronto.

Would anyone bother watching? Had the Dubin Inquiry revelations killed interest in Johnson's drug-free career?

In fact, Johnson commanded world attention at the Hamilton Indoor Games. About five hundred reporters, photographers, and TV crews from fourteen countries attended. A Canadian indoor meet attendance record was set at seventeen thousand, about double the usual ticket sales. Thousands of $10 Johnson posters, with "Back on Track" printed across them, were sold out before the race. Canadian national broadcaster CTV televised the race to a reported four million viewers, along with panel discussions and an interview with Francis.

Johnson was slimmer, not as bulky as before, but still sharply cut. The race was close, a thriller for the big crowd. American Daron Council, a last-minute replacement for Olympian Dennis Mitchell, won in 5.75 seconds. Johnson was second in 5.77, a reasonable effort considering it was his first race since Seoul.

Paul Gains, the meet director, remembered an awkward moment during a post-meet athletes' reception at a local hotel. He held out his hand as Johnson approached. "Ben wouldn't shake my hand at first," Gains said. "He was angry that the field was so strong and that he'd come in second."

Gains reminded Johnson that it was his job as meet director to assemble the strongest field possible and that Johnson's strong run against a world-ranked indoor sprinter after a two-year layoff was remarkable. The two then shook.

Johnson was paid $10,000 for his Hamilton appearance. Later in the month, he received a $30,000 appearance fee for the Sunkist indoor meet in Los Angeles.

Seagrave quit at the end of January to return stateside. The American coach said the split was amicable and he would continue to advise

Johnson if needed. Johnson carried on, aided by friends, including Desai Williams, who had tried to turn him in for doping. "After a while, it didn't bother me," Johnson said of Williams's snitching. In fact, he paid Williams about $25,000 to coach him during the 1991 indoor season and was pleased with the partnership. That spring, Johnson hired former Arizona State University coach Clyde Duncan for the outdoor season and also began working with Percy Duncan.

Johnson resumed speaking with Francis, by phone and at the York track after the Dubin Inquiry wrapped. He held no animosity. The two kept their repaired friendship quiet because of the sanctions imposed on the former Optimist group. Neither wanted more scandal to scuttle the sprinter's return nor Francis's foray into coaching non-Canadian athletes. They talked about training and competing, but they also chatted about life, just like the old days.

Johnson's competition schedule over the next two years had been set by Heidebrecht. Including appearance fees and bonus agreements, Johnson would earn about $1.6 million (US) through the 1992 Summer Games in Barcelona—enough money for the sprinter to retire if he invested properly, said Heidebrecht. "I said, 'Perfect, Larry, this will be my plan. I don't need to come back and run fast times anymore. I don't care. People just want to see me run, so this is what it is,'" said Johnson.

By the time he'd sorted out payments for all his handlers, Johnson figured he'd end up with about half of Heidebrecht's tally. "So $1.6 million becomes about $800,000. This is how my life goes, but I was okay with it." He could afford to pay his entourage to look after his affairs while he trained, traveled, and competed. He still owned real estate and estimated he had more than $2 million in his trust fund (the ARF account overseen by Athletics Canada) and felt financially comfortable.

There was also potential to make money from offtrack activities, too, such as corporate appearances, endorsements, and even media interviews. A British reporter has a fax in which Futerman stated the fee to interview Johnson in 1990 while he was still suspended was $10,000 (US). The reporter chose not to pay.

With revenue flowing in again, Johnson enjoyed his money. And why not? He earned it. Post-Seoul, he was still spending on five-star vacations, brand-name clothing, and pricey jewelry for girlfriends. He also supported his mother, Gloria, and was generous with his family.

Johnson was better at earning money than at keeping track of it. Like many athletes before and after him, he didn't monitor how and why money was leaving accounts, and he'd authorized others to access his accounts to pay bills and invoices. In addition, he didn't deposit all the cash accrued from appearances into his ARF account, leaving him vulnerable to an income tax hit.

Very soon, to his horror, the sprinter would realize that he was going broke. In a few years, a court would be told Johnson was "impecunious."

* * *

On the track throughout 1991, Ben Johnson was more of a crowd-pleaser than a record-smashing star. His times were ho-hum, never breaking the ten-second mark, but he was still in demand.

Johnson lived out of hotels for nearly six months, on and off, during this tour. He was left homesick and physically exhausted by the grind. He traveled often with Percy Duncan, a respected sprint coach who'd previously competed for Guyana. Duncan had known Francis and Johnson for years. He first coached Francis during his Canadian national team career and impressed Francis so much that he often asked Duncan for advice when Johnson was in his prime. Then, in his mid-seventies, Duncan became the new coach that Johnson trusted.

Still, traveling wasn't like the old days, the fun days, when Johnson would hang out in teammates' hotel rooms and shoot the breeze, crack jokes, drink beer, play cards, smoke the odd cigarette, or spend a day shopping. All that pre-Seoul camaraderie was gone. And he was drug tested, frequently. He passed them all.

Montreal's Bruny Surin was then Canada's fastest man. He had been since 1989. That didn't sit well with Johnson, and Surin was never free to enjoy his accomplishment without constantly being compared to or asked about Johnson. Surin, who sometimes seemed exasperated by the questions, would answer with restraint.

The highlight of Johnson's summer was a rematch with Carl Lewis, their first head-to-head race since Seoul. A reported prize of about $500,000 was at stake in Lille, France, but American Dennis Mitchell stole the show. On a cold, rainy day, Mitchell was first in 10.09 seconds. Lewis was second in 10.20, and Johnson showed up in seventh at 10.46. He walked away with $106,000 (US).

That same year, Johnson was paid $25,000 (US) to compete in Osaka, Japan. Organizers wired the fee to Canada, which Johnson accepted. He then drove to his bank and deposited two hundred and thirty crisp $100 bills in his account. The branch manager made a note of the unusual transaction in one of the athlete's bank files.

Johnson failed to qualify in the 100 meters for the 1991 world championships in Tokyo but was added to the Canadian relay team as the lead runner. The Tokyo meet did not hold the megawatt allure of Rome four years before, although Carl Lewis won the 100 meters (in 9.86 seconds). Johnson returned home without any hardware.

It seemed his career was waning. He was getting older, getting injured. Younger guys were beating him. But Johnson was on a mission to restore his name and redeem his career. He wanted another Olympic shot. He was not quitting.

A year later, Johnson finished second to Surin at the Canadian Olympic trials, clocking a decent time of 10.16 seconds, which qualified him for the 100 meters at the Barcelona Games, a rather extraordinary accomplishment after all he'd been through. He would be competing in his third Olympics at the age of thirty.

His improved performances raised suspicion.

* * *

The smooth set of arrangements in Seoul that allowed Ben Johnson to prepare physically, mentally, and mindfully for the 100 meters in 1988 did not transpire in Barcelona. Apart from the fact that Carl Lewis had failed to qualify in the 100 meters for the US team, almost nothing went smoothly in Barcelona.

Right away, Johnson clashed with his manager, Kameel Azan, whom he asked to book a high-end hotel close to the Olympic venues. None were available, so Azan rented a house. Johnson insisted on a hotel, but the only one with vacancies was about forty-five kilometers from the Olympic hub. Johnson lost the $6,000 (US) rental deposit on the house and paid hotel accommodations for himself, his mother, Azan, and Percy Duncan. In addition, taxi fare into the Olympic village was about $100 (US) each way, and Johnson would make that trip daily to train, get massages, attend meetings, pick up accreditations and team swag, and so on.

Then, Canada's anti-doping police, as distinct from the Olympics' anti-doping police, leapt into action. The afternoon before the men's 100-meter heats, Johnson sat down to order lunch with his mother at the hotel. The concierge hurried over to tell Johnson there was a phone call for him at the front desk. Johnson was told by a Canadian team official that he'd been among a small group of Canadian track-and-field athletes selected to provide a random urine test, immediately.

"I told them I was about to eat lunch, and they said, 'A car is on its way to come and pick you up in about half an hour,'" Johnson recalled. He was stunned, but knew he had to go, leaving his lunch order behind.

He waited outside the hotel with Duncan, a man then pushing eighty, under a blazing sun. The van arrived at around 3 p.m. "It's hot, like 110 degrees outside, and it's about 250 degrees in the van," Johnson said of the ride into Barcelona. He was also hungry.

"[Olympic officials] had blocked off the entire perimeter, and I had to walk in, me and Percy, like fifteen city blocks. People start recognizing me, and stop me for pictures and autographs. I get there, leave my bag with security, and keep walking up to the Canadian lab, where Andrew Pipe and his colleagues were."

Dr. Andrew Pipe, a respected anti-doping and fair-play advocate, was Canada's chief medical officer in Barcelona. He was a longtime volunteer with sports medicine organizations in Canada and, in 1992, was the chair of the Canadian Centre for Drug-Free Sport (later renamed the Canadian Centre for Ethics in Sport, CCES).

Johnson was not upset at the test itself, but at its timing. He was in the village every day, so why could he not have been randomly tested when he was already physically there?

He was also surprised to see four-time Canadian 100-meter champion Bruny Surin had been selected, as well as thrower Peter Dajia. "Everybody was pissed. I was pissed. Bruny was pissed. Peter was pissed."

Pipe said in an email that in 1992, "IOC testing was 'in-competition' only" and that in Barcelona, Canadian anti-doping officials collected urine samples from some Canadian track-and-field competitors following their arrival. Pipe added, "it had been impossible to locate some of them in the weeks prior to the Barcelona Games," meaning random testing for those hard-to-find athletes had to be done in Spain.

As Johnson recalls the day, Surin and Dajia delivered their samples relatively quickly and left. Johnson, feeling dehydrated, was drinking water but couldn't pass urine until around 7:30 p.m. A collection officer used a dip stick in the urine to measure its specific gravity and said it registered as too diluted. He'd have to pee again.

"They said, 'Why are you drinking so much water?' and I said, 'I have to run tomorrow, and I need hydration. I need to hydrate my body, or it gets tired.'"

At this point in the evening, Johnson was about twelve hours away from warming up for his first round of heats. Duncan was still with him. Johnson recalled that he gave a second specimen around 10 p.m., but that, too, was rejected as diluted. The officials, including Pipe, said they'd have to go back to his hotel. "I said, 'Come back to my hotel? For what?' and they said, 'So we can get another sample because this urine is too diluted.'"

They all drove to the hotel. Johnson said when he unlocked his door, Pipe and a colleague pushed their way in and rifled through the room: they looked under the bed, the pillow, behind the toilet bowl, under the sink, and in dresser drawers. He claims they were looking for banned drugs.

He delivered a third sample at around 1 a.m., which was again too watery. A fourth around 2:30 a.m. seemed to be satisfactory, and Pipe and his colleague left. Johnson said he had no option but to comply with the marathon session.

Pipe explained in his email that "as is normal practice, when an athlete is unable to provide a sample of sufficient quality, a sample is too dilute, or a sample cannot be provided" due to dehydration, the process is continued under supervision of a doping control officer "at the athlete's place of residence." The physician added: "Given the difficulties in locating Mr. Johnson in the period before the games, it was appropriate to complete the sample-taking process once it had commenced," and as soon as "an appropriate sample was obtained, the process was concluded."

By the time Johnson "calmed down" and was relaxed enough to sleep, it was 3:30 a.m. on the day he was to race. He awoke at 6 a.m. to eat breakfast, pack his gear, say goodbye to his mother, jump in a taxi, and head to the warm-up track. He tried to sleep in the cab.

When he got to the track, he tried to sleep again under the Team Canada tent, cutting his usual two-hour warm-up in half to preserve energy. But he knew he was in trouble. "I tried to recharge the batteries, but the body was already beaten up. Emotionally, I was beat up," he said.

He was tired but advanced through the heats to the semifinals, where he delivered a disastrous effort. His toes caught the track surface coming out of the blocks, and he finished dead last. "I felt my body start to lose a lot of energy [over the morning], and . . . I came out of the blocks and stumbled," Johnson said. "Weak legs, weak body, I stumbled and could never recover from that, and it cost me going forward."

Shattered, he watched the final from the stands as thirty-two-year-old Brit Linford Christie, the oldest man ever to win the Olympic 100 meters at that time, took the gold. Johnson thought that medal could have been his. "I was in good shape to win the Olympic Games. And when Linford Christie won it in 9.96 seconds, I cried. I knew I could have won it."

Four days later, Johnson had recovered physically and mentally for the 4 × 100-meter relay heats. He wanted a medal. Johnson ran a fast leadoff leg of just under ten seconds flat around the first curve; he believed that translated into a 9.90 on a 100-meter straightaway. But a handoff blunder between other runners disqualified the team.

Barcelona was a bust. No medals and more public contempt, the gist of it being that he was no good without steroids. As for the marathon urine sample experience, Johnson described it as an emotional rubber-hosing that crippled his 100-meter chances. He took time to reflect on his Olympic experience after the botched relay. "I was thinking it was time for me to get out [of track] because they don't like me, they don't want me being around anymore, and they are trying to discredit my name," he said, referring to a wide array of Canadian and international track officials. "They were just trying to break me emotionally and mentally, so I'd commit suicide or something like that."

If that sounds paranoid, it didn't feel so to Johnson. He believed then, as he does now, that no one expected him to qualify for the Barcelona Games, and when he did, he wasn't considered a worthy Olympian but a constant reminder of Canada's doping embarrassment.

* * *

For the balance of that Olympic year, Johnson cut back on competition and traveling. He'd thought hard about his future and how much was left in him to compete at track's highest levels. Maybe one more year? Maybe 1993 could be a rewarding finale?

The world indoor championships were in Toronto that spring, a special incentive. And with his spectacular, one-of-a-kind start back in working order, 50-meter and 60-meter races might be worth their weight in gold over the indoor season. He'd have Percy Duncan again in his corner, which was reassuring. Johnson could see his way to leaving the sport on a high note, hopefully with a gold medal in hand.

The thirty-one-year-old committed to the 1993 season, and it started well, too well, for some watchers. He had a superfast outing in Grenoble, France, on January 7, winning the 50 meters in 5.65 seconds, just 0.04 shy of the world record.

Was he back doping? Johnson said no. He swore on his mother's grave that he was not using any banned substances. He was randomly drug tested so often that it wasn't worth risking a repeat of Seoul. Besides, his racing results, though improving along the way, didn't reflect artificial boosting. "If I was taking drugs back then, I would have been running [world record] times."

After returning from Grenoble and before heading back to Europe, Johnson was tested three times over eight days in Canada. He'd come to expect this frequency; it was his price for being back in the game.

Johnson was tested at the Hamilton Spectator Indoor Games on January 15 and again two days later at a meet in Montreal, the city with Canada's lone IOC-accredited anti-doping lab. In Toronto on January 22, Johnson was asked to give a random urine sample and complied.

He was also part of a January news conference to promote the world indoor championships in Toronto's SkyDome, to be held in March. "I'm ready to do something this year," he told reporters. "I'm going to shock the world again one more time."

There was shock, all right. It surfaced on February 10 during a meet in Ghent, Belgium. Johnson recalls warming up when an organizer told him there was a phone call from Canada waiting for him in the meet office. Johnson feared it was a family matter but soon realized it was trouble: an Athletics Canada official told him he'd tested positive after the Montreal meet.

Johnson was stunned. No way, he thought. He'd had three tests conducted over eight days. He was negative in Hamilton and negative in Toronto. How was it possible to flunk a test in the middle of those two negative results? And why was he learning of this so late? It was nearly three weeks after he'd run in Montreal. It only took two days to boot him from Seoul.

"I said, 'You gotta be kidding me. It's impossible'; then I said, 'I guess I can't run in this meet,'" he recalled. But it was a provisional result: the A screening showed a high testosterone reading, Johnson was told, and the B sample had yet to be opened, and he was allowed to compete in the interim.

"I decided to run," he said of the 60-meter race, which he won in 6.60 seconds. "I just didn't care, I eased off [near the tape]. And then, I was back in turmoil."

He packed and caught the first flight home. He was expected at the indoor nationals in Winnipeg, Manitoba, later that month as a pre-world championship meet. He flew to Winnipeg, then out the next morning without competing. He said it made no sense to be there with another drug positive hanging over him, news he kept to himself.

When the Canadian team was selected for the indoor worlds soon after the Winnipeg meet, Johnson was not on the roster. He was nowhere to be found. Manager Kameel Azan didn't know what to tell reporters because he didn't know what was going on either.

* * *

The *Toronto Star*'s Randy Starkman broke the story on March 3, 1993, that Ben Johnson had failed his second drug test. It wasn't stanozolol this time. A high testosterone-to-epitestosterone ratio was detected in his urine, a measure that according to IAAF anti-doping rules likely meant he'd been using banned synthetic testosterone.

A testosterone/epitestosterone (T/E) ratio lower than 6:1 was considered a negative. If the T/E ratio was between 6:1 and 10:1, the IAAF would consider reviewing extenuating circumstances put forward by the athlete that may have contributed to the abnormal readings. A reading of 10.1:1 or higher was an automatic fail. Johnson's T/E ratio in his B sample was measured as 10.3:1, positive for doping again.

The sprinter didn't attend the opening of his B sample at the lab in Montreal two weeks before the news broke. He'd retained Dr. David Black, the American forensic toxicologist from Nashville, as his expert witness, and Toronto lawyer Terry O'Sullivan to represent him. On arrival, both men were disturbed to learn their client's identity was widely known among lab workers who referred to Johnson by name. His numerically coded sample was supposed to remain anonymous during testing. The breach of confidentiality was the first in a sequence of troubling due-process events for the Johnson team.

Canadian journalist and author Gare Joyce did a deep dive into this story's background for a *Saturday Night* story headlined "Was

Ben Cheated?" He reported on several critical moments over two days of testing, February 15 and 16, in Montreal. Joyce wrote:

> For twelve hours spread across two days, Dr. Christiane Ayotte tested the corresponding "B" sample: three separate tests produced varying readings, all showing high levels of testosterone, but fractionally lower than the "A" sample. O'Sullivan and Black required the officials in the lab to preserve the remainder of the "B" sample, in case they [were] asked to retest it. After granting the request, the officials in turn asked O'Sullivan and Black to sign a prepared statement that they had witnessed the lab work.
>
> O'Sullivan stroked out a clause that stated: "The witness is in agreement with the confirmation methods used to analyze this urine sample." This wasn't a bit of lawyerly nuisance-making. Black strongly disagreed with the hard-and-fast interpretation of the test results; an athlete was going to be banned from the sport on the basis of what many biochemists consider an inadequate clinical analysis in the absence of supplementary investigation.

During the testing of the "B" sample, Black noted the "turbidity of the sample," which "raised the question of the possibility of bacterial microorganisms generating testosterone post urine-sample collection from Ben Johnson, which could lead to an elevated testosterone-to-epitestosterone ratio greater than 6, which was then the definition of a positive test for the use of synthetic testosterone."

O'Sullivan and Black were prepared to travel to an IAAF doping commission meeting in Paris on March 5 to make submissions on Johnson's behalf, but that plan died when Starkman's scoop was published on March 3. The IAAF refused their request to meet.

For a second time, Canadian and international sports officials weighed in quickly to denounce Johnson, some doing so before the IAAF confirmed his doping failure and lifetime suspension on March

5 and, again, before the sprinter had a chance to defend himself. Sweden's Arne Ljungqvist, then chairman of the IAAF's doping committee, told reporters that "this is a clear case of testosterone doping."

Johnson was destroyed. He was now irredeemable.

* * *

Terry O'Sullivan held a press conference alone on March 7, 1993, a Sunday, in his law office. His client could not bear to be part of it. Ben Johnson had parted ways with Ed Futerman by then. With O'Sullivan, who'd been discus thrower Rob Gray's Dubin Inquiry counsel, the sprinter's disastrous situation was at least in experienced, capable hands.

O'Sullivan came out firing at the assembled media, including me and *Toronto Star* colleague Joe Hall. What we didn't grasp was that O'Sullivan was raising questions about deficiencies in due process, a claim that should have merited further investigation. It fell on very deaf ears.

He blamed Johnson's second doping offense on faulty testing procedures, breaches of confidentiality, and loose-lipped officials who complicated the matter by declaring the case closed before it had been formally announced. In an echo of Seoul, the IAAF refused to provide O'Sullivan with the detailed lab report that he'd urgently requested on his client's behalf. "All of you know, who have followed this story during the past week, that neither procedural fairness nor confidentiality were respected in the case involving Mr. Johnson," O'Sullivan said. "These leaks came from anonymous informants said to be associated with the IAAF, the athletic bureaucracy in Canada, and even the government of Canada itself."

The IAAF and Athletics Canada each banned Johnson for life. He immediately retired, knowing the public would interpret that decision as a doping admission. He insists he never used drugs again after 1988 and simply wanted to avoid the costs of a lengthy appeal, which might have run to $200,000. "I don't have the money to go and fight this case," he told Gloria at the time. "The money I have left is for our family to have, to have a roof over our heads."

"I never wanted to leave the sport like that," said Johnson more recently. "But there was nothing I could do. [The track sanctioning bodies] have all the power, they have all the tools . . . they just did what they needed to do to get me out, ruin my reputation again, and ban me for life."

O'Sullivan said it wasn't just the cost that convinced the sprinter not to appeal. He was also thirty-one years old, he didn't want to put his family through the public wringer again, and he was devastated by the ban.

The word "appeal" is critical here. It would become one of many due-process matters that riddled Johnson's doomed attempts to clear his name in 1993. In March, neither O'Sullivan nor Johnson realized that the sprinter had been misled, in writing and apparently by accident, by Athletics Canada officials. The IAAF rule in place was that Johnson had the right to an independent hearing, where the onus was on the athletic body to prove its doping case against him. In a hearing, Johnson would have had some power and protection: he could ask for more information about his test, including the opportunity to review the detailed analytical report on his abnormal T/E readings produced by the Montreal lab, and challenge the accuracy of those findings. Essentially, he and his legal team could study the disclosed evidence against him and prepare a defense in a hearing.

He didn't get that opportunity.

Instead, Johnson was told by Athletics Canada he could appeal, a much different endeavor. In an appeal, the onus is on the athlete to prove his or her innocence, and it can be an expensive proposition requiring expert testimony fees, legal representation, affidavit

212

collection, accommodation, and travel costs. One had to have deep pockets to finance a top-of-the-line appeal, making it an almost impossible option for most athletes. (Although in 2020, the Court of Arbitration for Sport overturned US long jumper Jarrion Lawson's doping ban after his legal team successfully argued he'd consumed steroid-riddled meat and that the analysis of his urine sample, produced by the accredited Montreal lab, was flawed.)

Because Johnson chose to retire, the matter lay dormant after 1993. The incorrect information furnished by Athletics Canada went unnoticed until, by chance, there was renewed interest six years later. The mistake would then become one of several focal points in an arbitrator's legally binding decision to reinstate Johnson, which caused panic at the highest levels of the IAAF.

CHAPTER FIFTEEN

TRAINING MARADONA AND RACING HORSES

In the years after his lifetime ban was imposed, Ben Johnson's fancy cars were gone. Fair-weather friends vanished when his cash ran out. His financial distress strained family relationships. He needed work—he had a mortgage, and he was still supporting his mother. And he wanted to remain in sports. He could still make appearance money at the odd event, often in Europe or Japan, but he needed a more reliable income.

Reinventing himself as a personal trainer was an obvious path, but Johnson's doping history made him toxic to amateur athletes. No aspiring Olympian wanted to be tainted by association. Fortunately, some people aren't as judgy as others.

An Italian friend connected to the Ferrari company called Johnson in June 1997. Would he talk to Diego Maradona's agent about training the aging World Cup legend in Toronto for a return to football?

Maradona? Hell, yes. How fast can he get here? Johnson asked. Right away, was the answer.

Johnson, Maradona, and the football star's agent met at the York University track-and-field facility that had once been central to the Canadian's Olympic dreams. They discussed what Maradona needed to accomplish his return-to-play goals. One challenge obvious to Johnson was that the Argentinian was obese. "I thought, wow, he's big," Johnson said, recalling that Maradona was about forty pounds overweight.

"I told them it was not going to be easy, but we can get the job done. We had to train twice a day for the entire program, which was over nearly six weeks."

There was a reason Diego Maradona had flown thousands of miles to train with a disgraced track-and-field star in the suburbs of Toronto. He had problems of his own. FIFA, soccer's world governing body, suspended Maradona for fifteen months in 1991 after cocaine was detected in his urine (he also faced subsequent charges for cocaine possession, causing him to flee Italy for Argentina). Three years later, he was booted from the World Cup in the United States when a urine test yielded traces of stimulants. They were humiliating public episodes, much like the shaming Johnson had experienced.

The Canadian had sympathy for the midfielder, and a deal was struck: $25,000 (US) for six weeks. Maradona didn't want the media around, but it was hard to keep the superstar's presence on a university campus quiet for long. The fact that football's bad boy wanted back in the beautiful game and that the Olympics' bad boy was training him made for engaging international news.

Johnson and Maradona got along well, which made sense: they were close in age and, in their prime, were massive global celebrities. A scroll through archival 1980s newspapers shows their respective exploits were often captured together on the front pages of sports sections.

Through a Spanish interpreter, Maradona, who agreed to speak to reporters a few times, explained why he came to Toronto: "I want to be the best in the world again," Maradona said. "Ben's the fastest man in the world—a powerhouse, an animal."

The footballer stayed with his entourage—his agent and an American nutritionist—in a modest hotel in Toronto's Downsview neighborhood, not far from where Johnson grew up. He threw a party one evening with dancing, catered food, and a large guest list. Johnson described his client as a generous and thoughtful person. He once casually complimented the basketball shoes Maradona wore, and, shortly after, a new pair arrived as a gift.

"He was a guy who would do anything for you. If you need something done or if you ask for something, he will come and surprise you and say, 'Here it is,'" Johnson said. "But if he doesn't like you, he cuts you off. When you were as good as he was in sport, too many people wanted a piece of you. There are too many hands in the pot when you are that good. People just take, take, take, take. One of the reasons why we got along is because we come from the same type of family background and the same lifestyle."

Sometimes they'd goof around at the track. Maradona asked Johnson to prove he had world-class speed. The sprinter obliged: "I was still in great shape." He warmed up, then blasted from a standing start over 60 meters in impressive form. Then, he asked his client to show "some of your magic" with a soccer ball. "It was incredible what he could do. The ball stuck to his feet like glue. It was like his feet were like hands."

A name from the past, Waldemar Matuszewski, soon joined the small team. Maradona and Johnson flew to Ottawa for sessions with the sports therapist, who worked to heal the stocky footballer's battered body, especially his lower back issues. Matuszewski assessed the damage, then treated the area with the same regeneration skills he'd used on Johnson while with the old Mazda Optimist track club.

Johnson said there were no hard feelings between Matuszewski and himself after Seoul. He said they kept in contact, and decades later, he can still rattle off Matuszewski's landline phone number from memory.

After the Canadian leg of his training, Maradona invited Johnson to Argentina to continue their sessions. He flew Johnson to Buenos Aires first class and put him up in a five-star hotel. It was a return to the jet-setting lifestyle Johnson had enjoyed, and he appreciated the consideration. Maradona, suddenly not so camera-shy, invited the local media to see him work out with his Canadian conditioning coach. "When the media came to check him out, they went, 'What the hell happened to him? He looks great,'" Johnson said. "Diego explained that we trained hard. Ben is a great coach and a great guy, and the media was wrong to pick on him."

To have Maradona suit up again as a Boca Junior, his old club team, was a major event in Argentina. Johnson was among the VIPs the player invited to watch from his private box that summer. The media noted the national hero showed flashes of his younger brilliance, which fanned renewed adulation.

Maradona also asked Johnson to his family's farm for a barbeque, a sign of a deepening friendship. He drove them there in a Porsche. The Canadian loved fast cars but didn't expect he'd be gripping the armrests in fear for three hours. "The highways were huge, like seven lanes, and Diego is driving fast. Like, 260 kilometers an hour," Johnson said. "The whole trip I kept saying, 'Easy, easy, Diego, you're going too fast.' And he would say back, 'Easy, easy' and laugh. My heart is going boom, boom, boom, and every time he overtakes somebody, he steps harder on the gas, and the car keeps flying. Then he'd laugh and go, 'Easy, easy.' When we got to the farm, I just said, 'Thank you, God.'"

The drive was worth the terror. Johnson recalled the beauty of the family estate, framed by tended grounds and an azure pool. The acreage was big enough for one of the Boca Juniors' owners to land his personal helicopter there to join the fun.

As their contract neared its end, Maradona asked Johnson to remain in Buenos Aires as his full-time personal trainer. The Argentinian was in a better emotional and mental health space but wanted the Canadian near him to stay focused on healthy habits. Though the two had grown close, Johnson couldn't stay. He had an important court date back home. He was taking Athletics Canada and the IAAF to court in a bid to have his lifetime ban overturned.

"Diego didn't want me to go. I could see it in his face, he wanted me to stay. I almost missed my flight," Johnson said. "I would have kept him in line because I'm very strong mentally and he didn't have that mental toughness. . . . He would not have done anything [like using drugs] if I was there."

Not long after, Maradona faltered. The thirty-six-year-old who led Argentina to World Cup glory failed a postgame urine test in August 1997. It was just two months after he reinvented himself with Johnson. The Argentine Football Association stated that he tested positive for "prohibited substances" at the time.

Maradona retired from competition that fall, his drug habit and illnesses taking an aggregate toll over the following years. He died in 2020.

* * *

Johnson's important court date back home was a direct result of his relationship with Morris Chrobotek, the man who took up Ben Johnson's fight when no one else in Canada would touch him.

A loud-talking, quick-thinking, self-deprecating, self-promoting, name-dropping, deal-making Toronto businessman, Chrobotek, against all odds, repeatedly charmed his way into the inner sanctums of the IOC and the IAAF despite having no sports management background whatsoever. "I may be ugly, but I'm not stupid" is one of Chrobotek's favorite lines.

It was Chrobotek who led a successful arbitration challenge of Ben Johnson's 1993 failed drug test and lifetime ban to secure his domestic reinstatement in the spring of 1999, an accomplishment that never received the attention it deserved.

Chrobotek's path to Canada and the politics of international sprinting were not straight lines. He was born in 1948 to Polish-Jewish parents who immigrated to Israel when their son was an infant. The family lived in Tel Aviv for a decade before moving half a world away to Toronto. Chrobotek learned English, attended public school, and then in 1968 trained in England with Vidal Sassoon to work in the famous hairstylist's first Toronto salon. His interests were the arts, especially music, theater, and opera. Sports were not his thing.

By the mid-1990s, Chrobotek had sheathed his scissors and established a successful business in the airline and hotel industries. When a mutual friend introduced him to Johnson at a Yorkville restaurant in the summer of 1996, Chrobotek said the sprinter struck him as a lost soul in desperate need of income and support. "Honestly, I felt sorry for Ben," he said. He gave Johnson his business card, thinking they would later set up a meeting about working together. "I told him to call me in three weeks because I was busy," Chrobotek recalled. "He called me the next day."

According to Chrobotek, their partnership began with Johnson asking for money to put gas in his car and the new agent lending Gloria Johnson $1,700 to pay their mortgage. Johnson disputes this recollection. In fact, they disagreed on several points about their working relationship regarding contracts, payments, and who ripped off whom before their acrimonious split around 2001. But in the beginning, Johnson was hopeful; he'd been living with his mother, spending too much time watching TV in the basement, and he wanted help rebooting a career.

The sprinter has his own recollection of the conversation that convinced him to team up with his new agent.

"Do you believe in me?" Chrobotek asked him.

"Yes. I will walk with you through fire. This is not going to be easy, but don't try to screw me," Johnson replied.

"I won't try to screw you. We are going to do this together."

"Good. I just want to clear my name."

In August 1996, they shook hands. Johnson turned over his personal files to Chrobotek, who quickly figured out whom in the sports world to contact for information or, more accurately, who to badger and who to bribe. Incredibly, Chrobotek would talk his way into private meetings with IOC president Juan Antonio Samaranch and IAAF president Lamine Diack of Senegal to drum up support for Johnson's reinstatement.

Chrobotek was intrigued by Johnson from the start. He knew who the sprinter was but, not being a sports fan, didn't know what the acronyms IOC and IAAF meant. Yet he sensed Johnson had been wronged by a hierarchical sports system that held enormous power over athletes' lives. "And I enjoy challenges," said Chrobotek.

The unlikely partnership, before it completely curdled, returned Johnson to the international limelight and got him within spitting distance of ending his lifetime ban.

Morris Chrobotek is not and never was a lawyer, though he was often erroneously described as Ben Johnson's attorney. He was a rookie sports agent adept at reading the fine print in business contracts. He easily absorbed sports governance anti-doping rules and policies as they pertained to Johnson and developed a premise: the lifetime doping ban was a restraint of trade, and Johnson was unfairly prevented from making a living as a sprinter. Johnson filed an application through lawyer Axy Leighl in an Ontario court to lift the bans imposed by Athletics Canada and the IAAF.

In July 1997, Leighl argued before Madam Justice Moira Caswell that Johnson was not trained for any other career; he was essentially penniless and could only earn a living on the track. Johnson was 35 years old.

The lawyer representing the IAAF countered that Johnson made money as an athlete while cheating, had been properly sanctioned, and compared him to a criminal: "It's a little like saying a jail sentence imposed on a jewel thief is a restraint of trade."

Athletics Canada argued the bulk of Johnson's earnings came from contractual endorsements, not prize money at meets, and that the federation hadn't prevented him from making a living.

Caswell agreed with the defendants. Although she found the lifetime ban was a restraint of trade, she didn't believe it applied in Johnson's case. She also concluded he'd not exhausted all sports-related avenues open to him to challenge the ban before turning to the courts.

In language that likely would come under fire today, Caswell framed part of her written decision in a patronizing tone that went unremarked in news stories about the case:

It is necessary to protect Mr. Johnson for the sake of his own health from the effects of consistently using prohibited substances. It is necessary to protect the right of the athlete, including Mr. Johnson, to fair competition, to know that the race involves only his own skill, his own strength, his own spirit and not his own pharmacologist.

Johnson was angry. "Since when does the government of this country care about my life or my career?" he said of the judge's decision. "What she is saying to me, as a Black man, is, 'we are not going to give you your license [to compete] back, we are shutting you down.' That's it. That's what happened."

He added, "if I was white, I would get my clearance to compete or even make a living [as a coach]. . . . They didn't give me a chance to clear my name. They shut me down, and that really pissed me off."

Chrobotek was furious at the ruling. Johnson appealed, but a three-judge panel upheld the decision and dismissed the case in September 1998.

* * *

Despite occasional lucrative training contracts with the likes of Diego Maradona, Ben Johnson struggled financially in the 1990s.

He was forced to sell some possessions, including his Corvette, his Porsche, a Mazda that he'd bought for his mother, and his Markham "dream home" property, which was under construction (some of the proceeds went into his ARF trust account when he was still competing).

He hadn't realized until 1993 that his collective funds, which he believed should have topped $2 million, were closer to $450,000. Of course, $450,000 is a lot of money to most, but to Johnson, with a pile of bills, a mortgage, a line of credit, and dwindling moneymaking opportunities, it was a shockingly low amount. And it depleted quickly.

Over the years, Johnson alleged and failed to prove he'd been swindled by various parties and handlers after the Seoul Games. Others suggested his spending habits and bad litigation outcomes contributed to his financial hardship. For example, he was ordered to pay about $50,000 in legal costs to Athletics Canada and the IAAF after losing his 1997 reinstatement bid.

Painfully, Johnson could not hold on to his beloved Ferrari Testarossa. In the summer of 1996, he used the 12-cylinder, $275,000 Italian beauty as collateral for a $30,000 loan but couldn't repay the lender by the deadline.

While Morris Chrobotek searched on his behalf for paying contracts, the agent also set about repairing his client's reputation through charity work. Much of the do-gooding was what you'd expect:

speaking with children about the risks of using drugs and donating his time to work out young athletes in non-track sports like soccer. He and Chrobotek traveled to Israel for eight days in the fall of 1998 to give anti-drug talks. But one charity event was so wacky, it overshadowed all his other work.

Ben Johnson would race two horses and a stock car to raise funds for a children's charity in Charlottetown, Prince Edward Island, one of Canada's Maritime provinces that, through its gaming commission, had asked him to participate. Pundits on sports panels across the country called it a spectacle, a joke, and another public humiliation for a washed-up athlete. Veteran *Toronto Star* columnist Rosie DiManno argued the sprinter was being exploited in an opinion piece headlined, "Johnson demeans blacks by racing a horse."

Johnson didn't see it that way. "If I could use my ability to raise money for kids who didn't have long to live, I say let's do it," he said. The people of Charlottetown took a similar view and welcomed the help.

The night of the October 15, 1998, race was frigid, rainy, and windy. The small harness track was packed with four thousand hardy souls who paid $2 each to watch. Johnson recalls being as cold as he's ever been. His shoes were almost pulled off his feet by the muddy track as he warmed up.

It was a staggered start, with the four contestants covering different distances to the finish line. The human would run 80 meters; a seventeen-year-old Morgan saddle horse (and rider) would race 100 meters, a harness horse and driver would run 120 meters, and the stock car would drive 140 meters.

Johnson finished third. The Morgan won, followed by the harness horse and driver. The stock car was last, mired in mud at the start. More than $10,000 was raised for PEI children, and according to news accounts, the soaked Charlottetowners went home happy.

* * *

That an Ontario court judge had upheld his lifetime ban in 1997 and an appeal court had concurred did not stop Ben Johnson and his agent, Morris Chrobotek, from seeking justice.

The lifetime ban had been imposed by Athletics Canada and the IAAF after his 1993 Montreal urine test found him to have an unduly high testosterone-to-epitestosterone ratio. Johnson had decided against appealing primarily because of the expense. Chrobotek applied instead for an early reinstatement hearing under the "doping control standard operating procedures of the Canadian Centre for Ethics in Sport." He was successful. This meant Johnson would get an independent arbitration hearing regarding the Montreal test.

Johnson's case would be heard by a Canadian arbitrator, Graeme Mew. This time the sprinter had an unexpected anti-doping expert in his corner, Professor Arnold Beckett, a long-serving member of the IOC medical commission and a man who had voted for his Seoul expulsion. The Englishman had since resigned from the medical commission and was now an advocate for athletes fighting doping violations.

Chrobotek had tracked down Beckett after finally acquiring Johnson's detailed lab report. The IAAF never released the document, but the Canadian Centre for Ethics in Sport delivered it to Chrobotek in 1998. Beckett reviewed how the B sample's T/E ratio was calculated and provided Johnson's team with an alternative T/E ratio conclusion, one that was lower than an automatic fail and based on "simple mathematics," said Chrobotek.

It was not Graeme Mew's role to reconsider Ben Johnson's doping failure in Montreal. That positive T/E ratio finding would stand. The Toronto lawyer's task as arbitrator, in a nutshell, was to assess ten criteria pursuant to the sprinter's application and weigh them as neutral, positive, or negative factors in his reinstatement bid.

The hearing was chock-full of witness testimony, exhibits, scientific documents, and other submissions, all presented over an aggregate six-week period in early 1999. In addition to the Johnson team, Athletics Canada, Sport Canada, and the Canadian Centre for Ethics in Sport had seats at the table. Athletics Canada did not support the athlete's application.

As Mew described the proceedings, Johnson bore "the onus of proving, on a balance of probabilities, exceptional circumstances justifying reinstatement" under a section of Canadian policy on doping penalties in sport. Johnson did just that.

In a legally binding decision released in April 1999, Mew concluded Johnson met the standard of exceptional circumstances and that the Athletics Canada life ban was an excessive punishment. The strongest reason for his decision was that Athletics Canada had made a mistake, albeit inadvertently, by incorrectly advising the sprinter he was entitled to an appeal after the IAAF and Athletics Canada had imposed their lifetime bans. In fact, Johnson had a right to a hearing before his own federation under IAAF rules. In such a hearing, the onus was on the IAAF's anti-doping commission to prove Johnson had committed an offense.

Mew wrote in his fifty-seven-page decision:

Athletes are held, quite properly, to high standards of conduct. By the same token, athletes are entitled to expect from their sport governing bodies a high standard of procedural fairness. Sport governing bodies must obey their own rules, just as they expect athletes to. Here, though, through inadvertence, Athletics Canada failed to meet the appropriate standard in 1993.

In my judgment, Ben Johnson was prejudiced by this failure. While the measure of that prejudice is hard to gauge, the integrity of the process of adjudication in sport penalty cases can only be maintained if athletes can be confident that the rules will be properly applied and that they will be judged by a process that is just and fair.

Mew also believed Johnson's testimony that he hadn't used banned drugs since 1988 because he knew he'd be tested regularly. Mew wrote that the positive test result was likely "inadvertent" since he'd produced negative T/E results two days earlier and five days after the Montreal sample was provided.

As for producing an alternate T/E ratio, Chrobotek averaged a series of smaller ratio values attached to the scientific "confidence level" he and Beckett saw in the original lab report. In the new calculation, the T/E ratio was fractionally lower than 10.1:1, not a negative result, but it fell within a range that would have allowed Johnson the opportunity to try to explain the reading six years earlier in a hearing.

Mew wrote: "Mr. Johnson's submission, simply put, is that had the detailed test data been available [in 1993], it could have been concluded that Mr. Johnson's T/E ratio was, in fact, lower than 10.1. Whether or not this is so, had there been a hearing . . . no matter how imperfect it might have been, there would have been at least some consideration of the data."

Mew reinstated Johnson's eligibility to participate in track and field in Canada. When the decision was rendered, Athletics Canada was obliged to assist Johnson in applying on his behalf to the IAAF for his return to the sport. The IAAF sent the case to a subcommittee, and Johnson, at age thirty-seven, appeared poised to make a second comeback. It was an extraordinary development, albeit with a catch. Johnson still needed the IAAF's approval to compete against other runners, including Canadians in Canada, to protect their international eligibility pending the IAAF decision. Until then, the sprinter could only race against the clock, not people.

The written decision hinted that the man-versus-horse gambit had worked out in Johnson's favor. Mew noted Johnson's charitable resumé as a factor in the outcome: "Although there was a suggestion that Mr. Johnson's appetite for community service increased as he laid the groundwork for his application for reinstatement, I am satisfied that Mr. Johnson's commitment in this regard is genuine. . . . On balance, I find that the application of this criterion weighs in Mr. Johnson's favor."

The arbitrator sent Johnson on his way in the final paragraph with a reminder of his good fortune: "Mr. Johnson should appreciate that by this decision he has been given a rare opportunity to redeem his reputation and to renew his ability to make a significant contribution to his sport. Many of the people who wrote in Mr. Johnson's support have expressed their trust, confidence, faith, and hope in him as an athlete and a human being. He knows that he cannot let them down again."

The trust, confidence, faith, and hope recognized by arbitrator Graeme Mew vanished just six months after Johnson's Canadian reinstatement. He was on his way to having the IAAF consider reinstating him internationally, perhaps becoming the first amateur athlete in history to overturn a lifetime sport ban after a second doping offense, when he failed a third doping test.

As part of his Canadian eligibility conditions under Mew, Johnson had agreed to submit to random urine tests until the IAAF ruled on his case. In October, after providing a random sample at a Toronto doctor's office, he screened positive for a diuretic, a masking agent athletes often use to hide the presence of performance-enhancing drugs. Diuretics were also a banned class of drug.

Johnson swore, yet again, that he didn't know how this happened. He said pills he'd recently taken for a stomach ailment may have been a contamination source. The innocent victim excuse fell flat.

Morris Chrobotek was apoplectic at the third failure but rallied to salvage what he could. He claims to have used a third party to grease the IAAF's president, Lamine Diack, with $75,000 (US) sometime around December of 1999 to restore Johnson's eligibility. Diack, now dead, was found guilty by a French court in 2020 for taking millions of dollars in bribes in a scheme to cover up Russian doping cases. Diack, says Chrobotek, took the $75,000 but failed to reinstate Johnson.

Track's rejection of him was now absolute.

CHAPTER SIXTEEN
THE SON OF A TYRANT AND THE RCMP

The son of Libyan dictator Colonel Muammar Gaddafi, Saadi Gaddafi was a notorious party boy who fancied himself an elite-level football (soccer) player. Already the Libyan national team captain, he was looking for a fitness coach to get him to the next level. His target was the Italian Serie A level, where he would play with the best professionals in the world. Gaddafi had invited Diego Maradona to Libya for a visit in 1998. Maradona spoke of Ben Johnson's talents as a conditioning coach, praising him effusively. A year later, Gaddafi's representatives reached out to hire the disgraced Olympian. Morris Chrobotek handled the deal.

It was December 1999, and the Gaddafi offer was controversial. Among other reasons, Col. Muammar Gaddafi had only months before handed over two Libyan suspects for trial for the 1988 terrorist bombing of Pan Am Flight 103 over Lockerbie, Scotland. The airborne explosion killed all two hundred and forty-three passengers, mostly Americans, and sixteen crew members (plus eleven residents on the ground). US President Ronald Reagan dubbed the Libyan leader "the mad dog of the Middle East." He was similarly viewed in other Western nations, including Canada.

Chrobotek laid out the pros and cons for his client. Johnson's reputation could be further harmed by his choice to work with the Gaddafi family. On the other hand, the sprinter would be dealing with the son, not the "mad dog" father. The money was excellent, and the job was right up Johnson's alley in terms of personal training. The sprinter thought about it for a few weeks, not sure what to do. Then, Chrobotek called him around Christmas. "Morris says: 'Guess what? You're going to Libya.' I said, 'when?' He said, 'Now.'"

The financial details are disputed by the two, but it seems the total Libyan deal was worth about $350,000 (US) for about three months' work. Johnson was hired as Gaddafi's conditioning coach and would be part of a three-person Canadian training contingent sent to Tripoli.

When Johnson got to Toronto's Pearson airport on December 27, he was met by reporters. They wanted to know why the sprinter agreed to work in a country that Canada considered politically unstable, risky for visitors, and ruled by a man who deployed deadly terrorist tactics. "I told them, 'I can't make a living here, so what am I doing here?' I said, 'I'm not afraid to go anywhere in the world. I just go. People have a great love for me. I'm a Jamaican-Canadian, and everybody knows my background, so I'm not afraid to go anywhere.' They were all stunned when I said that."

The Libyan experience would be unlike training Maradona, a low-key, collegial affair. Working with the dictator's son and his heavily armed guards was off-the-charts unpredictable. When Johnson landed in Tripoli, he was taken by Gaddafi staffers to a nondescript hotel. He and the others, a soccer coach and a nutritionist, were told not to unpack their luggage and to remain in their suites—they might be going to Benghazi to meet The Big Man. The Canadians understood that Saadi Gaddafi was "The Big Man."

Johnson said they waited in hotel rooms, luggage zipped up, for most of that day. When the order to fly to Benghazi arrived, they climbed aboard another plane. In Benghazi, Johnson met his client.

"He was very friendly; he was overweight too. I'd say he was about two hundred and thirty-five pounds," Johnson said. "I'd heard from friends we met that he had bags of chocolate under his bed."

For the first few days, the group discussed nutritional and conditioning strategies with Gaddafi, so he understood what was expected. It became quickly apparent, said Johnson, that Gaddafi had a sense of humor, was serious about a pro soccer career, and was deadly serious about security. Gun-toting guards were everywhere. Car travel was by convoy, and on one future flight to Malta with the player's entourage, a cache of military-grade firearms made the trip, carried by men who knew how to use them.

Gaddafi was also an accommodating host, Johnson said. When the sprinter mentioned December 30 was his birthday, the Libyan had a sumptuous cake made for him.

The group returned to Tripoli after the "strategies" week to check in at the same suites they had waited in upon landing. Johnson said it was a "one-star" hotel that played the same saxophone music endlessly. "All day, every day, every week, every month, it was Kenny G," he said, "no offense to Kenny G."

If nothing else, the no-frills hotel was well-located. It was near the soccer stadium where they'd train. And security was tight. Always. "We had a chauffeur and bodyguards with guns, and they'd say, 'Mr. Ben, do not leave the room without us because if The Big Man finds out, we are going to be in big trouble,'" he was told.

Johnson said he and the soccer coach snuck out once in the early hours, just to get away from constant surveillance, but were caught upon their return. "They said, 'Mr. Ben, that's not very nice,'" he recalled. That ended the unaccompanied outings.

Another way Johnson unwound was by telephone. In his pre-Seoul days of travel, he'd spend at least an hour a day chatting with his mother, Gloria, sharing his adventures from fabulous cities like Rome, London, Seville, Tokyo, or New York. He found comfort in hearing her voice, listening to how her day went, and catching up on news from home. In Tripoli, he dialed Gloria often and for hours at a time. He quickly ran up a $20,000 long-distance bill, and the Kenny G hotel manager, shocked at the amount, cut him off. According to Johnson, Gaddafi found the situation funny when informed and soon had his phone privileges restored, with the proviso that he keep his calls shorter.

On the pitch in the early days of training, Johnson was puzzled at Gaddafi's slow conditioning progress. The would-be football star was not losing weight, even though he was doing all the physical work, putting in his mileage, sprints, and weight-room reps. The suspicion was that Gaddafi's personal chef was not sticking to the diet plan.

The nutritionist spoke to the chef while Johnson gave "The Big Man" a pep talk about short-term pain. "I told him the first two weeks are going to be hell, but you have to eat this way," he said in explaining the menu of egg whites, veggies, salads, non-meat proteins, and no carbs. Gaddafi was game, although he'd complain at times about how hungry he was. Johnson said, "Trust us."

"He trusted us, and he started seeing results," said Johnson. "Then he'd be able to eat a bit more each week, and when I was finished with him, he was an athlete. He looked like a guy who'd been training for 15, 20 years. He got in shape; he had muscles in his arms, back, and a six-pack. He could run faster than he ever did. He was pleased with the training. He was happy, and he could see the results within ninety days."

Did Johnson advise Gaddafi to use anabolic steroids or any other banned substance to achieve this improved fitness level and musculature in three months?

"No."

Johnson, who would work with Gaddafi on and off into 2003, swore his client was not using. He would not suggest steroid use to anyone, he insisted, including Gaddafi, because the risk of being tied to drug schemes would destroy his new line of work. Gaddafi nevertheless ran into doping trouble after signing with Italian Serie A club Perugia. In a postgame test in November 2003, Gaddafi's urine was positive for an anabolic steroid, nandrolone.

After his first Libyan contract, said Johnson, he was invited to train Gaddafi three more times. One of the engagements was a two-week minicamp in Malta to touch up the soccer player's fitness.

Johnson flew to Tripoli and joined the Gaddafi entourage for a midnight flight into Malta. As they deplaned, Johnson noticed bodyguards in the back of the plane transferring armfuls of guns from a box into a carrying bag. The large men were stopped by a customs agent who cautiously peered into the bag of weapons, said Johnson, who watched without saying a word. A discussion ensued between the customs agent and the Libyans. Phone calls were made. The bodyguards insisted they needed guns to protect their client and his friends. "Somehow, the guns made it through, and when we were on the soccer field [the next day], we practiced with four [armed guards] all facing the outside walls for three straight hours," he said. "As long as it takes for us to train, they stay there."

Johnson had spent most of his life in Canada, where guns are not as plentiful as in other cultures, nor as fanatically embraced as a right to possess. He said it was shocking to see that amount of weaponry at first, but since it was his new normal, he rolled with it. "I was safe; I did my job as a sportsman, as a coach, and that was it. I didn't have to worry about anything, and they took good care of me."

* * *

Getting robbed on the streets of Rome would not be headline news for most people. Ben Johnson is not like most people.

It was summer 2000. Having just finished another training camp with Saadi Gaddafi, Johnson planned to meet his new Venetian girlfriend at a Marriott hotel in central Rome. He was flush, having just been paid by the Libyan. He took $7,000 in cash to Rome. He recalled thumbing through the wads of greenbacks as he checked into the hotel before sliding his wallet into a pocket.

Johnson loves to shop in Rome. It is where he bought his chunky $9,000 gold chain and a $20,000 gold watch during a 1987 visit to a Cartier store. He and his girlfriend planned to shop along the Via Veneto, one of his favorite streets. Clothes were on the morning agenda. "The $7,000 was just fun money to go shopping in Rome. You can pick up a lot of clothes for that amount, brand-name clothes you can't get at home, and they are cheaper in Italy," he said, mentioning Versace as one of his favorite labels.

The couple began strolling when a little girl, about six or seven, ran up, rubbing her stomach like she was hungry. Other children swarmed him. A woman was with them. The girl quickly took Johnson's hands into hers, distracting him. He walked a few steps and realized his wallet was gone. He grabbed the girl and looked around frantically for the woman. He couldn't spot her. "I was so pissed," he said. "I held onto the kid."

Police arrived on the scene and stopped Johnson from further roughing up the girl—he admitted to slapping her head a few times. The sprinter asked his girlfriend to return to the hotel. The sympathetic *polizia* knew who he was and took him and the girl to the police station. They pulled out binders with mug shots of local street thieves. Johnson thought he recognized the female pickpocket but couldn't be sure it was her. He left the station and the child behind.

His time with his girlfriend was ruined, so Johnson decided to fly home sooner than he planned. He might have been a disgraced athlete, but he remained famous, and news of the robbery was broadcast far and wide. "Ex-sprinter Johnson Loses Dash for Cash," read one headline.

In Libya, Saadi Gaddafi heard of his trainer's encounter with the gang of pickpockets. Next time they met, Gaddafi prodded Johnson for details about the theft and needled him about the old lady giving him the slip. "I lost $7,000, and he just started laughing about it," Johnson said.

* * *

His involvement with Gaddafi would later haunt Ben Johnson for years. On March 22, 2012, for instance, he found himself peering nervously through the curtains of his townhouse in Markham, just north of Toronto. The cops were outside.

Two Royal Canadian Mounted Police officers were sitting in a rented car on Betty Roman Boulevard. One was a member of the RCMP's International Anti-Corruption Unit who dealt with "financial integrity," according to the business card he'd stuck in Johnson's front door.

The officer, a corporal, had called Johnson that morning to request a chat about his relationship with Saadi Gaddafi, whose opulent lifestyle and ability to grant favors were interrupted when he fled the Libyan uprising in late 2011. Interpol was after Saadi Gaddafi. And in Canada, he was linked to a corruption case involving employees of Quebec-based engineering giant SNC-Lavalin and the awarding of Libyan projects. The Mounties also had questions about Gaddafi's lavish spending in their backyard, including his 2008 purchase of a $1.6 million Toronto waterfront condo.

Gaddafi wasn't talking. He'd sought asylum in Niger after his father was deposed and killed during the rebellion. The police were knocking on Johnson's door and sitting outside his house because he knew the man they were investigating.

Although their coach-and-client relationship ended in 2003, Johnson and Gaddafi had kept in touch. Johnson even broached a business deal with his friend's assistance during a 2005 visit to Tripoli, something regarding the Libyan oil industry. Nothing materialized, but whenever Gaddafi visited Toronto, they would get together. The last time was about eighteen months prior to the Libyan government's overthrow.

When the RCMP corporal sitting outside called Johnson earlier in the month to arrange a meeting, the retired sprinter said he'd only do it at his lawyer's office. Now Johnson didn't know what to do. He stayed at home all day, wondering if he could simply outwait the stakeout. Or would the Mounties get even more aggressive if he refused to cooperate?

Documents later acquired by Johnson (with some help from me) through a federal access to information request suggest the RCMP was probing his financial interactions with Saadi Gaddafi. It was while investigators were nosing around the Libyan's Toronto condo purchase that Johnson's name arose as one of his buddies.

The RCMP named their investigation "Paris" for reasons unclear in the eighty-two pages of heavily redacted documents released under the access request. Even with so much of the text removed, it is apparent the Mounties had plenty of reasons to zero in on Johnson. The following are drawn from the documents and Johnson's recall of events. Some file information and notations were compiled *after* officers visited Johnson, which will explain entries dated later in 2012 and 2013.

- At least one person told police that Johnson and Saadi Gaddafi were friends and that Johnson may have been using the waterfront condo when the Libyan was out of the country. Johnson said he never stayed or lived in it.
- Other witnesses suggested Johnson was pimping for Gaddafi by supplying female escorts for parties in Toronto. There are large redactions around these statements, although there is more than one reference to "hookers." Johnson flatly denies ever recruiting sex workers.
- Officers did research on Johnson by reading Wikipedia entries and a *Los Angeles Times* article from May 2012. They checked his

criminal history—Johnson had none—and conducted a Teranet property search of his Markham home.

- A $5,444.25 limousine invoice linked to SNC-Lavalin in September 2009 caught officers' attention. So did a $594.56 tab from Niagara Falls to Markham, with Johnson listed as the passenger. No more details were available. Johnson says these receipts are not related to him.

- There's an oblique reference to Johnson and Gaddafi using burner phones to communicate. Johnson said he never owned a burner phone and that he and Gaddafi "never talked on the phone, never." It was always in person or through a third party using a phone "because Saadi knows the system, he knows what's going on" regarding surveillance, he said.

- On March 22, 2012, two Mounties flew from Ottawa to Toronto, landing at 9:40 a.m. They drove a rental vehicle to Betty Roman Boulevard in Markham. There is a big blanked-out space after this, with the next entry noting the officers were back in Ottawa by 16:00 hours.

- A later note states an officer contacted Johnson's longtime friend and manager, Di-anne Hudson, "to clarify issues about [sic] contract and payment from Gaddafi to M[r.] Johnson."

The Johnson file may have been closed or become dormant in late 2013; redactions make it impossible to know for certain. But Johnson believes the Mounties' interest in him didn't end when they drove away that day. He's convinced his phone was tapped for years. He would hear clicking sounds on the line, which was an indication to him that his calls were being listened to. The claim has not been proven.

And what of Gaddafi, the flamboyant, free-spending would-be football star who was, at least for a time, in the RCMP crosshairs? Niger shipped Gaddafi back to Libya, then under a new regime, in 2014. He was kept in a Tripoli jail until 2021, when he was cleared of all criminal charges against him, including the murder of a soccer coach in 2005. The former dictator's son then flew directly to Istanbul.

In 2023, Gaddafi began the complicated process of selling his Toronto waterfront condo, which had been temporarily seized as an asset by the Libyan government, from abroad. According to news reports, he needed the money.

* * *

While training the son of a vicious despot and a World Cup legend fighting addiction were the highlights of Johnson's oddball, if enterprising, post-ban employment record, they were far from his only endeavors. There was film work: he had a cameo in a Finnish movie as an angry cabbie with a few lines and a fight scene. He starred in Japanese reality programs, having to outrace contestants in goofy scenes and, occasionally, acting out a role in costume—once as a white-hatted chef who runs down a dine-and-dash customer. He joined Australian businessman Jaimie Fuller on a Seoul twenty-fifth anniversary world tour. Closer to home, Johnson continued to develop his personal training business with athletes, mostly from ice hockey, soccer, or lacrosse.

His desperation to keep himself afloat financially led him to consider a range of business proposals, like a sports bar in Ukraine, that either didn't happen or were unsustainable. And it led him into ill-considered projects, including a regrettable self-published memoir in which a spiritual advisor claimed Johnson and Carl Lewis crossed paths in ancient Egypt in previous lives. Nothing, however, matched his venture with Frank D'Angelo, an actor/singer/writer/filmmaker/restauranteur/talk show host/brewery owner/Toronto mayoral candidate with a strong entrepreneurial bent.

In 2006, D'Angelo operated a beverage company called D'Angelo Brands. It produced an energy drink called Cheetah Power Surge.

D'Angelo had dreams of competing with market leaders Red Bull and Monster with his caffeine-free product. One day, he called his advertising partner with a wild idea for a TV commercial. "You know what we're going to do to get everybody to shit their pants? Get Ben Johnson," said D'Angelo: a cheater endorsing Cheetah.

D'Angelo also bounced the commercial idea off his close friend and sometimes backer, Barry Sherman, the generic pharmaceutical billionaire. Sherman liked the cheeky approach. D'Angelo took that as a green light. "So, I said, 'Let's get hold of Ben. I heard he's down on his luck.' I'm not going to make fun of him, [and] everybody knows who Ben Johnson was—the fastest man in the world."

D'Angelo had actually encountered Johnson years earlier at a Toronto waterfront nightclub called The Guvernment. They shook hands in passing, Johnson more interested in the dance floor action. They now met in much different circumstances, with Johnson pulling up to D'Angelo's office in a Honda Accord. "He's not the same Ben Johnson as at The Guvernment. He's extremely humble. I said, 'I'm not going to fuck around here, I'm going to shoot [this] commercial.'"

Johnson listened as D'Angelo outlined the project. Johnson knew "Cheetah" was a loaded word. He thought it over for a week, then said, "Screw it, I'm in."

"I was silent [on the world stage] for five years," he said, laughing. "Nobody knew where I was, so I thought, well, why not make some noise?"

They filmed the thirty-second spot at D'Angelo's former restaurant, the ForgetAboutIt! Supper Club on King Street West, near the TIFF Bell Lightbox that anchors the annual Toronto International Film Festival. The commercial's setting was reminiscent of the *Being Frank* television show D'Angelo produced and hosted in a west-end studio. In the ad, he was a late-night host, and Johnson was his guest.

"Ben, I want to ask you, when you run, do you Cheetah?" D'Angelo asks.

"Absolutely," says Johnson, as the audience gasps. There's a pause. He then holds up a can of the energy drink, looks into the camera with a wide grin, and says: "I Cheetah all the time."

D'Angelo said he spent about $1 million airing the spots across Canada, often during broadcasts of National Hockey League games. There was a second shorter commercial shot, too, with the pair acting as teacher-and-student sensei characters and a slight twist on Cheetah-ing.

The international reaction to Cheetah's new pitchman was a frenzy, according to D'Angelo. He was bombarded by global media requests to chronicle the sprinter's participation in the defiant ad, and he obliged them all.

Many Canadians were taken aback. The belief of some, and it came up often and without prompting during interviews for this book, was that D'Angelo preyed upon Johnson to sell a drink. "I should slap him for doing that Cheetah commercial," said retired boxer Tony Morrison, angry at Johnson for agreeing to do the ad. "I didn't like that commercial. People were making fun of that commercial. The man has done his time."

The backlash didn't bother Johnson. He stands by his decision. "Some people thought it was funny. Some people didn't think it was right for me to do it because of my past, but I said, 'I don't give a shit,'" he said. "The media was always trying to scold me, tell me what I can and can't do. . . . They asked, 'Are you making fun of the situation, of what happened to you?' and I said, 'Yeah. I'm turning a negative into a positive.'"

Johnson adds that Cheetah was "just a drink;" the commercial was an opportunity to earn a payday, and he harbors no ill will toward D'Angelo, who at least gets credit for memorable branding. His company is long gone, but for a certain generation of Canadians, Cheetah and its Olympic pitchman are burned into the collective memory.

The fee he received from D'Angelo was $12,500, which Johnson considered decent for a day's work. It was little help in his ongoing efforts to remain solvent, however. He further complicated his affairs with his litigiousness. A $37-million lawsuit against former lawyer Ed Futerman and Futerman's estate was summarily dismissed in 2012. Johnson's claim that his athlete's trust fund overseen by Athletics Canada was improperly governed went nowhere. He also had to catch up on years of unpaid taxes. In late 2012, he filed for bankruptcy protection, stating that he had liabilities of $463,100 and assets of $3,001.

D'Angelo would go on to write, direct, score, produce, and star in a range of small-budget films with veteran actors, including James Caan, Paul Sorvino, Daryl Hannah, Margot Kidder, Daniel Baldwin, and Danny Aiello. All of them were funded by his buddy Barry Sherman until, in 2017, the billionaire and his wife, Honey Sherman, both in their seventies, were found dead in their Toronto mansion. Their bodies were found in semi-sitting positions beside their indoor swimming pool, with belts looped around their necks and secured to deck railings. Despite millions of dollars in reward money and an ongoing investigation by police, the killings remain unsolved—another bizarre footnote to Ben Johnson's Olympic afterlife.

CHAPTER SEVENTEEN
MYSTERY MAN SPEAKS

Ben Johnson has some wild threads running through his life. But the one connecting him and the Seoul "mystery man" in a four-decades-long relationship is the most mind-bending.

When Johnson accused an American of sabotaging him in 1988, he did so without proof, and the story was subsequently dismissed at the Dubin Inquiry. Johnson didn't discover until late 1989 that the mystery man's name was Andre Jackson and that he was a track fan and a close friend of Olympic sprint champion Carl Lewis. By then, Jackson was pursuing a career in the African diamond mining industry.

One might assume that Johnson would want nothing to do with the man he believes is responsible for his positive test in Seoul. If he truly believed he'd been grievously wronged by this friend of Carl Lewis, why on earth would he speak to him again? "Keep your enemy close," explained Johnson. "Maybe something might spill [to] use down the road. I kind of used that as leverage to see if [Jackson] is going to open up."

They have spent time together since the mid-1990s. Once, they met in Dubai while Johnson was on a business trip. Another time, while watching New Year's Eve fireworks atop a Las Vegas hotel. And they chat periodically by text and WhatsApp.

But where Andre Jackson sees a friend, Ben Johnson sees an answer. The Canadian stubbornly believes Jackson has inside information on his doping failure, and that's why he keeps the man in his life. Jackson counters that he is simply being a good friend, despite Johnson's repeated assertions of skullduggery. "I'm into friendship maintenance [which] is why my friendship endures," he wrote in an email.

Johnson doesn't buy this explanation. He believes Jackson harbors a white-hot secret about tampering with his urine sample. "I think his conscience is killing him."

* * *

The pills-in-the-beer scenario would likely have died long ago had not a dogged English filmmaker, Daniel Gordon, tracked down Andre Jackson for his award-winning documentary, 9.79.*

Gordon's film was one of several media projects to mark the twenty-fifth anniversary of the 1988 men's 100-meter race in Seoul. Its full length-version debuted at the 2012 Toronto International Film Festival and later aired in North America as part of ESPN's 30-for-30 documentary series. I was one of the talking media heads in 9.79*, and I attended the premiere in Toronto.

I thought I knew the Ben Johnson saga quite well, but two points in 9.79* made me sit bolt upright. First, Carl Lewis's manager, Joe Douglas, confessed on camera that "we" figured out a "sneaky" way to get Andre Jackson a doping control pass in Seoul to keep an eye on the new gold medalist.

"We wanted somebody in the room in case [Johnson] took a masking agent," Douglas tells Gordon. "Do you know what a masking agent is? That covers up the [positive] results of the test. And he had a camera, and if Ben took any pills or liquids, he was going to take a picture."

Secondly, Gordon asked Jackson about the sabotage claim but was unable to get him on camera. This was his response to the allegation, shared in writing on the screen for the audience: "Maybe I did, maybe I didn't."

My interest in Ben Johnson's story was cautiously revived. The race was a quarter-century old, and surely every aspect had already been investigated. Or could Charlie Francis and Johnson have been right all along about things like lax doping control security and American shenanigans in Seoul?

I began speaking with Johnson more often. During one conversation, he casually mentioned that he and Jackson kept in touch and had also met in person several times. I was floored.

Johnson identified two specific short-notice meetings, the first around 1994 and the second in 2004, in which Jackson said he'd "tell me something important" about Seoul. It was Johnson's pie-in-the-sky hope that the "mystery man" would confess to spiking his beer with stanozolol in 1988. Johnson brought witnesses each time.

The initial rendezvous was at a Toronto Pearson airport terminal, the first time they'd seen each other or spoken since Seoul. According to Johnson, friends told him Andre Jackson wanted to connect. One of these friends passed along Jackson's phone number. Johnson called, and the American said he'd fly to Toronto. Johnson said they were to discuss the events surrounding his drug test in Seoul.

In Jackson's telling, Johnson hunted him down and asked to meet. Jackson agreed and chartered a plane the next morning.

Johnson brought his trusted high-school friend, the pro boxer Tony Morrison, to the Pearson meeting. Unbeknownst to Jackson, the Toronto buddies had devised a sting operation. There was bumbling involved. Johnson planned to surreptitiously record Jackson, hoping to catch a shocking "I did it" confession on tape. He and Morrison decided the boxer should wear "the wire" in case Jackson became suspicious of the sprinter. Morrison purchased a mini tape recorder to slip into his shirt pocket, and he positioned himself beside the visitor, edging closer each time he spoke.

Johnson said he greeted Jackson with, "Hey, I'm here, what do you want to talk to me about?" and that Jackson, pointing and laughing, responded: "Son of a bitch, I got you."

In an email, Jackson recalled their interaction like this: "If he accused me of doing anything in the drug testing room that day, it was not in my presence. If there is any regret I had that day at the airport, it was failing to give him the gift of premium Soju that I brought for him. I ended up leaving it in the aircraft after the Customs [*sic*] officer advised me not to bring it in." Soju is a grain-based Korean liquor.

Jackson, who can come across as pompous and evasive in written communication, claims Seoul didn't come up at Pearson: "On that particular day, he did not say what he wanted from me, because I wasn't really there to entertain anything that he wanted. I looked him in the eye and fearlessly spoke my peace (sic) with a level of conviction he had never heard before."

The conversation lasted about forty-five minutes. The Canadian sleuths managed to record almost none of it. Morrison's shirt pocket rubbed against the microphone, and only the rasping of the material could be heard on tape, Johnson said.

Morrison has only a faint recall of the long-ago airport meeting. He was seriously injured in a 1994 car crash that ended his boxing career. It also destroyed part of his long-term memory. He can only remember buying a tape recorder at a now-defunct Radio Shack and going with Johnson to meet somebody at Pearson. He apologized for not remembering more.

Like the Pearson rendezvous, there are different memories of how and why the second short-notice meeting in September 2004 occurred. Johnson says Andre Jackson called him "out of the blue," saying he had something "really important" to discuss about Seoul, and could Johnson come to California to hear it in person right away?

The decision to fly out was a difficult one, Johnson told his caller, as his 71-year-old mother, Gloria, was terminally ill and in palliative care at Toronto's Sunnybrook Hospital. "My mum didn't have much time to live. She was slowly dying from cancer," he said. What began as stomach cancer had spread to Gloria's lungs and beyond. She was weak. She could barely speak. Her son was by her side round-the-clock, calming her when frequent nightmares of her childhood kidnapping attempt in Clark's Town surfaced. "She had a fear in her mind that people were coming to kidnap her now that she couldn't move [from the hospital bed]. Every time somebody came in the room, she'd look around, and I'd say, 'Mum, you're okay, I'm here, and no one is going to come for you.'"

Johnson sought out his mother's pastor to ask for guidance as he was torn about traveling to meet Andre Jackson. He wanted to hear what the man had to say, but his guilt at leaving his mother was overpowering. The pastor suggested that since he could not help his mother recover, he should make the trip if it was that important. Johnson fashioned a compromise. He would take an early-morning flight to LA, meet with Jackson the next day, and get the red-eye back that same night. He'd be gone about forty-eight hours.

He didn't inform his mother of the trip, lest it upset her. He said he needed a short break and would return soon. "But she knew I was up to no good," he said, noting that even in her critical state, she sensed her son was trying to pull something past her.

Johnson and his longtime friend, Di-anne Hudson, flew to LA, then drove to a motel in Irvine. Jackson met them there.

Again, Johnson tried a secret agent ploy. Hudson had a tape recorder running in her purse when Jackson arrived at the hotel room. Johnson and Hudson said the visitor showed up carrying a six-pack of beer as a sight gag about Seoul. Jackson denied bringing beer and said in an email that "anyone who knows me is well aware that I don't drink beer, so if there was a six-pack in the room, it wasn't purchased, brought, consumed, or seen by me."

Jackson remembers the visit this way: "We met in California because both he and Di-Anne [sic] wanted to speak with me. I was a bit pressed for time because I had plans to travel overseas. Nonetheless, I had no objection to them coming to [California] because I was preparing to return to my chateau in Kasai-Oriental province of the Democratic Republic of Congo a day or two after I spoke with them in Irvine."

At any rate, the discussion was not what Johnson had hoped for. He said they chatted about how their paths had crossed in the past, including the nightclub outing in Zurich. Jackson said it was 1987; Johnson said it was 1986. Hudson described Jackson as speaking in riddles, not answering questions directly, and being coy about events in Seoul.

Again, alas, the tape recording of the chat is garbled and unintelligible. It's also of no consequence since Johnson said there was no confession. "He didn't come out and say, 'Yes, I'm the guy who made the test positive, I set you up, I put steroids in your drink'—he didn't admit it. He didn't want to say he did it. He just toyed with me."

For Johnson, the trip was a bust. It was time to go home to his mother. That evening, he and Hudson packed their carry-on luggage and were about to drive to the airport for the overnight flight to Toronto when Hudson's cell phone rang. She answered, thinking it was Jackson who had forgotten something in the room and was returning to pick it up. It wasn't. It was Johnson's sister, Clare.

Johnson had his shoe propped on a table and was lacing it up when Hudson hung up. She quietly told him his mother had died. Johnson slid off the edge of the bed in disbelief, then cried, inconsolable.

Relating that moment years later, Johnson broke down again. "I didn't even get to see her pass," he said, hands covering his face and tears flowing.

When he returned to Toronto, his sisters told him their mother intuitively knew he'd gone somewhere on an urgent matter, "and she was waiting for me to come back, but she couldn't hold on."

He joined his siblings to prepare their mother for burial at the funeral home. They made sure she wore her most beautiful dress and delicate white gloves on her hands. Johnson leaned over and kissed her cheek a final time.

The family tried to keep Gloria Johnson's passing from becoming public, but on the morning of the funeral service, it was in the news. Reporters and camera crews showed up outside the church to record the proceedings. Johnson's pain was mixed with fury. He could not privately mourn the most important person in his life.

* * *

Ben Johnson and Andre Jackson have not met up in recent years, there has not been a lot of WhatsApping. Johnson said he's finished trying to learn anything more from the "mystery man."

Jackson, when asked why he kept in touch with a man who repeatedly accused him of spiking his beer in Seoul, wrote: "What my friends benefit most from me is loyalty, truth, reality-check, and a clear understanding of consequence. I may not always tell my friends what they want to hear but I do make it a habit of telling them what they need to know . . . and for many, they are forever grateful, and some even consider it to be an unusual luxury."

He signed off as "Andre Jackson, a limelight-shunning and no-nonsense global powerbroker, who just happens to be a very dear and supportive friend to Team Canada, USA Track & Field, and Santa Monica Track Club."

CHAPTER EIGHTEEN
LOSING CHARLIE

Ben Johnson was in his car, about to run an errand, when his cell phone rang on May 12, 2010. It was Angela Coon, wife of Charlie Francis, calling from Sunnybrook Hospital. "Ben, where are you? Charlie is asking for you. He's not going to make it, and he doesn't have much time left."

Francis had been privately fighting cancer for several years. Only family and close friends were aware of his illness and how determined he was to beat the disease. Now, unexpectedly, he was slipping away. "I can be there in twenty minutes," Johnson said.

Tires squealed as he turned the car around and sped to the sprawling hospital complex in North Toronto. He arrived in just under twenty minutes, sprinted from the parking lot to the patient wing, where his coach was being given end-of-life care.

A week or two earlier, Francis had enjoyed the company of good friends at his home in a small, lively gathering. Johnson was there, as was Rob Gray, the discus thrower-turned-lawyer, and others who'd been invited to have a bit of fun. At one point, Johnson recalled that Francis collapsed, complaining of pain and being too weak to get up. He and Gray carried him to a couch to recover. When he was strong enough to return to the party, he did.

Johnson and Gray were the last two stragglers that night. The trio laughed uproariously at years of shared memories. Johnson said it was a magical time, with Francis enjoying the companionship of people he cared about. But Johnson was silently worried. "I knew when he collapsed that Charlie really wasn't well," he said. "His body was just worn out."

* * *

Not all the memorable Charlie Francis-Ben Johnson moments occurred at the track's finish line, with world-record times flashing on time clocks.

As tough as Francis was, he was a nervous flyer, and he couldn't hide it, especially when turbulence hit. Johnson, who could sleep through a hijacking, said Francis's in-flight fear was one of the few opportunities he had to poke fun at him. "When the plane started rocking," said Johnson, "Charlie would pick up the airline magazine in the pocket flap in front of him, then start flipping through it, but he wasn't reading shit. The worse the turbulence was, the faster he'd flip through the pages. It cracked us up because we knew he wasn't reading a word."

"Sometimes he'd hold the seat in front of him and go, 'Fuck me.' That was his favorite phrase: Fuck me."

Francis's own sense of humor could be wielded as a weapon. His athletes had to be at the training facility for 3:15 p.m. sharp and work hard the entire session, no excuses. Johnson said he was feeling under the weather one day and wanted to stay home. He decided to tell Francis he'd be a no-show. "I phoned Charlie, and I said, 'I don't feel too good. I think I have a cold,'" he said. "And Charlie said, 'Your legs aren't sick. Your legs don't have a cold. Come to practice.'"

Johnson went to practice and logged a strong workout despite having the sniffles. Francis was skilled at motivating athletes to commit to his program that required a total buy-in.

The coach and sprinter both loved cars. Winning the 1987 world championship earned Johnson the Mazda international athlete of the year award from the Japanese automotive giant. The prize was a new, fully loaded Mazda convertible. "It was a really nice red color, and Charlie loved it," Johnson said. "I only enjoyed driving it for a day or two, and when Charlie saw it, he said, 'Give me that car, let me buy it from you.'"

Johnson sold it to him for $25,000. When asked why he didn't just give it to his coach, the man hugely responsible for the sprinter's wealth and achievements, he said Francis insisted on paying because Johnson had wanted to keep the sporty vehicle.

"I'd do anything for Charlie," said Johnson who, when he was in the money, frequently gave his coach gifts—$5,000 here, $20,000 there—because he wanted to. Francis was one of the few people around him who neither asked for money nor expected it.

Francis was fortunate, after he was banned from coaching in Canada, that his technical skills and speed training methods were in demand in other nations. He worked with American sprinters Marion Jones and Tim Montgomery in 2003—his most high-profile stars, both of whom were later caught up in the infamous BALCO doping scandal. His training advice was sought by major league pros, especially NFLers, recalled *Toronto Sun* sports columnist Steve Simmons, who developed a rapport with Francis.

Francis kept in touch with individual members of the media, like Simmons and a few international reporters he respected. He was a rich but anonymous source for background information on doping stories.

Even though Francis told Canada's sports officials to "go fuck themselves" rather than apply for reinstatement, he was crushed by the ignoble end of the Optimist club, Johnson said. Not just because the Seoul fallout killed the elite sprint team, but because it also destroyed a program that assured quality coaching, competition, and training for young runners. It was a low-cost entry for financially strapped families, subsidized in part by the bingo revenue raised by club founder Ross Earl. All that died.

"What really hurt Charlie was that he spent so much time building the club, doing what he loves, only to have people come in and dismantle it because we were independent," Johnson said, referring to Francis's defiant streak that defined the club and its members. "Whatever happened to me in Seoul, he never recovered from it. All the things that he wanted to be, and could have been, it disappeared in a second . . . Charlie was bitter about that for years, even though off the [Canadian] tracks he was doing very well with his own coaching company and in using my training program to make money. But deep down, that really hurt him."

Francis wrote several books, one of which was the candid 1990 memoir *Speed Trap*. Rob Gray recalled getting frequent phone calls while Francis was writing, bouncing ideas off him. Gray said the coach was convinced Johnson was framed in Seoul, an unshakeable belief he held until his death.

The memoir is full of Johnson moments. Asked if he'd ever read his coach's book, Johnson's responded: "I never read his book because I lived it."

Even now, Johnson can outline the three main planks of Francis's coaching philosophy from memory: methodology (athletes must believe in the program's effectiveness), recovery (strategic use of longer rest periods during training so muscles aren't overworked), and regeneration (through recovery and injury prevention practices like deep muscle and tissue massage, as Waldemar Matuszewksi provided).

Francis discusses doping throughout his memoir. He argues that the small group of in-house scientists who banned steroids never engaged in open, transparent discussions as to why they were banned. Nor were the drugs clearly defined as medical, moral, or ethical infractions, further muddying the reason why steroids were declared off-limits.

Francis's other works, including sprint training manuals, are offered online. Angela Coon, the former Canadian team hurdler-turned-coach, personal trainer, and motivational speaker, operates the website.

* * *

Ben Johnson began to spiral after his mother died in 2004. Things got worse when he learned Charlie Francis had cancer.

He had been living with his sister, Clare, then moved out to buy his own place in Markham. He was bitter over losing the fortune he'd once possessed, the millions of dollars never to be recovered. He began to drink heavily, not in bars, but at home, by himself. "I started getting depressed because, for the first time in my life, I was living alone, no more nieces and nephews around, no sisters," he said. "I didn't know how to cook. I bought all this food and didn't know how to make it, so I'd call my friends on the phone [for instructions]."

He'd only leave his house to train clients, coach teams, or hit the liquor store to buy wine. "I'd come home, lock my doors, I didn't want to see nobody. Then I started drinking hard," he said. "I didn't care about anything. I didn't travel at all. I just trained, coached, made money, and paid bills. It was pretty tough."

Three years into this emotional limbo, Johnson wondered what his parents would think of him in this empty state. It moved him. "I used my mum's words and my dad's words in the back of my mind. 'Try to get through this,' and I thought, 'Mum, you don't want to see me this way.'"

Around that time, he ran into a friend who had turned his life around by seeing a naturopathic doctor who promoted a holistic approach to well-being. Johnson was impressed and became a client of the same naturopath. He stopped drinking cold turkey in 2008 and hasn't had a belt since. He began self-care practices. Meditation. Proper sleep. He turned to natural whole foods and herbal supplements to detoxify— no more junk food.

He also re-examined his spiritual side and returned to church. "It took me twenty-five months to heal my body, but I believe it saved my life because I was going down the wrong path," he said.

It was a new Ben Johnson, but a little of the old Ben Johnson ego played into his recovery: he didn't want his detractors to know he'd fallen into a bad place. "I had to try to climb out of that hole after all those years, and I wasn't going to roll over and give the enemy that satisfaction."

* * *

Charlie Francis was lying very still in his hospital bed when Ben Johnson stepped into the room. There were a few people there, including Angela Coon, who was crying.

Johnson saw an empty chair beside the bed. He walked over, sat down, and took Francis's hand in his. "Charlie, I'm here. It's Ben."

Francis's eyes fluttered open. Johnson looked into them, a final connection, one mind. "I could see Charlie's eyes dimming. I kissed him on the neck. I said, 'I love you. I will always love you, and I'll always be here for you.'"

He continued to hold his coach's hand as he wept. "Tears were flowing down my face, onto the floor. Everybody was crying." Francis passed away peacefully later that day.

Johnson cried twice during interviews for this book. Once for his mother, the second time for Francis. When he recovered, the first thing he said was: "We worked so hard to do what we do best."

Johnson didn't speak at Francis's funeral—"it was too emotional"— but was a pallbearer, and he attended the burial site with the family.

Francis was like a second father to Johnson. He genuinely loved the skinny boy, who trusted him implicitly and loved him back. He was the man who discreetly bought him meals when Johnson had no money, helped him pay for his first car, fought to get him government funding, and sought sponsorships for him before Johnson had a big-time agent and millions rolling his way. In that time, all Charlie Francis ever asked of his superstar sprinter was that he show up on time for practice and work his ass off.

It's been many years since the sprinter held his coach's hand in Sunnybrook. But the memory of the man is strong. "I think of Charlie every day," said Johnson. "Every day."

CHAPTER NINETEEN

COLD CASE IN SEOUL

In a cold case, as any true-crime buff knows, police review long-forgotten files and dig up new clues to crack unsolved crimes.

Ben Johnson did not break any laws by failing a urine test in 1988, but in the court of public opinion, he was pilloried as a fair-play fraud who cheated his fans, his fellow athletes, and the public in an epic foot race, resulting in the Olympic Games' most explosive and enduring doping scandal.

And, let's be frank, after two more positives in 1993 and 1999, sabotage theories put forth by Johnson and Charlie Francis seem absurd. Their claims that the runner was framed in Seoul and that the IOC's medical commission overstepped its authority have been widely dismissed as nonsense.

But was it nonsense? Is any of Johnson's story worth a second look as the only track and field Olympian in Seoul to fail a drug test? Is it possible to railroad a guilty man?

"I came in clean and came out dirty," Johnson maintains to this day.

After hearing Lewis's manager, Joe Douglas, reveal in the 9.79* documentary that Andre Jackson was sent to spy on Johnson in doping control, I decided to revisit the 1988 Olympic 100-meter sprint final. I wanted to review the whole story of Johnson's disqualification to see if something, anything, had been missed the first time around.

I asked Johnson for a copy of his original drug test from Seoul. He looked in his files but couldn't find it. I tried a few lawyers from back in the day, but no luck there, either. Then, I remembered that the test was entered as a Dubin Inquiry exhibit, courtesy of Manfred Donike, who produced it. With the help of Canada's Library and Archives staff, the test and other materials were tracked down in boxes stored off-site for decades. I had the exhibit paper trail in hand by 2017.

Reading much of it for the first time was like seeing Johnson's Olympic disqualification with new eyes. The information contained in the old documents was shocking. The actions described were troubling. Johnson had clearly been denied due process in Seoul.

I couldn't help but wonder if Johnson might have kept his gold medal if he'd had a fair hearing.

* * *

Richard Pound, a lawyer, not a chemist, declined to attack the science during his defense of Ben Johnson in Seoul. He trusted the IOC's lab work was bulletproof and felt no need to look at the comprehensive screening data supporting the anabolic steroid analysis. But Canada's chief medical officer in Seoul wanted to see it. William Stanish asked for it, twice. He was refused each time by the IOC medical commission.

Stanish's efforts are outlined in the orthopedic surgeon's hand-written fax to the commission dated September 29, 1988. In the fax, Stanish states he asked Arnold Beckett at 11:30 a.m. on September 26, right around the time Johnson's B sample was being opened for testing, for the lab urinalysis of both the A and B specimens, and that he was now making the request again. The urinalysis data was never delivered.

Pound confirmed he was not given any lab documentation by the IOC medical commission panel. "We didn't have the paper result," Pound said. "We were simply advised [Johnson] had tested positive, and the compound was stanozolol; did we have any explanation for it?"

Canadian Olympic Association president Roger Jackson recalled getting a printed page or two with a graph showing the "chemical constituents," but no one from the Canadian delegation clapped eyes on the crucial supporting analytical paperwork that doomed the most famous athlete on the planet. As one former teammate put it, it's like going to court to fight a drunk driving charge, but the police won't hand over your breathalyzer readings as evidence.

One didn't need to be a chemist to notice unusual aspects of Johnson's lab report. Unsigned handwritten alterations riddle the thirty-one pages—a series of revisions, deletions, question marks, switched lab codes, calculation doodles, and, oddly, the name of a different anabolic steroid, oxandrolone. The records of an IOC-accredited lab were expected to be of the highest integrity and beyond reproach. A few examples:

- Johnson's anonymous sample code was noted on the document bundle as 24-066. Then it became 24-66. Why?
- A sample code other than Johnson's was scratched out on one page, and Johnson's code, 24-66, was handwritten over the deletion. Why? Who was the other athlete with sample number 22-46?
- Oxandrolone, an anabolic steroid, is printed on three different pages and crossed out three times. I've since learned it's simply a reference to testing for this substance, not that it was detected. But why the unsigned deletions?
- The word "stanozolol" is handwritten in the corner of one page with a question mark beside it. Why?

Perhaps officials could have explained the marked-up pages if the document had been questioned at the time. Perhaps not. When Pound was asked if Johnson's fate might have been different had the lawyer seen the lab report, he cautiously allowed it was possible but also offered this: "I would have been really embarrassed that through some lawyering, you got somebody off who was guilty. All the information eventually gets out."

I went to an original source to clear up some of the questions regarding the paperwork. In 2018, I telephoned Dr. Jong-sei Park, the man in charge of Seoul's Olympic doping control operation. He confirmed he conducted the testing on Johnson's sample but couldn't remember the name of the steroid or technical details. Then, in his seventies, Park said he was concerned his recall of 1988 may have faded and that he might provide incorrect information working just from memory. No helpful explanations about sloppy paperwork, then, from the Seoul lab director.

Sloppy paperwork was a serious issue for a medical commission subcommittee that awarded or removed IOC lab certifications. In fact, it partially stripped Canada's second lab, in Calgary, of its accreditation for that reason. After the 1988 Winter Games, the Calgary facility was sent a set of samples to screen as part of the subcommittee's ongoing reviews of certified labs. The Calgary team aced the science portion, correctly identifying substances, but allegedly flunked the paperwork portion. At the Dubin Inquiry, lead counsel Bob Armstrong asked Pound for an explanation:

> [The Calgary lab] detected the right substances in the sense that they properly analyzed the samples that were given to them but the documentation of those results was not sufficiently clear or precise to enable them to really stand up against the scrutiny that might come from a man of your ability representing somebody affected by those samples.
>
> So [commission assessors] said until we are satisfied with the quality of the supporting documentation that go with your results, we're withdrawing the accreditation.

After months of fighting with assessors over perceived deficiencies, Calgary lab officials ended their reaccreditation pursuit, citing, in part, the subcommittee's many conflicts of interest that defy "common standards of public accountability."

Charles Dubin was not impressed with the proprietary way IOC-accredited labs shielded anti-doping testing results from scrutiny. After hearing testimony from scientists who ran some of those labs, the inquiry commissioner raised concerns about athletes' rights in defending a doping violation without having full screening disclosure. This was not specifically about Ben Johnson, but concerned any athlete producing a positive test who may want to examine the evidence against them.

"IOC-accredited laboratories are reluctant to have the accuracy of their tests challenged," Dubin wrote in his 1990 commission report. "They have a legitimate concern that releasing technical information would allow athletes interested in cheating to benefit from that information. Athletes whose futures are affected by drug testing should, however, be allowed to know the criteria used to judge them."

* * *

Not only was Ben Johnson's detailed lab report withheld by the IOC medical commission, but a second similar event occurred that same night in Seoul. An additional doping screen was conducted on the runner's urine sample without his knowledge or consent. It was the endocrine profiling test, a pet project being developed by Manfred Donike. Outside of his commission confreres, few in sport had heard of endocrine profiling.

The German chemist declared that his work proved Johnson was a longtime steroid user prior to the Seoul Games, therefore making his race-day sabotage excuse moot. It was a shattering moment in the hearing. It was also an abuse of due process.

Neither the test's existence nor its results were disclosed to the Canadians in advance of Johnson's hearing in Seoul. Endocrine profiling was not an authorized IOC anti-doping tool at the time. What's more, endocrine profiling had never before been used to confirm a positive doping result. Johnson was singled out as the lone athlete out of more than eight thousand in Seoul to be subjected to the test. As Charlie Francis would later muse, if Donike's test was so reliable, why wasn't it used on every Olympic athlete? And if it was not reliable, why use it only on Johnson?

Not even Donike's colleague on the IOC medical commission, American Don Catlin, approved of this grandstanding. Catlin wasn't convinced Donike's endocrine profiling methods were sufficiently accurate at that time. "I just didn't think he ought to have told the IOC that, because he couldn't prove it," said Catlin, a professor emeritus of molecular and medical pharmacology at the UCLA School of Medicine, among many other distinguished titles.

Science aside, the shock value of the endocrine test was undeniable. The Canadians did not argue against the validity of the test or its findings, a mystifying failure to ensure procedural fairness for Johnson.

In his memoir, *Speed Trap*, Francis discussed Donike, whom he called the "J. Edgar Hoover of dope busters," and was angered by the chemist's sly move. "Only an endocrinologist could have countered the commission's eleventh-hour tactic. But Pound had no way of knowing he would need such an expert, since the commission failed to disclose its purported evidence in advance. The endocrine profile was a card they kept in their pocket until they were about to lose the hand."

Maybe Francis was correct. Perhaps Pound had been scoring reasonable doubt points when Donike unilaterally intervened with the profiling. Johnson said that if Francis had attended the hearing, he would have called out Donike. "Charlie, with his brilliant mind, would have known exactly what was going on," Johnson said. "He would have said, 'No, this is wrong,' and tried to stop it."

In the end, the unprecedented deployment of Donike's endocrine profiling helped cement Johnson as the Olympic Games' most notorious drug cheat, and Donike was applauded for his enterprise. Along with its official disqualification announcement, the IOC made public that Johnson was also a longtime doper. That a test could show historical steroid use was astonishing news in 1988.

* * *

In the days, months, and years after Ben Johnson lost his gold medal, more information surfaced regarding the circumstances of his positive test. Much of it speaks to an ongoing lack of due process that would continue to plague him long after 1988.

A document titled "IOC Medical Commission, Games of the XXIVTH Olympiad in Seoul" is a rich source of information that was kept under seal by the commission for 31 years. It contains written notes of meetings, decisions, and discussions conducted within the private world of the in-house IOC scientists who had enormous power over athletes' careers, especially in that era. Its revelations are among other pertinent Johnson disclosures to surface since 1988, all listed below:

- In an interview for this book, Sweden's Arne Ljungqvist, a medical commission member and longtime IAAF official, explained the IOC's sole decision was to remove Johnson's medal, and after that, the international federation took over Johnson's case. Ljungqvist said the IAAF's independent arbitration panel was empowered to assist an athlete in overturning another body's rulings if an appeal was successfully argued. "It had happened before [1988], and it happened later," Ljungqvist said of medals being returned to athletes after a winning arbitration. "If it could have been proven the [Johnson disqualification] decision was wrongly taken, it would have been referred back to the IOC for a change in decision." Johnson was not told by Canadian sports officials that he could have immediately appealed his Olympic disqualification to an IAAF arbitration panel of legal experts.

- Grigory Rodchenkov, the former head of Russia's national anti-doping agency, attended the Seoul Games. He had official access to the main doping control lab and chronicled his observations about the state of the Seoul testing equipment when discussing Johnson's doping violation in his 2020 memoir. "This was not a cut-and-dried case. I saw the [Johnson] test results from the laboratory—the fact that halfway through the Games, their instrumentation was in desperate need of cleaning and maintenance. The detected peaks of stanozolol metabolites looked a little dubious to me, but it did seem that there was stanozolol in Johnson's system."

  Rodchenkov, who spilled lab corruption secrets in the 2017 documentary *Icarus*, claims "the Johnson bust" had been "years in the making. . . . South Korean analysts, trained by experts from Donike's laboratory in Cologne, reported the positive result, and Donike himself, as head of the IOC anti-doping sub-committee, reviewed the evidence."

- Other lab-related troubles flared in Seoul. There were reports of the wide-necked urine sample bottles leaking. On September 25, the day Johnson's urine was first screened, Donike reported that "four instruments had broken down" in the main testing lab, and it was running at capacity. After the Johnson camp complained about lax security, Ljungqvist told members "regarding the entry of unauthorized persons to the dope control station" that "a large sign had been placed on the entry to the station at the athletics stadium."

- Doping control entry records from Seoul no longer exist. Even the collected urine specimens are gone, according to the IOC. Its media team confirmed that following standard procedure, "the samples collected in 1988 as well as the relevant documentation, including the entry logs to the doping control stations, have now been destroyed. It is therefore impossible to tell who approved the presence of observers [in doping control] at the time."

- Behind closed doors, Richard Pound was savaged for defending Johnson. Australian Kenneth Fitch didn't feel it was "correct for an IOC vice president to appear before the IOC medical commission in order to protect an athlete from his country." The members "unanimously requested that Prince de Merode speak with the IOC President [Juan Antonio Samaranch] . . . to ensure that such a situation did not occur in the future."

- While there was no leniency for Johnson, there was for other Olympians with potential doping infractions hanging over them, according to information within the medical commission document. Eight unnamed Americans who were tested during competition prior to arriving for the Olympics were not sanctioned in Seoul after their cases regarding "over-the-counter herbal preparations containing ephedrine" went before IAAF officials in Korea. The Americans' identities were protected, unlike almost every other athlete in the document.

  As previously noted, British sprinter Linford Christie escaped disqualification from the 200 meters for a stimulant violation. Manfred Donike called the amount of pseudo-ephedrine in the urine a "clear case of doping," but Christie was given "the benefit of the doubt" and cleared by a majority vote. It was accepted that he'd consumed a ginseng preparation that produced the flagged result.

- Johnson was told 80 nanograms per milliliter of steroid metabolites were found in his urine. It's a relatively large amount to appear in a race-day sample, especially for someone adept at clearance times. According to Charlie Francis's research at that time, Johnson's reading was sixteen times higher than a typical competition-day steroid metabolite finding in other athletes.

- During Donike's brief 1989 Dubin Inquiry appearance, he testified that he'd retested Johnson's negative urine sample from the Zurich meet prior to the Olympics. This is the meet where Carl Lewis won the sprint and Johnson faded. But when it came to athletes' rights, a negative "A" sample meant the athlete passed the screening and should have remained anonymous. Yet Johnson's urine specimen was retained, and Donike knew it was his. This raises questions about how and why testers were able to identify an athlete attached to a clean urine sample.

* * *

Dr. David Black, the American forensic toxicologist, has testified as an expert witness in anti-doping cases around the world. Most famously, the Nashville scientist was a witness for American Olympic 400-meter medalist Butch Reynolds, who was falsely accused of doping in 1990. Black's expertise helped identify a list of errors made at the accredited lab in Paris, including a stunning mix-up that confused Reynolds' negative sample with another athlete's positive specimen.

Black also knew Jong-sei Park, the Seoul lab director, from their days as colleagues at the office of the chief medical examiner in Baltimore prior to the 1988 games. Before Black joined Vanderbilt University in 1986, South Korean lab technicians traveled to Baltimore to be trained, in part, at the toxicology lab Black directed at the Maryland Medical Laboratory. In addition, Black traveled to Manfred Donike's IOC-accredited lab in Cologne, Germany, in 1986 and 1987 to study anabolic steroid testing.

In 2023, Black reviewed Johnson's 1988 urine screening documentation from Seoul. He'd never previously seen the paperwork and gamely ploughed through six hundred and one scanned electronic pages to assess eighty-two pages of drug testing data linked to Johnson. He provided a detailed scientific report. As part of his review, Black noted several issues of fact related to the 1988 Johnson test that were familiar to him from his work with Butch Reynolds:

> During the Butch Reynolds' case it was revealed that Dr. Park, when testing the Ben Johnson sample for banned androgenic anabolic steroids . . . the Seoul laboratory technicians had actually added the parent drug [s]tanozolol as an Internal Standard (IS) to the sample processed. Although the use of internal standards is good laboratory practice for forensic and clinical drug analysis, it is not good laboratory practice to add to an actual athlete sample being tested one of the very drugs included in the analysis and identified as a targeted and prohibited drug.
>
> It needs to be noted that the testing for [s]tanozolol use by an athlete was focused not on the parent drug but bio-transformed metabolites that appear in the urine. Nevertheless, this is an unacceptable practice in a laboratory testing for prohibited drug use where sanctions will be applied with a positive test finding.

Black also found it disturbing that in evaluating the "positive urine test reported by the [IOC] regarding Ben Johnson," no documentation was provided, like a signed attestation, to prove that the sample analyzed belonged to Johnson and that the sample number was given as 24-066, then 24-66. He wrote that there is no analytical evidence of the presence of stanozolol metabolites in the urine sample tested, and "the data and information are so poorly marked and referenced, that [it] is impossible to conclude the testing was conducted properly."

Black summed up his findings in an email accompanying his report: "My succinct expert opinion is that this data is unacceptable under current laboratory requirements and should have been unacceptable in 1988."

* * *

Not everyone is warm to the idea that Ben Johnson was denied a fair hearing in Seoul. "What good would it have done if he'd kept his gold medal after failing a drug test?" demanded an experienced anti-doping expert who wishes to remain unnamed for fear of reprisals. "That means a longtime cheat would have gotten away with it. How fair is that to other athletes who don't touch banned drugs like steroids?"

Solid point. It's the counterargument that polarizes the Ben Johnson story. He was a cheater who broke doping rules and was suitably punished.

At the same time, is it fair to ask if a cheater can be cheated by the system when deprived of due process? The answer is yes, even for some who are unflinching anti-doping advocates. The Hon. Hugh Fraser was not part of the proceedings in Seoul. He said while hindsight is beneficial when reviewing decades-old decisions, he felt Canadian sports officials fell short of aggressively protecting Johnson's right to due process during and after his Olympic disqualification proceedings.

"You're talking about the highest profile event at the games," said Fraser, "the gold medal winner, the world-record holder, [and] you think that you would pursue every possible avenue of appeal that there was until every door was slammed shut, and then, finally, you would accept that result. To me, that's not an endorsement of 'we support' Ben Johnson or anything else. That's just part of the due-process rights that every athlete is entitled to."

Fraser recalled arbitration cases he handled that, at first blush, looked hopeless for the athlete but would turn if procedural deficiencies were found. "I've seen some cases that on the face of it, [one asks] 'Why are they even bothering? They've got this athlete dead to rights. Then you get into it and you realize, 'No, we are upholding this appeal and restoring [the result] because there have been screwups in the process, or [there's] evidence in a [urine] contamination case that clearly would not be attributed at all to an athlete.' You have to explore all those things because you can't just jump to conclusions at the front end and say, 'It must be *this* because *this* is the finding.'"

Athletes have far more protection these days, especially after the advent of the World Anti-Doping Agency. Athletes' rights, including the right to hearings before an independent panel, were enhanced under WADA.

Johnson did not get an independent hearing in Seoul. Nor were the conflicts of interest of medical commission members sitting in judgment of him challenged in any way. Canadian lawyer John Barnes provided one of the few assessments of the Seoul situation in the 1991 *Ottawa Law Review*:

> Johnson's urine was certainly tainted, but no more than the summary proceedings he faced.
>
> In any other walk of life, the defects in due process would fatally flaw the disciplinary action. . . . The accused does not have full notice of all the elements of the charge, and it is not clear what constitutes evidence of knowing use.
>
> A particular abnormality in Johnson's case was the ad hominem use of the endocrine profile to prove repeated steroid application; use of the profile is not expressly authorized in IOC rules, and the evidence was introduced as an unprecedented surprise. The hearing process denies an adequate chance to rebut the allegations and evidence, and particularly gives rise to the apprehension of bias.
>
> Doping control requires IOC officials to act as testers, prosecutors, and judges (and Johnson further muddled the roles by

asking an IOC vice president to serve in the very difficult position of defense counsel). There may also have been serious breaches of security rules in the presence of unauthorized persons at the doping control office and in the publicity given to Johnson's positive "A" sample.

Barnes argues that "Johnson might have relied on the numerous irregularities in the IOC's proceedings to challenge his disqualification. A delegation and [a Canadian] government fully committed to athletes' rights might well have encouraged him in this course."

Had Johnson been able to keep his Olympic gold, he'd be just another tainted champion on a growing list of world-class sprinters with doping histories and Olympic medals. Of the Seoul 100-meter finalists, Carl Lewis, winner of four golds in 1984, was absolved of stimulant infractions weeks before he was awarded the 1988 gold; Linford Christie tested positive for the steroid nandrolone in 1999, seven years after racing to Olympic 100-meter gold in Barcelona and eleven years after narrowly avoiding a stimulant violation in Seoul, where he earned a silver; and Dennis Mitchell retained his Barcelona bronze after high testosterone levels were detected in his 1998 urine sample. And it's not only late-twentieth-century sprinters on this list. American Justin Gatlin, for instance, failed two drug tests (in 2001 and 2006) and won Olympic medals (gold in 2004, bronze in 2012, silver in 2016) before and after serving his four-year doping ban (from 2006 to 2010).

Ben Johnson's aunt, Laura Case, has her own read of track-and-field politics. Sitting on her Clark's Town porch, fanning herself under a blistering Jamaican sun, she put her nephew's fate in blunt terms: "They sentenced him to life before they tried him."

CHAPTER TWENTY
ONE MORE BATTLE

Ben Johnson is not finished trying to clear his name and restore his reputation. Since 2019, he's been working with an experienced sports lawyer to research his legal options. These include possibly filing a claim against World Athletics, formerly called the IAAF. Details are not clear, but it's likely any litigation would involve restraint-of-trade and due-process allegations.

Johnson doesn't have a winning record in seeking redress through the courts, but he believes this attempt, unlike the others, is solid. His energy to keep fighting is rooted in his belief that he was set up in Seoul and that his "enemies" expected he would go away quietly.

"Over the years, when I reflect on what happened in Seoul, sometimes I use it as a great positive," he said of his motivation. "All the sacrifice I made since I was fourteen years old and all the hard work I put in over that twelve-year span, the pain, the suffering, the anxiety, and the depression, it was all for my mother, to give her something back in this world. And my father, [who] saw his youngest son become the best athlete to ever run the 100 meters."

He often refers to his mother's prediction of his redemption. "I won't live to see the day, but you will get your gold medal back," Gloria Johnson told her son.

Johnson remains angry with sports officials, especially in Canada, who didn't run interference for him in Seoul. "All those people who screw me over the years, go on to have better paychecks, better job opportunities, and make a name for themselves." They had the power to advocate for him, "but they put me on the chopping block."

He is also angry about what he perceives as a double standard in 1988: "None of the American athletes ever tested positive. It's a no-no, it can't happen."

Does Johnson have any remorse for having used steroids? Not at all. That five other runners in that 100-meter-medal final in Seoul were later linked to doping infractions tends to support Charlie Francis's argument that many were using, and in the decades since, countless athletes across many sports have been caught up in drug violations. It's hard to keep the body count straight. Johnson's head-on-a-pike was supposed to clean up doping in sport forever, but it never came close.

"If that is my destiny, I'd do it again," Johnson said of doping. "I wasn't the only one out there using steroids."

He wears his defiance on a vanity license plate affixed to his Cadillac SUV: Ben979. Pedestrians call out or wave to him when he motors past. Drivers stop at traffic lights and roll down windows to shout the familiar, "Hey, world's fastest man!" Johnson revels in it. "It makes me feel good in a lot of ways because people respect me. They know what track and field is all about and what athletes need to do to get [to the elite level] or even win the gold medal.

"It's nice when people come up and say, 'I remember where I was, I saw the race, you are still the best and the fastest man on Earth.' That makes me feel good, to have great fans out there who believe in what I accomplished."

That said, he wants a fresh start. And it won't be in Canada. Johnson is planning to make Jamaica his home base and visit Toronto periodically. The move isn't solely to escape cold winters, although the glorious Caribbean weather is a factor. Toronto holds less appeal for a man deciding where he'd be happiest when he retires.

Estrangement is part of the issue. Johnson is not as close as he'd like to be with family members—many relationships are strained or broken—and often he spends holidays or birthdays alone. In reflective moments, he'll admit how much this hurts him. Johnson still has plenty of friends in Canada and abroad, and he's big into social media chatting. Some people from his competition days keep in touch. Others have moved on without looking back.

Two of the most cherished people in his life in Canada are gone: his mother, Gloria, and Charlie Francis. In recent years, more have followed. Former Optimist club and Olympic teammate Desai Williams has passed, as has Toronto lawyer Terry O'Sullivan, one of Johnson's fiercest supporters. Johnson counts off other contemporaries who have died, including American Olympian Harvey Glance and Canadian Olympians Angela Bailey and Marv Nash, and is alarmed by their relative youth, too many jolting reminders of his own mortality.

After the pandemic, which shuttered gyms and arenas for many months, Johnson got his personal training business back on track. When travel was still restricted, he was unable to get to his paid overseas gigs, which became a bigger problem for him than most because he refused to get a COVID vaccination. He didn't believe in the vaccination science or the government's reasons for shutting down borders.

Now that he can travel freely again, getaway flights to Jamaica have also become reconnaissance missions to study floor plans, check out beachfront properties, and ponder business ventures on the island.

"Look at this," he said excitedly, opening his tablet. He plays a video of an open-concept, three-bedroom condo not too far from his Falmouth hometown. The gated complex, complete with grocery stores, banks, and restaurants, has not yet been built, but Johnson is smitten. It's the type of condo lifestyle that would ease his transition from Canada back to Jamaica.

He understands that Jamaica is transitioning too. The harbor in Falmouth, once the domain of sugar freighters, now docks cruise liners. Tourists can spend their money in the large new malls on the edge of town, bypassing the British-engineered streets where, long ago, young Ben Johnson raced his friends for pennies.

* * *

The drive to Napanee, Ontario, is about a two-hour trip from Toronto, a straight shot east along Highway 401. On a warm June day in 2023, Ben Johnson visited Bubby Kettlewell at her Napanee studio. Kettlewell was the commissioned artist who in early 1988 photographed Johnson from all sides, measured his face and head with old-school calipers, and sketched him on paper before sculpting his image. All that remains of her extraordinary work are four mini versions of her series. And that's only because she retrieved them when the owners walked away.

The two hugged when Johnson walked into her studio in a Victorian home atop a leafy ravine. He listened carefully as Kettlewell shared the project's genesis and how it was scuttled in the fall of 1988.

Kettlewell won an open competition offered by the University of Toronto and the Ontario Science Centre to do figurative sculptures of Johnson. Four life-sized sculptures depicting four sprinting stages were to be cast in bronze and installed on the grounds of Ottawa's National Sports and Recreation Centre. Kettlewell sketched and sculpted in public view as a live participant in the OSC sports display. She recalled that Gloria Johnson came by to meet her and was pleased a woman had been hired for the task.

One of the larger pieces sculpted in clay—Johnson blasting out of the blocks—was completed by the time he was disqualified in Seoul. Kettlewell was rattled by the news but kept working since her $40,000 contract ran through October. During that time, she created the four smaller wax models, called maquettes, for each sprint stage. The larger clay pieces would have been based on them.

She also felt "massive anxiety" after the scandal broke. Angry people called her at the OSC, attacking her personally for sculpting the sprinter, and vilifying Johnson in the process. The once-ambitious project quietly folded.

Questioning her path as an artist, Kettlewell traveled through Europe for a few months, then returned to Canada to earn a PhD in science. In the meantime, her Johnson art and sketches were shipped to a storage facility where, over the years, the larger clay sculpture was subjected to cold temperatures and crumbled to dust.

Around 1998, Kettlewell, who had resumed painting and sketching, contacted the storage facility to inquire about her pieces. The ownership rights had expired, and she claimed the maquettes, a clay bust of Johnson, and a series of drawings and anatomical sketches that were part of the 1988 exhibit. She paid to have the maquettes cast in bronze and kept them in her studio, to Johnson's delight. "This meeting today was meant to be," he said.

Kettlewell brought out the four pieces, each about a foot high and much heavier than they looked. Johnson held them as gently as a newborn, studying them intently, and marveling at the detail. Not a man given to excessive chatter, he repeatedly told Kettlewell how beautiful they are and how much he loves them.

There's a poignancy to the scene. Kettlewell captured Johnson at his athletic zenith, his youth and power carved into wax, then encased in bronze. It's her best work. It's his best year.

He asked if he could buy the miniatures. She is kind and cautioned that they would be expensive, meaning tens of thousands of dollars for the one-of-a-kind set. Johnson is unfazed. He said that when he gets sorted out financially, he will purchase them. He wants to open a "Ben Johnson" museum near Falmouth. The maquettes would be the showstopper display visitors would see upon entering, bathed in spotlights and anchored to a marble mount. Kettlewell heartily approved of his vision.

She photographed Johnson holding the maquettes on her back deck before he returned to Toronto. He is smiling widely. The former sprinter babbled happily all the way home, calling his good friend Di-anne Hudson three times to tell her about his day.

* * *

Ben Johnson's story has staying power. Love him or hate him, he remains a compelling historical sports figure whose downfall retains a stubborn wisp of mystery.

His post-Seoul decades are peppered with documentaries, essays, and books that feature his "fall from grace." Most media offerings have news hooks, meaning they are tied to an event or a special date, like the twenty-fifth anniversary of his 1988 Olympic win and disqualification. But some projects break that mold.

One that veers sharply from tradition is a Canadian-based television series called *Hate the Player*, which began development in 2023. It's the brainchild of Toronto's New Metric Media founder, Mark Montefiore, and it's written by showrunner Anthony Q. Farrell, who has writing credits with the NBC sitcom *The Office*. The twist in *Hate the Player* is that it uses humor to tell Johnson's tale but is anchored to the facts of his dramatic history.

"[We] are obsessed with the outrageous scandal-behind-the-scandal of Ben's story that we have no choice but to convey it as a comedic series, or we will be forever lost in the one-sided tragedy that we think we know," Montefiore said. "He went from 'hero to zero in 9.79 seconds', and we as a country disowned him even faster without truly knowing the circumstances surrounding the event. The series aims to bring a bit of shine back to Ben's name and shed more light on 'the dirtiest race in history.'"

What is it about Johnson that remains so fascinating? There have been many champion male and female sprinters tripped up for doping since 1988, so why is Johnson the go-to guy and the ultimate steroid villain?

Richard Pound, who estimates he's been interviewed more than fifty times for Johnson-themed projects, offered a simple explanation. "Probably because he's the first [superstar] Olympic champion to have been caught [and] disqualified," Pound said. "Then the US PR apparatus, in and around Carl Lewis, didn't help. Carl was pretty much able to paint Ben as a villain, unlike his own radiant self."

* * *

Sangster International Airport in Montego Bay was jammed. Lines snaked through the check-in area, with passengers pushing massive luggage sets or jauntily holding a single carry-on bag over a shoulder.

Ben Johnson was in the Toronto-bound queue. Fellow passengers had spotted him walking in, giving nuanced head nods or sometimes a hearty backslap and an arm-pumping handshake. He juggled two passports and a couple of cell phones, like an amateur James Bond, and tried to remember which passport, Jamaican or Canadian, to use at the counter.

Directly behind him in line, a good-looking, sharply dressed woman about his age cheerfully asked: "Ben, do you remember me?"

Johnson spun and gazed at her with a deer-in-the-headlights look, an awkward pause. "You look familiar," he ventured politely. Bored people in the slow-moving line began listening.

The woman was a good sport and gave him major hints, like her first name, and where they used to spend time together in Toronto. He clued in: they dated in the late 1980s, and yes, of course, he remembers her. The people in line were now deeply engaged in the scene, watching the world's fastest man backpedal as chivalrously as he could, while the woman was equally courteous, filling in the blanks. The two shared a few laughs and parted ways on good terms.

In the departure lounge, Johnson is again recognized. He gets fist bumps, finger points, high fives, and "hey, Ben!" One chap button-holes him about a business venture, and they talk for a while.

When it's time to board, Johnson hangs back. His seat is at the front of the economy section, and there's no need to rush while people are cramming bags into the overhead storage. When he gets to the Jetway, he teases two beautiful young women ahead of him. They are carrying boxes of duty-free rum—maybe they could spare a bottle? The women laughed and chatted with him for a few minutes. One asks, rather earnestly: "Does it ever get old being recognized all the time?"

At that moment, a man from Vancouver has his arm around Johnson's shoulders and his cell phone in front of their faces.

"No," Johnson answered, as the Vancouver man snapped a selfie of the two smiling into the camera.

"It never gets old."

NOTE ON SOURCES

I was fortunate to have a long list of primary sources for research, with Ben Johnson at No. 1. I relied on first-hand accounts from others who were not just witnesses to events but often, key players with front-row seats to Ben's drama as it unfolded. They were at the Seoul race, in the main testing lab, in the IOC Medical Commission hearing room and later, subpoenaed to give testimony at the Dubin Inquiry.

Those primary sources include written material like books and contemporaneous notes, such as those recorded by the IOC's medical commission in Seoul and Dubin Inquiry exhibits. Information from memoirs and biographies are reflected in this book, including but not limited to: *Speed Trap: Inside the Biggest Scandal in Olympic History*, by Charlie Francis (with Jeff Coplon); Angella Issajenko's *Running Risks* (as told to Martin O'Malley and Karen O'Reilly); *The Dirtiest Race in History* by Richard Moore; *Ben Johnson: The Fastest Man on Earth* by James Christie; *Inside Track: My Professional Life in Amateur Track and Field* by Carl Lewis (with Jeffrey Marx); *Doping's Nemesis* by Arne Ljungqvist; *The Rodchenkov Affair; How I Brought Down Putin's Secret Doping Empire* by Grigory Rodchenkov; *Inside Dope: How drugs are the biggest threat to sports, why you should care, and what can be done about them* and *Inside the Olympics* by Richard (Dick) Pound.

Newspaper, magazine, radio and television archival material from around the world provided useful news and context of the times. I have tried to credit sources throughout and I sincerely apologize if I have fallen short anywhere.

I also reviewed my original work on Ben published in the Toronto Star newspaper from the 1980s through 2019. My investigative reporting regarding Ben's failed drug test in Seoul, from 2016 through 2019, included interviews and information used in this book.

Last but not least, I'd like to thank award-winning British film-maker, Daniel Gordon. His excellent documentary, *9.79**, provided inspiration to dig deeper. And to use the asterisk.

Toronto, 2024

ACKNOWLEDGMENTS

A small army of people, including those who were in Seoul during the 1988 Summer Games, helped to tell Ben Johnson's story. They gave interviews in person, by phone, video and email. They dug up old documents, records, correspondence, legal files, and photographs. Their insights into Ben ranged from sympathetic to hostile to dryly factual and I am grateful for every precious morsel. Others supported the book behind-the-scenes and wanted no credit. I owe everyone my sincere thanks.

There are too many thank individually but I am especially indebted to the following for their candor: Richard Pound, Arne Ljungqvist; the Hon. Robert Armstrong; the Hon. Hugh Fraser; Tony Sharpe; Rob Gray; Ross Earl; Roger Jackson; Jean Augustine; Paul Godfrey; Steve Simmons; Morris Chrobotek; Paul Gains and Jean Hanlan.

I also want to applaud two exceptional people. Nashville's Dr. David Black exhaustively reviewed hundreds of pages of Seoul Olympic anti-doping records, then provided a written expert opinion on Ben's lab-produced urinalysis screenings, all on his own time. Canadian photographer Claus Andersen, who camped overnight in Seoul's Olympic stadium to reserve his shooting space for the gold-medal sprint final, shared his stunning Ben Johnson portfolio for the book. Thank you, both, for your generosity.

Sutherland House Books made *World's Fastest Man** possible, from the moment publisher Ken Whyte said "I'd read that book" to his phenomenal edits. To Ken and his team of managing editor Shalomi Ranasinghe; marketing director Serina Mercier; editorial assistant Leah Ciani and publicist Sarah Miniaci, endless respect.

To my family, who handled my physical and mental absences with good humor and lots of takeout, I love you for sticking this out with me. Paul, Sam, Will, Reilly, Rob, Tatyana, baby Tommy and Malto the Wonder Dog, take a bow.

Finally, Ben Johnson.

The steely mindset that made him fearsome on the track remains. Ben shied from nothing when interviewed for hours, even when discussions were painful and upsetting. He was also endlessly cheerful, courteous and always up for adventure. He once drove through a snowstorm to do an in-person interview at the appointed time, despite my protests, laughing into his cell phone that "Mary, I'm the world's fastest man" and that a blizzard couldn't stop him. It didn't.

I am deeply grateful to Ben for asking me to write *World's Fastest Man**. I hope, as he does, this book provides a richer, more accurate depiction of one of sport's most fascinating and polarizing athletes.

INDEX

Dreams of fame, fortune drive athletes to drugs

By Frank Dolson
Knight-Ridder newspapers

SEOUL — The news spread through the Olympic Village so fast — as well, as fast as Ben Johnson.

The world's fastest human, it now appears, needed help to beat Carl Lewis in the phenomenal 9.79-second 100-metre dash.

A shock? Yes, of course. The single biggest event in these Olympic Games is tarnished.

A surprise? Only in that the Canadian was caught — the seventh athlete, and third gold-medal winner, to test positive in the Summer Games of '88.

There has been a cloud of suspicion hanging over these Games — a belief that the use of performance-enhancing drugs has become commonplace and that their use has been successfully exploited.

Lewis said suggested as much in an interview on British television after Johnson beat him in last year's world championships in Rome.

More recently, in an interview with Runner's World Magazine, Lewis was asked to comment on the growing suspicion that Johnson's seasonal improvement was a product of steroid use.

"I don't want to point fingers," Lewis said. "People want me to say Ben is on drugs because they can't say it. You can't say it. They want to get it out. I cannot say yes, but ... what we have to be instead of going after Ben, go after everybody."

There seems little doubt that Olympic athletes caught so far put the tip of the iceberg.

American sprinter Dawn Fanmore told the Atlanta Journal and Constitution last March, "Everybody thinks track and field is quiet, but it's one of the biggest drug rings you can imagine ... and they get away with it. Everybody's playing Russian roulette, and nobody even dies."

German heptathlete Birgit Dressel died last year, allegedly after receiving massive amounts of performance-enhancing drugs.

Before competing in the men's pentathlon last week, Mike Gostigian, a member of the U.S. team, talked about how discouraging it was to compete against athletes who were using drugs and getting away with it.

'Everybody wants to have an edge. I mean you're not trying to come in tied.'
Dr. Alan Richardson

Moment of glory, lifetime of anguish

Medal was worth $10 million

TORONTO — Canadian sprinter Ben Johnson...

Drug scandal shatters Canada's Olympic glory

Stripped of gold medal Johnson banned for life

By William Walker Toronto Star

OTTAWA — Ben Johnson will never again compete for his country.

The federal government last night cut off funding for Johnson, and he was suspended from the national team for life, just hours after he was disqualified from the Olympics in Seoul and stripped of his gold medal for failing a drug test.

Prime Minister Brian Mulroney said the decision by the International Olympic Committee was "a moment of great sorrow for all Canadians."

"It's a personal tragedy for Ben and his family."

But the decision — reached after an anabolic steroid, was found in Johnson's urine sample — was certain, Mulroney told reporters.

Johnson had electrified millions of Canadians with his world-record run of 9.79 seconds in the 100 metres on Friday night when he crushed his arch-rival Carl Lewis of the U.S.

But now Canada is left with a "national embarrassment," said Sports Minister Jean Charest.

A grim-faced Charest told reporters that he...

INSIDE
☐ Olympic officials rule out claims of sabotage. Page C1
☐ Parade cancelled; our athletes hide in shame. Pages A16-A17
☐ Steroid dangers don't deter some athletes. Page A22

Big Ben's career in ruins

By Al Sokol Toronto Star

SEOUL — Ben Johnson's world-come crashing down yesterday, leaving the entire Canadian track and field program in ruins and a country in mourning.

Big Ben, our flag bearer of this showcase sport of the Olympic Games, failed a drug test for anabolic steroid use, according to the International Olympic Committee.

Less than 72 hours after win...

A champ tu

Canadian daily newspaper editorial comment on the Ben Johnson affair:

Thunder Bay Chronicle-Journal: Ben Johnson, it appears, didn't get tricked, he got caught. If it were otherwise – if only it were – the test results taken after his breathtaking victory would have shown it.

But still we don't want to believe it. Johnson has been tested for drugs eight times since February of last year, including just after setting a world record of 9.83 seconds last August in Rome. All were negative.

They say the whole story hasn't been told. We sincerely hope it hasn't and that clear evidence to support the theory he was tricked into drinking steroid-laced substances can be offered.

Even better would be evidence that the testing apparatus could be inaccurate in terms of the time steroids were present, and that the test results are not necessarily conclusive.

Montreal La Presse: Ben Johnson is a victim . . . His gold medal was his passport to financial success but also to his recognition by his adopted country. We cannot avoid noting that for many this Jamaican-born athlete didn't really become our countryman until he delivered the merchandise – the medal.

In this story of anabolic steroids should be seen first the human drama and then yet another indication of the Olympic illness.

From one year to the next in most disciplines, so-called amateur sport goes from record to record when we know very well that the human race is not evolving as fast.

Highly sophisticated training techniques play a major role. But amateur sport also counts on the support of two scientific disciplines more commonly used to produce better milking cows – an extreme selection process based on the study of characteristics of the human body and biotechnological discoveries.

There is a general use of steroids and other crazy ways of improving athletic performance. So we are entering a universe where athletes, trainers and authorities play cat and mouse – an auction where the trick is to outdistance and avoid detection. Ben Johnson's mistake was to get caught.

Montreal Gazette: The International Olympic Committee did what it had to do quickly and well. It weighed fully the evidence of drug use by Ben Johnson, and then took back the gold medal he had won in the 100-metre dash.

Let us hope this shocking affair is a stark lesson to other athletes who may be tempted to cheat their competitors and cheat themselves by pushing their bodies to dangerously unnatural lengths.

Yet the more one looks at the sanctions against athletes for violating anti-doping rules, the weaker those sanctions appear.

Brantford Expositor: Ben Johnson now holds a new world record and one that will long endure: fastest-ever transition from idol to infamy. Never has a track athlete from Canada reached such heights of adulation and glory as Ben Johnson did last Friday night in his spectacular showdown with Carl Lewis, when he proved beyond any shadow of a doubt that he was the fastest man alive. Then came the thunderbolt. The tests showed, beyond doubt, that Ben Johnson had taken steroids to give an artificial boost to his performance. Our hero had been caught cheating. Instantly, he lost everything.

Winnipeg Free Press: Ben Johnson, a somewhat lonely and isolated figure even...

Johnson's C

By JOHN HUXLEY

SEOUL, Tuesday: Thirteen thousand athletes and officials here are still in shock tonight after the disclosure that Canadian Ben Johnson – "the world's fastest man" – cheated by using a dangerous drug.

There was speculation in the Olympic Village tonight that other athletes could be banned for using the same drug as Johnson – or decide to withdraw from competition rather than risk detection.

A disgraced Johnson was due to arrive with his mother and coach in New York last night, before flying on to Toronto.

He fled Seoul early today, after being stripped of the 100m sprint gold medal, won in world record time on Saturday, by the International Olympic Committee.

"He was shocked and not able to comprehend and totally unable to respond," Carol-Anne Letheren, the Canadian chef-de-mission, said of Johnson's reaction to the findings.

An IOC official, Mr Michele Verdier, said: "He gave us his gold medal, but he didn't seem to understand all of the facts or the consequences."

First place in the men's 100m was awarded to Carl Lewis, who now has an opportunity to repeat his performance in Los Angeles in 1984 when he won four gold medals. He won the long jump yesterday, is in the 200m sprint tomorrow, and the 4x100m relay on Saturday.

The American learned of Johnson's disqualification for drug use in a telephone call from brother Cleve and Houston-based coach Tom Tellez at 3.30 am Seoul time.

"It confirms what we've been saying all along," he is reported to have replied.

Athletes call for immediate drug tests

By Randy Starkman
Special to The Star

SEOUL — Many Canadian track and field athletes and officials are calling for immediate on-the-spot drug testing to clear the team's name in the wake of the Ben Johnson drug scandal.

Upset over the negative image given the team by Johnson's stunning disqualification for steroid use, they want the Canadian Track and Field Association (CTFA) to administer the tests before the Summer Olympics continue.

Head track coach Gerard Mach said that wholesale testing was one option, though he was not certain the CTFA is empowered to do it.

"We've talked about that, but we don't know yet if it's possible or not," Mach said. "I personally don't have the authority to do that. We will be discussing that tonight."

Team meeting set

A team meeting was originally scheduled here for last night, primarily to convince Johnson's victory in the 100 metres.

Instead, it was postponed a day and many athletes and officials are expected...

that they've received in the past.

The Canadian athletes are disheartened that Johnson's nature has reflected badly on the team and the sport.

'No problem'

The public will tend to see it as track and field is dirty," said steeplechaser Graeme Fell of Vancouver. "It has to be to be reiterated that it's a small minority.

"I know that I'm clean and that it's no problem for me. It's a personal choice. And if you make that choice you use drugs and you get caught ... It's sad that it affects the sport as a whole."

Fell said the athletes hoped some good would come out of the incident.

"I think everybody's disappointed, upset," he said. "At the same time, they're sort of happy in some ways that if they weren't playing the game, they got caught."

Can athletes win without drugs?

Steroids and similar substances destroy the heart and soul of sport

By Al Sokol Toronto Star

AL SOKOL

SEOUL — Is it possible to compete at the Olympic Games level without performance-enhancing drugs? Some longtime observers are now saying no.

They argue that everyone cheats, intuit that controlled drug taking is not dangerous and, in any case, the world-class athletes are prepared to pay almost any price for Olympic medals.

From 0 to 100 in 9.83 seconds

252